Cooking With Baja Magic Dos

More Mouth-Watering Meals
from the Kitchens and Campfires of Baja

© 2005 Janna Kinkade

Ann Hazard

Cooking With Baja Magic Dos is dedicated
to my mother, Dottie Hazard who passed away in 2001.
She was truly the queen of culinary plagiarism
and the inspiration for this book.
In addition to teaching me to cook and collect recipes,
she and my dad, Togo Hazard, took my sister Nina and me
all over Baja as children - igniting our spirits of adventure.
During every trip she would remind us
to lock the memories up tight in our hearts -
where we would never lose them.
¡Gracias, Mami!

A portion of the profits from sales of this book will be donated to Baja charities.

Author: Ann Hazard
Cover and three other credited paintings: Janna Kinkade
Photo/Artist: Terry Hauswirth
Artist with two credited paintings: Gayle Hazard
Book Designer: Colleen Taylor
Cooking With Baja Magic Dos
Publication Date: December 2005

Printed in Hong Kong

Hazard, Ann L.
Cooking With Baja Magic Dos
ISBN O-9653223-4-3

Baja Map - by Mike McMahan
Courtesy of Baja Source

Fiesta en la Playa - by Janna Kinkade

ACKNOWLEDGEMENTS

Obviously, my gratitude is first and foremost to my family. Without my husband, Terry this book never would have happened. After all, 95% of the art in here is his! My dad, Togo Hazard and my sister, Nina Hazard Baldwin have always been a support and inspiration to me. It is our father's lively sense of humor and passion for living life to its fullest that truly inspired Baja Magic. Nina's input and ideas are always invaluable. Without her many contributions to the seafood section, this book would be a joke. I am so grateful that my kids, Gayle and Derek love Baja as much as I do and come to visit so often. I thank my mom, Dottie Hazard, my Uncle George and Aunt Hope and Pappy Hazard up in heaven for infusing me with an obsession for this amazing peninsula.

I thank Janna Kinkade for painting us the perfect cover! I'm also grateful to Janet Howey of Tecolote Libros in Todos Santos for hooking us up with Janna. This is the second book I've worked on with Colleen Taylor, the book designer and Greg Zarcoff, the printer and it was an even more enjoyable and smooth experience than with *Agave Sunsets*. I thank Chuck Potter, who's been distributing my books down here since the beginning. He also graciously allowed us to use his father-in-law, Mike McMahan's famous Baja map in this book. I will be forever grateful to my next-door neighbor and amiga, Harriet Purkey, who was a godsend as my editor/proofreader, as was her husband Ben. Whenever my computer acts up, Ben comes over and makes things right! I thank my new Baja book distributors, Jim and Judy Tolbert who are amazing, fun, creative, helpful and enterprising. Dick VanBree and Ray Lieberenz collaborated with me to get the recipe for Fish Meuniere. Kudos to Sabrina Lear, publisher of *Discover Los Cabos*, who introduced me to restaurateurs in San Jose and has done a terrific job of advance promotion for this book. Mónica and Armando Montaño of El Chilar went beyond the call of duty as my "Mexican eyes" in reviewing the contents herein. Finally, a big gracias to Susan Leptich who runs our stateside business.

I thank all the restaurants and hotels here in Baja who shared their best-known recipes with me. New recipes from old favorites from the first Baja Magic include Tío Pablo's in Los Barriles, Pancho's in Cabo, Caffé Todos Santos and the Buena Vista Beach Resort. Eighteen of Baja's hottest hotels, restaurants and bars are contributing for the first time here. They are: Hussongs and Taquería Mexico (Ensenada), Pueblo Bonito (Cabo), Posada la Poza and Hotel California (Todos Santos), El Chilar, Hotel Tropicana, Brisas del Mar and Buzzard's (San Jose del Cabo), El Corral and Rancho Buena Vista (Buena Vista), Tacos Los Barriles (Los Barriles), Ray's Place (Mulege), Isla Loreto (Loreto), Mr. Azucar's (La Paz) and the Giggling Marlin (Bahía de los Sueños). The chef on the *Spirit of Endeavor*, a small cruise ship that sails between Cabo, La Paz and Loreto shared a recipe. My favorite stateside Mexican restaurants, Las Olas (in my former hometown of Cardiff, CA) and Chapala (in my current summer hometown of McCall, ID) also inspired recipes.

I thank my amigos and neighbors who have contributed their personal specialties to this book: Christine and Leo Duwell, Kimberly Ford, Ben Purkey, Suzanna Colyer, Suzanne Morrison, Hugh Kramer, Sue Graham, Kit Worthington, Carol English, Vee Webber, Leslie Eady, Kathy Alward, Laurie Hunter, Gina Valdez, Rich Falleti, Debbie Robertson, Susie Giacalone, Debbie Havens-Wren, Leigh Arrington, my husband Terry and of course my sister Nina.

Finally, thanks to the thousands of you who bought and enjoyed *Cooking With Baja Magic*, *Cartwheels in the Sand* and *Agave Sunsets*. Terry, Nina and I hope you are at least as happy with *Cooking With Baja Magic Dos*. ¡Viva Baja!

TABLE OF CONTENTS

TABLE OF CONTENTS

TABLE OF CONTENTS

TABLE OF CONTENTS

TABLE OF CONTENTS

Cabo Pulmo on the East Cape

WHAT IS BAJA MAGIC?

Travel as far south and west as you can in this country without leaving the mainland and you end up in San Diego. Head further south, cross the world's busiest border and you're in Tijuana - Baja California - Mexico.

My sister, Nina and I grew up on this bicultural piece of real estate. So did my dad, and his father before him. My grandpappy raised cattle on ranches spanning both sides of the dotted line, back in the early part of last century when there was no line, when immigration wasn't legal or illegal and the only thing that divided our two countries was a lonely outpost on a dirt road going - as Jimmy Buffett would say - south.

When I was a child, Baja was Never-Never Land, a place where I felt more at home than in my own hometown. It was a place of endless empty hills, sunny skies and see-through aquamarine water teeming with fish. A smiling, brightly colored place of leather-skinned cowboys who tossed us high into the air, sang mariachi ballads and danced to songs like "La Bamba." Nina and I ate tacos before we ate hot dogs. We ate them every day for breakfast on our first trip to La Paz, back in 1961. We learned to speak Spanish before kindergarten. And we loved it all. Still do.

Why? Well, let me tell you a couple of secrets about Mexicans. They believe life is to be enjoyed, that integrity is paramount, and that God and family are more important than money. They may live in what snooty gringos call a third world country, but guess what? They don't think they're deprived. They think we're ridiculous with our obsession to hoard and discard possessions. Raise the hood of any ancient (but roadworthy) Baja troque (truck) and you will instantly appreciate Mexican ingenuity. These folks are more resourceful than you could ever imagine. They've raised recycling to an art form. And - they will use even the lamest of excuses to throw a fiesta. From gray-haired grannies to Pampers-clad toddlers, everyone gets into the spirit of revelry. Food abounds, cerveza (beer) and tequila flow and music blares. Do they count carbs? Hardly. They consider it just another example of our gringo (that's us, we're the gringos) lunacy. And one more thing ... I believe Mexico is the only second world country on the planet - on the cutting edge of a better life for all.

Back in the mid-fifties when my parents first took my sister and me to Baja, most of their friends thought they were nuts. We were sure to be robbed by banditos, they said. If not, we'd ingest toxic amoebas and come down with Montezuma's Revenge. But my dad has some serious cowboy blood in him, and even though my mom swore she never stepped off Wilshire Boulevard in Beverly Hills until she graduated from high school, she was part renegade too. (She just didn't like to admit it.) We spent our vacations traveling in Baja and mainland Mexico every year when I was growing up - and nothing bad ever happened to us. We visited cities and seaside resorts; we took our camper to remote beach and mountain villages where we were the only gringos for miles.

My mother let me loose in the kitchen early on. We became partners in culinary crime, plagiarizing together as we recreated our favorite meals from trips south of the border. Over the years we collected recipes and kept them in a file box I made myself. Later on I spent time in Spain, the Imperial Valley of California, Colorado and New Mexico. Each time it was back to the kitchen. More trial and error. My file box eventually outgrew itself and I typed up my first cookbook in 1981. This was a good move on my part, because I was tired of being the designated chef whenever a fiesta was called for. Soon my friends were inviting me over for dinner. (Yes!)

From 1993 until 2003, my family had a second home in La Bufadora, a few miles south of Ensenada, at the tail end of what the L.A. Times has labeled, "Baja's Romantic

Gold Coast." La Buf (pronounced Boof) is a gringo colony of homes on a private ranch owned by the Toscano family. It is (like every other gringo enclave in Baja) to its expatriate residents, an antidote to 21st century civilization - a place where everyone knows your name and an outback where kids can run free. When I wrote Baja Magic Uno, La Buf epitomized Baja Magic for me, because it's raw and remote. It drew me in like a magnet and helped me reconnect with the essence of who I am. Like everyone else whose soul has been captured and held prisoner by Baja, I am humbled by the vastness of its emptiness, its mountains that rise up right out of the desert - stark and adamant against sea and sky. The face of the desert, with its profusion of blooming cacti and surprise oases, enraptures me. Nowhere am I happier than walking down a deserted beach and slipping into the water for a quick swim.

The original **Cooking With Baja Magic** was published in 1997 and reflected my life and travels up to that point. In the intervening years, I have had the opportunity to further explore this magnificent peninsula and meet some amazing people. In 2003, my husband Terry and I sold our houses in San Diego and La Bufadora and moved to Buena Vista, midway between La Paz and Cabo San Lucas on the Sea of Cortez. Since then, we have traveled extensively and learned much about our adopted country. The life here suits us perfectly.

I always felt more at home in Mexico than in the US and for years I pondered why. Now I know. I now know that my heart is Mexican. Mi corazón es Mexicano. That is why I am here and I believe that because I am in Baja, the experiences I share now in **Baja Magic Dos** are more authentic. I've also added 80 new recipes - some that I've created, many that I've discovered and several that were given to me by talented Baja chefs. There are lots more surprises too ... more stories, all new art, and more historical and culinary information. There are now 50 restaurant recipes from 31 Baja eateries and two from our favorite US Mexican restaurants.

I will remind you again that Baja Magic isn't just about cooking - it's about creating and maintaining an attitude where we can focus on the beauty in God's creations - not our own. To cultivate it is to kick off your shoes, put on some festive Latino music and heave a huge sigh that casts off the cares of our crazy, mixed-up world. To cultivate it is to imagine yourself in a simpler, gentler place, celebrating life and beauty with people you love. Baja Magic is about savoring life. It's about sharing. Caring. Laughing. It's about accepting life as it presents itself and not minding that you don't have all the answers.

This cookbook has one purpose - to tip your perspective to the south by injecting you with some Baja Magic. So, hey - come on! Dare to throw a fiesta! It can be a dinner for two, a party, a backyard barbecue or a meal for your family. Just kick off those shoes, crank up the mariachi tunes and remember to dance while you cook! ¡Ole!

LA COMIDA MEXICANA

Now that we know what Baja Magic is, I thought you might appreciate a little historical background on Mexican cuisine, since it's one of the world's most extensive and diverse. This richness comes from the fact that it is basically the offspring of the Spanish-Moorish and Native American cultures, which have distinctly different culinary tastes, traditions and ingredients. The Orientals and the French have also subtly influenced it.

In 1492, after the discovery of America, the relationship between the European and Native American cultures began. European conquerors introduced plants, seeds and animals from their native lands. This made for both subtle and significant modifications to the American ecosystem. At the time the Spaniards arrived in the New World, the Moors (who are of Arabic descent) had been living in Spain for several decades. From the Moors they developed a fondness for citrus, such as lemon, grapefruit and orange, and exotic spices, including nutmeg, black pepper and sugar.

Mexico's indigenous contributions to the culinary world include corn, chocolate, peanuts, tomatoes, tomatillos, chiles, pineapple, papaya, nopalitos (paddle cactus), vanilla, avocado, squash, sweet potato, jicama and turkey. The union between these and Spanish staples like wheat, rice, barley, rye, sesame, oats, lentils, garlic, oil, carrots and meat has resulted in one of the most integrated and mysterious cuisines of the world.

Into the Caribbean port of Vera Cruz in Mexico came Spanish galleons with their gastronomic treasures from Africa and the Orient. Seeds of plants from far off places were planted in Mexico and adapted themselves immediately to its climate. These new plants included tamarind, mango, coconut, pistachio, clove, mustard and cumin. During the time that Emperor Maximillian ruled Mexico, French cooking, with its specific methods and ingredients, entered the mix.

Mexico is one of most diverse countries in the world, geographically and climatically. Because of this, each of Mexico's 32 states has its own specialties using products native to their region. The states most famous for their cuisine in Mexico are Oaxaca, Puebla, Veracruz and Yucatán.

Baja "cuisine" used to be an oxymoron, since it consisted largely of street tacos and seafood. Over the last two decades this has changed dramatically. The restaurants in Tijuana, Ensenada, Todos Santos and Los Cabos, in particular, offer up fare as varied, exotic and sophisticated as anywhere in Mexico. So, read on and see what's changed on the culinary scene down here since the original Baja Magic came out in 1997!

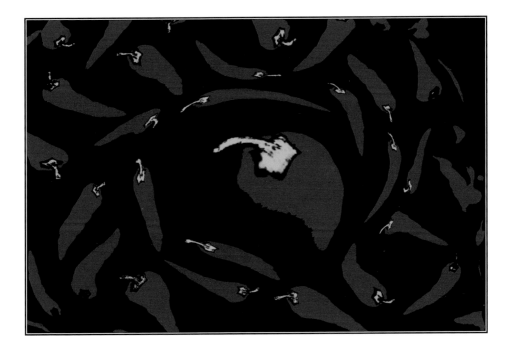

ALL ABOUT CHILES

There are over 60 varieties of chiles, ranging from very mild to fiery hot. All chiles derive their heat from oils concentrated in their seeds and membranes. The heat of a chile lasts six minutes before it dissipates, so even if you overindulge, rest assured that you'll be OK in six minutes! (If your mouth is on fire, try a spoonful of sugar or a bit of salt and lime juice. It helps a little.)

How to Avoid Chile Irritation
Wear rubber gloves or even small plastic bags over your hands when working with chiles. Don't touch your face or rub your eyes while handling hot peppers. Slit the chile lengthwise, rinse under running water, remove and discard stem, membranes and seeds. Chop or slice as directed in recipe. Wash your hands and utensils thoroughly with hot, soapy water afterward.

FRESH CHILES

Jalapeño Chiles
Jalapeños are the most recognizable and widely used of all Mexican chiles. Rarely do you see a Mexican table without a small bowl of jalapeños from a can, pickled in escabeche with carrots and onions. They are plump, about an inch or two in length, medium to dark green and fairly hot. They're used as a condiment, in salsa, nachos and many other dishes.

Poblano Chiles
Poblanos are used in chiles rellenos and most other stuffed chile dishes. They are dark green and about the size of a bell pepper (four to six inches long), but tapered at one end. They can be mild or quite hot. They're best fresh, but also available in cans.

Serrano Chiles
Serranos are hot! They're skinny, about an inch and a half long and bright green. They are used frequently in salsas. They're best fresh, but also available in cans.

Guero Chiles
Guero chiles are about an inch and a half long, plump, yellow and tapered on the end. They're sold either fresh or pickled and are medium-hot.

Anaheim or California Chiles
Anaheims are used in the US for chiles rellenos. They are thin, light green, mild, about four to six inches long and tapered at the end. Their flavor is similar to a poblano, but a little mellower.

Habanero Chiles
Also known as Scotch Bonnets, habaneros are the hottest chiles in the world! Usually less than an inch long, they're bright orange and look like a tiny bell pepper. Their flavor is delicious, if used sparingly. They are used widely throughout southern Mexico, particularly the Yucatán. Originally discovered by the Maya, they are said to have mystical healing powers and give a serious endorphin rush.

DRIED CHILES

Dried chiles are generally hotter than their fresh counterparts. All dried chiles are best if lightly toasted, then the veins and seeds are removed and they're either soaked in just enough hot water to cover them for about an hour or briefly boiled. Afterward, put them in the blender with water and add to your recipe.

Chipotle Chiles
Chipotles are made from jalapeños that have been dried and smoked. They are sold both dried and canned in adobo, a rich, smoky, dark reddish-brown sauce. Their flavor is uniquely delicious.

Ancho Chiles
Anchos are dried dark red poblano chiles. They're mildly flavored and used in many sauces.

Mulato Chiles
Mulatos are frequently used when ancho chiles are called for in a recipe. They're deep brown, longer and more tapered than the ancho and a bit more pungent.

Guajillo Chiles
Guajillo is a dried red chile that gives more color than taste to Mexican recipes. It's about four to five inches long, narrow and has a smooth skin.

Chile de Arbol
Chile de Arbol is also known as the Cola de Rata or Rat-tail chile and is about the size of your little finger. These are often dried, toasted and used to decorate Mexican dishes. They also make great salsa. They're fairly hot.

New Mexico Red Chiles
Ristras, or strings of dried New Mexico red chiles hang outside most homes in that state every fall. A rich, fairly hot chile, it makes an excellent enchilada sauce.

Pasilla Chiles
Pasillas are about seven inches long and very thin. They're dark reddish brown like the ancho, but have more fire to them.

Pequin Chiles
Pequins are tiny, dried red bullets of fiery heat. They add a unique flavor to many dishes. To use, crumble the dried pod between your thumb and forefinger.

BLISTERING AND PEELING CHILES

If you have a gas stove, lay the chiles over the open flame and char skins well, turning with tongs frequently until they're uniformly blackened and stop snapping. The more charred they are, the easier it is to remove the skins. I have an electric stove, so I do mine in a large skillet on high heat. It takes about ten minutes and I turn them frequently. After chiles are blistered, put them in a plastic bag, close it and let it stand for 10 minutes. Remove chiles from the bag, place in ice-cold water and remove skin, veins and seeds. Note: You can also blister chiles over a barbecue grill or under the broiler.

USING CANNED CHILES

When using canned chiles, be sure to rinse them, remove seeds and stems and pat dry with paper towels. Then use as you would fresh chiles that have been blistered in Mexican recipes.

MEXICAN COOKING TERMS

Achiote (Ah-CHEE-oh-tay)
Achiote is a bright red paste made from ground annatto seeds, spices and lime juice or vinegar. It originated in the Yucatán and has been used by the Maya on fish, chicken and pork for centuries.

Arrachera (Arr-ah-CHER-ah)
Arrachera is made from flank steak, marinated in fruit juice and spices, then grilled in strips over a hot fire. It's similar to carne asada, but is thicker and more tender.

Avocados
Avocados are delicate, delicious and healthy fruits that are used to make guacamole, or sliced and served as a garnish to many Mexican meals. They are oval in shape, with either a dark green, rough skin or a smooth medium-green skin. They must be used when they are slightly soft. Skin and peel, remove seed and use in your recipe as noted.

Bolillos
Mexican hard rolls.

Burritos
Burritos are made using warmed flour tortillas. They are stuffed with just about anything, including guacamole, tomatoes, onions, beans, cheese and either carne asada (grilled, marinated steak), shredded beef or chicken, carnitas (pork), or fish.

Carne Asada
Carne Asada is made from skirt steak, marinated in fruit juice and spices. It is grilled in strips over a hot fire, then diced and served in either soft tacos or burritos with an array of Mexican condiments.

Carnitas
Carnitas, which originated in the state of Michuacán are made from pork simmered in fruit juices or salsa. Sometimes carnitas are baked in the oven; sometimes they are deep-fried. They're served in soft tacos or burritos with an array of Mexican condiments.

Ceviche (Seh-VEE-chay)
Ceviche is made from raw fish, marinated until "cooked" in lime juice. It is then combined with tomatoes, onions, chiles and spices and served with chips or saltine crackers as an appetizer.

Chicharrones (Chee-cha-RRO-nays)
Chicharrones are deep fried pork rinds. They're a favorite snack (like potato chips) in Mexico.

Chiles Rellenos (Chee-LAYS Ray-YAY-nose)
Poblano chiles stuffed with cheese and either grilled or deep fried in egg batter and smothered in salsa ranchera.

Chimichangas
Chimichangas are deep-fried meat-filled burritos.

Chorizo (Choh-REE-soh)
A spicy Mexican sausage.

Cilantro
Also known as coriander, cilantro is an herb used all over Mexico to jazz up salsa and other dishes. Its lively green color and equally lively flavor are a great enhancement to many dishes!

Comal (COH-mawl)
Flat, cast iron griddle used to cook tortillas.

Enchiladas
Enchiladas are made from corn tortillas, lightly fried in oil, then stuffed with cheese, onions and most frequently, shredded beef of chicken. They can be vegetarian, or even stuffed with pork, shrimp or lobster. They are then rolled, heated and smothered in sauce, topped with melted cheese and sometimes sour cream.

Epazote (Ep-ah-SOE-tay)
Epazote is an herb indigenous to Mexico, which is used to calm intestinal disorders as a tea and to flavor certain dishes, including soups and frijoles. It does have de-gassing powers, which make it a desired addition to beans! Its leaves are best if used fresh, but dried epazote is widely used too.

Esprimador (Lime Press) (Es-pree-MAH-dor)
Similar to a garlic press, but used to squeeze the juice from limónes (Mexican limes) in Margaritas and any other recipe calling for lime juice. Usually made of pewter.

Fajitas
Fajitas are a fun, festive dish made with marinated steak, chicken, shrimp or mushrooms. They are then grilled on a sizzling hot skillet (comal) with onions, tomatoes, bell peppers and other chiles and served with flour tortillas burrito-style.

Flautas (FLOU-tahs)
Flautas are made from either corn or flour tortillas, filled with shredded beef or chicken, rolled into a thin cylinder and deep-fried, and often topped with guacamole.

Frijoles (Free-HOE-lays)
To make frijoles (refried beans), put desired quantity of dried pinto beans in a large pan. Cover with water and soak overnight. Drain and rinse. Add more water, to almost double the volume of beans. Cook until tender, season and serve.

Limón
Mexican lime. About half the size of the kind you see in the US. Similar to a key lime in size and flavor. Used in many Mexican dishes, sauces and beverages.

Jicama (hee-KUH-muh)
A white, lightly sweet and crispy root vegetable used as an appetizer or in salads. Widely available in the US.

Margaritas
Margaritas are historically made of equal parts tequila, Controy and fresh lime juice, served either blended or on the rocks in a salt-rimmed glass.

Menudo
Menudo is a robust, fairly spicy soup that is supposed to cure hangovers. Its key ingredients are tripe, hominy, onions and spices.

Molcajete (Mole-cah-HET-ay)
A bowl, usually made of stone, with four legs. Small ones are frequently used to serve salsas. Larger ones are used to serve double helpings of soup. In many Baja restaurants you will find Molcajetes on the menu. It will be the house special soup and worth trying.

Mole (MOH-lay)
Mole is a highly complex, dark sauce made from chiles, nuts, spices, fruits, vegetables, chocolate and seasonings. It takes a great deal of time and loving care to prepare and is served as a sauce in beef and chicken dishes for special occasions and holidays in Mexico.

Nopales or Nopalitos (Noh-PAH-lays or Noh-pah-LEE-toes)
Made from the paddles of the prickly pear cactus, nopalitos are used widely in Mexico, in salads, soups and just grilled as a vegetable. Delicious and exotic, they are known to help reduce cholesterol and control diabetes.

Pozole (Poe-SOH-lay)
A robust, fairly spicy soup that is similar to menudo, except that instead of tripe other meats or seafood are used.

Quesadilla
A tortilla with cheese inside, folded in half and cooked in a skillet, comal or griddle.

Queso (Cheese) (KAY-soh)

Mexicans do not use yellow cheese! For dishes calling for melted cheese, either queso Monterey (jack cheese) or queso Chihuahua are used. For a pungent, drier cheese to use as a garnish for tacos, guacamole and salads, try queso frescos.

Salsa

Salsa is the most basic dish in any Mexican meal, often served as an appetizer with chips and used to jazz up everything from eggs to main courses. Salsas can be made from fresh, raw vegetables or cooked. Every Mexican chef has his or her own particular way of making salsa. No two are ever alike! Basic ingredients are chiles, tomatoes, onions, cilantro and spices.

Tacos

There are two types of tacos: fried and soft. Fried tacos are made with corn tortillas, lightly fried, folded in half and stuffed with either shredded beef or chicken. Then they're topped with lettuce, tomatoes, cheese and a little salsa fresca. Soft tacos are not fried. Either flour or corn tortillas can be used. Tortillas are warmed and stuffed, with any of a myriad of meat, fish or chicken fillings.

Tamales

Tamales are made from corn masa dough filled with meat, vegetables and spices (or fruit) and wrapped in a cornhusk (or banana leaf) and steamed until hot.

Tequila

Tequila is the national drink of Mexico. Originally created by the Maya in the form of pulque, a less potent liquor made from the agave cactus, it was discovered by the Spaniards when they arrived in Mexico. After much experimenting with different types of agave, tequila was invented. It is made from the blue agave and about 80 proof.

Tomatillos (Toe-mah-TEE-yohs)

Tomatillos look like tiny green tomatoes. They are actually from the gooseberry family. They're flavorful and used in many sauces, particularly salsa verde (green sauce).

Tortas

Tortas are Mexican sandwiches made from a bolillo (hard Mexican roll) cut in half and layered inside with tomatoes, avocados or guacamole and carne asada, shredded beef or chicken, cheese and salsa.

Tortillas

Flat, thin pancakes made of either corn or flour, which are used in many Mexican dishes such as tacos, enchiladas, tostadas and totopos (chips).

Tostadas

Tostadas are made with fried flat corn tortillas, topped with a layer of beans, shredded beef or chicken, lettuce, tomatoes, cheese, avocado and salsa.

Totopos (toe-TOE-pohs)

Chips made from wedges of corn tortillas.

NOTE: If you can't find any of these basic ingredients and tools for Mexican cooking, go online. The most comprehensive selection of Mexican grocery items is found at www.mexgrocer.com. You can find anything nonperishable you need there, so you'll be able to cook like a native.

Buena Vista afternoon by Gayle Hazard

 # SALSAS

In the beginning there were chiles ... and then there was salsa. There are more varieties of salsa than you could ever imagine. Every Mexican chef has his or her own signature salsas.

No Baja meal is complete without salsa. You know it - it's a zesty sauce made from fresh or canned chiles, tomatoes, onions and spices that can be mild or it can be so hot it'll blow your head off. When you visit a Mexican restaurant, you're probably served a bowl of it to scoop up with totopos (tortilla chips) while you're waiting for your meal.

In the recipes that follow, I use several varieties of chiles. Fresh chiles can be found in markets all over the Southwest US, and of course anywhere in Baja and mainland

Mexico. However, in other parts of the US it may be necessary to go to a Latino market to locate some of the more exotic types. I don't use exotic chiles very often - too much hassle. But when I do, I offer substitutions or suggest canned chiles to keep you from going crazy if you don't live in an area with a large Hispanic population. I've also specified brands of prepared salsas that I like, for those times when you just don't have the time or inclination to make your own salsas. For online Mexican grocery shopping, check out: www.mexgrocer.com.

When you make a particular salsa, you can make it spicier by using more chiles and also by leaving the seeds and membrane intact. That is where the fire is. There are six new salsas in here too, and most recipes have been improved. I've also added my favorite street taco accompaniment, the chile toreado.

So go for it! You may become a salsaholic like my sister and me. Nina claims that salsa raises the metabolism and releases endorphins, thus burning fat while enhancing the diner's sense of well-being. Hey! That works for me.

Mural - Rancho Buena Vista Cantina

SALSA FRESCA

This is not the recipe from Baja Magic Uno. That has been renamed Vaquero Salsa and is next in line. This new salsa has all raw ingredients, and is called Pico de Gallo in parts of Mexico. However, in Baja when you get your drink or glass of water, you will get a bowl of fresh salsa just like this and some homemade totopos (tortilla chips) to munch on while you wait for your meal. Makes about two quarts.

10 large tomatoes, diced
2 medium white onions, diced
5 jalapeño (hot) or 5 serrano (hotter) chiles, seeded if desired for less heat, finely chopped
1 large bunch cilantro, stems removed and finely chopped
Salt to taste

In large bowl combine all ingredients. Add salt to taste. Refrigerate for two to four hours or overnight. This will keep in the refrigerator for several days.

VAQUERO SALSA

My lineage is solidly comprised of cowboys (on my dad's side) and artists (on my mom's). My dad's family found its niche in the twentieth century in the construction business. Every Christmas for 40 years I was invited to a construction company barbecue at my dad's office. In true Baja fashion, the meat was cooked over grills fashioned from split oil drums and served with homemade tortillas, salsa, beans and guacamole. The chef's name was Carlos and he lived in Tijuana. Every other day of the year he worked as a laborer, cleaning up jobsites.

He recited this recipe to me several years ago in Spanish during a Christmas party. The ingredients may be varied, depending on how hot you like your salsa. If you're unsure, experiment. If your salsa turns out too spicy, add more tomatoes. If it's too mild, add more jalapeños or yellow guero chiles.

Aside from being served as an accompaniment to nearly every dish in this cookbook, salsa can also be served as an appetizer with chips. If you don't have time to make your own salsa, Herdez Salsa Casera (Mexican red sauce) or Embasa Salsa Casera are good substitutes. I also keep Pico Pica Hot Sauce and Durkee Red Hot Cayenne Pepper Sauce on hand at all times because their flavors are unique. When in Baja, Salsa Huichol or Salsa Amor are my preferences. In-A-Pinch Campsite Salsa (recipe immediately following) can be substituted for Vaquero Salsa when fresh ingredients are unavailable. Makes about two quarts.

5 - 10 fresh jalapeño chiles
5 - 10 fresh guero (yellow) chiles
2 - 5 fresh poblano or Anaheim chiles

10 - 12 medium-sized tomatoes
2 medium white onions
4 garlic cloves
1 large bunch cilantro
1½ tbsp beef bouillon powder
Juice of 1 limón (Mexican lime) or key lime

Wash all chiles and tomatoes and remove stems. In a large Dutch oven, place chiles and tomatoes in about one inch water. Bring to boil and simmer for three to four minutes.

Remove from stove and cool for a few minutes. When you can handle the chile mixture, drain off about half the water and mince, by hand or in the food processor. Put all minced chiles and tomatoes in a large bowl. Dice onions and garlic in food processor and stir into chile mixture. Wash cilantro and cut off the longest portion of the stems. Chop the leaves and stir into salsa.

Add lime juice and beef bouillon. Stir well. Place in quart size jars and refrigerate. Depending on quantities of chiles and tomatoes you use, this should make two to three quarts of salsa. It's best if refrigerated at least six hours and will keep for several days in the refrigerator.

IN-A-PINCH CAMPSITE SALSA

Aside from being San Diego pioneers and builders, my grandfather, Pappy and his sons, Bruce and Togo were some of the first Baja Aficionados. My dad (Togo) loves to tell the  story of his first big fishing trip south. It was 1932 and he was ten years old. It took the trio over seven hours to traverse the 75-mile dirt road from Tijuana to Ensenada in their beat-up old Ford. Pappy's fish camp, which consisted of a tiny, completely primitive hut with an attached outhouse, was located at Punta Banda - another two hours away, at the southern mouth of Todos Santos Bay. The road there was accessible only at low tide, so on many of their trips over the years, they had to wait half a day for the tide to recede. No matter. They always hung out with the locals and the hours sped by.

This salsa is made for times like those, when the nearest store is too far away to even contemplate. Keep the ingredients on hand, like I do and you can always make it in a pinch - whether you're in a remote part of Baja or at home and craving something Mexican and too lazy to go to the store. My mom always kept a store of these goodies in our camper, so that on our Baja trips, we could make salsa whenever the urge hit us. The recipe calls for canned tomatoes and canned chiles, which means that it's as quick as it is easy. It's also tasty and can be used whenever the recipe or the mood calls for salsa. Makes about three cups.

1 - 1 pound, 12 ounce can tomatoes, drained
1 onion
3 cloves garlic (or 1 tbsp garlic powder)
2 - 8 canned jalapeño chiles,
(depending on how hot you want it)
1 tsp dried oregano
1 tsp dried cilantro
1 tbsp beef bouillon powder
2 tbsp American chili powder (mild)
2 tbsp lemon juice

Coarsely chop all ingredients, one at a time. Mix together in bowl. Place the salsa in a large saucepan and simmer for about 20 minutes. This will keep for about 10 days in the refrigerator.

SALSA RANCHERA - PANCHO VILLA STYLE

Rumor has it that
Salsa Ranchera was invented
by the vaqueros, or Mexican
cowboys. After a hard day working
the range, they would gather
around the campfire, whip up a batch
and spoon it over about anything. I believe that! Salsa Ranchera is wonderful over fried eggs (huevos rancheros). You can also pour it over omelets, chiles rellenos, grilled fish, chicken or turkey breasts.

At Pancho's Restaurant in Cabo San Lucas, where this particular recipe originates, owners Mary and John Bragg (by all means - check out "The Truth About Tequila" in the "From the Bar" section of this book) serve it over their chiles rellenos and use it as a key ingredient in their Pancho's Tortilla Soup. Read about Mary in the Soup section. And trust me, the mild, light and very tomato-ey taste of this salsa appeals to even the most sensitive palates. Makes about four cups.

6 whole poblano or Anaheim chiles, thinly sliced
2 large, white onions, thinly sliced
4 cloves garlic, minced
10 large, ripe tomatoes, thinly sliced
4 tbsp olive oil
1½ cups tomato purée
½ cup water
2 tbsp dried or fresh oregano, or to taste
4 bay leaves
4 - 6 tbsp powdered chicken bouillon powder
Fresh ground black pepper to taste
Salt to taste

Place chiles, onions, garlic and tomatoes in large skillet with the oil and sauté until cooked. Remove and let cool slightly, then add tomato purée and water. Add the seasonings and bouillon and cook about a half hour. This recipe makes enough for 12 servings of tortilla soup, huevos rancheros, chiles rellenos, etc. Mary recommends that you use half and store the other half in your freezer for the next time....

ENCHILADA SUIZA SAUCE

Nina and I plagiarized this enchilada sauce from a malecón front eatery in La Paz in the late '90s. It is a favorite of ours and can also be used over chiles rellenos, grilled fish or chicken. Makes about three cups.

1½ tbsp oil
8 large tomatoes
6 chiles de arbol, lightly toasted
1 pasilla or guajillo chile (pasilla is milder), lightly toasted
1 large white onion, quartered
6 cloves garlic, peeled
1 cup water
1 cup crema media ácida or sour cream
Salt and pepper to taste

In large skillet, heat oil and cook tomatoes until blackened and softened, about 20 minutes. Meanwhile, boil chiles in small saucepan for 15 minutes to soften. Remove stems, seeds and membranes if desired. In food processor, blend together tomatoes, chiles, onion, garlic, water and crema or sour cream. Season to taste with salt and pepper and pour into a large saucepan. Heat thoroughly.

ROASTED TOMATILLO SALSA

This green salsa has a rich but tangy flavor that comes from blackening the tomatillos and chiles. It's relatively mild but you can easily up the "bam" factor by adding more chiles! I know it may sound kind of weird to you if you're new to salsas, but you have to believe me when I tell you that it's really, really good. In fact, it's superb with pork entrées, enchiladas or virtually any dish. If you can't find fresh tomatillos in your supermarket, you can buy them canned. If you want to go with a ready-made version (good but not as good), then look for Herdez Salsa Verde, Embasa Green Jalapeño Sauce or any green salsa listing tomatillos as a key ingredient. This makes about two quarts.

3 cups fresh tomatillos, skinned and rinsed or 3 cups canned green Mexican tomatillos, drained
4 - 8 cloves garlic
5 - 10 fresh jalapeño chiles, halved and seeded if desired (to lessen heat)
1 tbsp chicken bouillon powder
1½ to 2 cups water (to desired consistency)
1 large white onion, puréed
1 large bunch cilantro, chopped

Place clean, skinned tomatillos, garlic and seeded jalapeños in large skillet. Cook over medium high heat until tomatillos are blackened and soft. (Do not use oil.) Remove from stove and cool for a few minutes.

When you can handle the chile mixture, put in food processor and purée. Put in a large bowl and set aside.

Pour the water into the skillet. Stir in bouillon. When boiling furiously, toss in onions. Cook, stirring constantly until mixture thickens to a good salsa consistency, about five minutes. Stir in cilantro. Pour in tomatillo-garlic-chile mixture and combine. Place in quart size jars and refrigerate. It's best if refrigerated at least three hours and will keep for several days in the refrigerator.

MARÍA'S SALSA DE ARBOL

My dad currently owns two fishing boats that operate out of Hotel Buena Vista Beach Resort. He named them both after his female Shih Tzu, Dusty. The new boat is Dusty B III and the first boat is the Dos. The captain of la Tres is Vicente Cosio - a great friend of ours. His mom, María has a restaurant called El Corral in their backyard where she and her sister Vicki serve baked potatoes filled with crema, butter and carne asada. She serves them with an array of salsas. Her red salsa de arbol rocks. This salsa is meant to be fairly hot, and it is, but it's one of my favorites! I love it over chiles rellenos. Makes about a quart.

20 - 25 chiles de arbol, lightly toasted
1 cup water
6 large tomatoes

1 tbsp vegetable oil
2 ancho chiles, slightly toasted
1 medium white onion, puréed
6 cloves garlic, puréed
3 tbsp cider vinegar
Salt to taste

In large skillet, lightly toast the chiles over medium high heat, about 5 minutes. Remove and place in one cup water to soak. In same skillet, roast the tomatoes over high heat in oil until blackened, about 20 minutes. Set aside in bowl. Do not clean the skillet! Loosen blackened pieces of tomato and stir in soaked chiles, onions and garlic. Boil over medium high heat about 10 minutes. Place tomatoes in blender or food processor and liquefy. Pour into bowl. Repeat with onion, garlic and chile mixture. Pour into bowl, add cider vinegar and salt and chill at least an hour. Will keep several days in the refrigerator, or part can be frozen for later.

MARC'S MANGO SALSA TROPICAL

Marc Spahr came to Todos Santos, then a tiny undiscovered town an hour northwest of Cabo San Lucas back in 1986. He came because he wanted to farm and the water there was sweet and plentiful. First thing he did was to buy a farm and plant every kind of tropical fruit tree he could get his hands on. Now he grows 20 varieties of fruits and berries, plus 12 types of bananas. Almost all the fruits he grows are used at Caffé Todos Santos, a one-of-a-kind gem of a restaurant he opened in '93.

With its totally tropical, spicy-sweet flavor, this salsa is incredible served with Marc's equally incredible Chicken Flautas (find them in the Appetizer section). Or you can try it spooned over grilled chicken breasts, red snapper, or with carnitas. I swear, you'll think you're in the little latitudes, serving dinner under a palapa at the edge of the Pacific or the Sea of Cortez every time! Makes about a quart.

½ cup mango, chopped
½ cup pineapple, chopped
¼ cup papaya, chopped
2 tsp vinegar
2 tbsp water
¼ tsp salt
2 cups tomatoes, chopped
½ cup white onion, chopped
½ cup cilantro, chopped
½ cup serrano chiles, chopped

Mix all ingredients and put in glass or plastic containers. It's best if refrigerated at least three hours and will keep for several days in the refrigerator.

SANTA FE
GREEN CHILE SALSA

This amazing sauce originated in New Mexico, back when it was part of Mexico. Like all Mexican food, its roots are both Native American and Spanish. However, its flavors are distinctly different. Try this and you'll taste the difference for yourself.

This salsa is mouth-watering spooned over grilled chicken breasts and can be substituted wherever enchilada sauce is called for.

12 - 14 fresh poblano, Anaheim or canned whole green chiles
2 - 4 jalapeño chiles
¾ cup chicken broth (or 1 tbsp powdered bouillon and ¾ cup water)
1 tsp oregano
1 large white onion, minced
3 cloves garlic, minced
½ cup crema media ácida or sour cream

Using fresh chiles
If you have a gas stove, lay the chiles over the open flame and char skins well, turning with tongs frequently until they're uniformly blackened and stop snapping. The more charred they are, the easier it is to remove the skins. If you have an electric stove, place chiles in a large skillet on high heat. Turn frequently as above. Remove chiles to plastic bag, close it and let stand for 10 minutes. Remove from bag, place in ice-cold water and remove the stems, skins, veins and seeds.

Using canned chiles
Rinse and pat chiles dry, discarding any seeds or stems.

Puree chiles in food processor. In medium saucepan, simmer chiles, oregano, onion and garlic in bouillon for twenty minutes, or until sauce has thickened. Immediately prior to serving, add crema or sour cream.

MAYAN SALSA HABANERO

Back when Europe was locked in the dark ages, the Mayans were thriving, their culture both sophisticated and diverse. The five Maya nations were originally located in Belize, El Salvador, Guatemala, Honduras and Mexico. Although their cities were abandoned approximately 450 years ago, they're still thriving as a people and today inhabit the Mexican states of Tabasco, Campeche, Chiapas, Yucatán and Quintana Roo.

When Terry and I visited the Yucatán a few years ago, our friend Antonio (formerly of Ensenada) acted as our private tour guide. We visited Chichenitzá and Tulum, swam in cenotes (underground rivers and lakes) and snorkeled in the Caribbean. If you ever visit the Riviera Maya, the Mayan people'll surround you. They still farm the land and live in small villages throughout the Yucatán peninsula - much as they did centuries ago. They own and work in the shops where you'll buy handicrafts or groceries, the restaurants where you'll eat and the hotels where you'll stay. They are a friendly and proud people. If you're interested, it's possible they will teach you a few words in their language.

For the Maya, eating is an act of spirituality. Their foods are different than the northern Mexican food most Americans and other tourists are familiar with. Their chile of choice is the habanero, the hottest chile known to mankind. It is revered for its healing powers and supposedly will ward off any number of diseases. I will personally attest that it gives the best endorphin rush of any chile.

When habaneros are combined with lime juice, they lose some of their fire. I invented this recipe after a trip to the Riviera Maya where I did much tasting and asked a lot of questions about the salsas. If your palate is very heat-sensitive, cut down on the habaneros, but don't be a pansy and leave them out altogether. This makes about a quart.

1 large red onion, finely diced
6 large tomatoes, finely diced
1 bunch cilantro, chopped
3 cloves garlic, minced
4 - 6 habanero chiles, minced with seeds and membranes removed
Juice of 2 limónes (Mexican limes) or key limes
1 tbsp Controy or orange juice
1 tbsp salt

Mix all ingredients together in bowl. Cover and refrigerate for up to three days. Use with chips, on tacos or as a condiment to any Mexican dish. It makes a wonderful, simple nacho dish, when you pour grated cheese over a plate of totopos (tortilla chips), microwave for a minute or until the cheese is melted, top with salsa habanero and serve.

SALSA CHIPOTLE

This salsa is one of my favorites because of its delicious, unique, smoky flavor. Chipotle chiles are dried jalapeños, usually sold canned and cooked in adobo. They're quite hot, but with deep, almost mesquite-like flavors that remind me of colonial Mexico, back in the days when Jesuit and Franciscan monks like Father Serra traveled up the peninsula building missions and converting Indians to Catholicism. These chiles can be found in California supermarkets, or in markets specializing in Mexican or Latino foods. Try salsa chipotle over grilled turkey or chicken breasts or spoon it over red snapper while it's baking. It's also great for dipping with chips. This makes about a quart.

1 - 1 pound 12 ounce can tomatoes in purée
1 onion, quartered
6 - 8 chipotle chiles, canned in adobo
¾ cup adobo sauce, from the can
2 cloves garlic, minced
1 tsp oregano
1 tsp cinnamon
1 tbsp distilled vinegar

Place tomatoes, onion, rinsed chipotles, adobo sauce and garlic into food processor. Process until coarsely puréed.

Place the salsa mixture in a large saucepan along with oregano, cinnamon and vinegar. Simmer for 15 minutes. Store for up to a week. Flavor actually improves after a day or two.

AVOCADO SAUCE

I love street tacos. Street food is internationally considered to be a defining element of a culture. (Think New York hot dogs) Mexico is famous for its street taco stands, where you can walk up, order and eat standing up right on the sidewalk. One of my favorite places for tacos is Taquería Mexico in Ensenada right next door to Hussongs Cantina. The chef there, Ricardo gave me his recipe for avocado sauce. Thick, rich and creamy, it's a staple of every street taco stand in Baja and to me, a carne asada taco wouldn't be complete without it. Makes about a cup.

1 avocado, peeled and seeded
½ cup milk
1 tsp garlic salt
2 tbsp cilantro, finely chopped

Combine all ingredients in a blender or food processor. Blend until uniformly liquid. If desired, add a bit more milk so that it has a creamy but not watery texture. Serve with tacos. This will keep about 24 hours in the refrigerator.

CHILES TOREADOS

Another street taco stand staple is the chile toreado. It's basically a jalapeño, guero or serrano chile, grilled on the griddle until slightly blackened on all sides and then marinated in Soy Sauce. Baja locals eat them with lime and more salt. I like them just the way they are and I have been known to eat 10 or so with my order of three tacos! Veronica, the chef at the Los Barriles taco stand, gave me this recipe. Whenever we stop in for lunch, if she doesn't have any of these ready, she makes me up a batch to eat with my tacos! She uses the yellow guero chiles.

24 jalapeño, guero or serrano chiles
1 tbsp vegetable oil
½ cup soy sauce

4 limónes (Mexican limes) or key limes, quartered
Garlic salt to taste

Heat the oil in a griddle or in a fry pan. Blister the chiles until cooked through and slightly blackened. Remove and put in a bowl of soy sauce. Sprinkle with lime and garlic salt. Let sit about 30 minutes or up to 24 hours, and serve. Warning! These can be pretty hot, so proceed with caution. They are great stuffed inside a street taco!

APPETIZERS

When I lived in San Diego, whenever I headed out on a Baja road trip, I stopped in Ensenada and stocked up at one of the local supermarkets. Not only did I save money, but it was a cultural adventure that got me totally in the mood to go south! Avocados cost about 50 cents apiece. They sell the biggest mangos and papayas I've ever set eyes on and their watermelons, tomatoes and limónes (Mexican limes) are luscious. In the big stores like Gigante and Calimax, you'll find entire deli cases filled with 30 varieties of queso (cheese). Don't forget the hot-off-the-grill tortillas and just-baked bolillos (Mexican hard rolls - oh yum). Much of Mexico's meat is from Sonora, it's range-fed and hand cut for you by a staff of smiling butchers.

If you've never traveled in Baja before, let me pass on a few tips. First of all, do some research before you go. Visit the many Baja web sites. I list many of my current favorites at the back of the book. Go to the library and AAA. Call one of the Baja travel clubs - Discover Baja or Vagabundos del Mar. By all means, get Mexican car insurance - it's not expensive but it's necessary. If you'll be traveling long distances, have your vehicle checked out stateside before you go. Ask fellow travelers about road conditions. Keep an eye on your map and gas up at a Pemex station (they're all Pemex stations) before you hit a long stretch of empty road. If you do run out of gas or have car problems in Baja and find yourself scratching your head wondering what to do next at the side of a deserted road, don't be surprised when a modern green troque (truck) pulls up behind you offering free assistance and gas for sale. The Green Angels, as they're known, exist solely to help tourists! They patrol all major highways in Mexico - supposedly passing by twice a day. Although most Baja aficionados I know subscribe to the theory that the "worst" roads (read that rutted, gnarly, washboard dirt roads) lead to the "best" places - the Green Angels aren't into off-roading. So be extra-well prepared if you have a hankering to find those "best" places!

One of the amazing things I remember from my growing up years about our camping trips to Baja (and my dad was into bad roads and best places) was the friendliness of the people - Mexicans and gringos alike. Labels and titles and status don't matter south of the border. Whoever you are stateside fades into insignificance as you reconnect with the basic "you." That would be the salt-of-the-earth, easy-going, outgoing, willing to help a stranger "you." Really. I wouldn't even want to count the times Dad got stuck, or ran over a sharp rock and got a flat on our camper and some kind-hearted Mexican rancher showed up out of the blue and helped us out. It was beyond cool. We returned the favor whenever we came upon someone needing assistance.

While you will likely be trying these recipes in the US and shopping at gringo grocery stores, your creations can still taste like you shopped in Baja. Starting with this section on Appetizers, pick out something that makes your mouth water. There's a lot to choose from and many can be easily modified to serve as a main course - especially the new ones like Champancha, Coconut Shrimp, Esquites Callos de Almeja, Sashimi, Seared Ahi and more. You can offer up any of a variety of munchies to your lucky guests while they're sipping cerveza (beer), Margaritas or just plain iced tea. If you're an expatriate like me, you'll have no problems finding everything you need down here. Of course, now that Costco, Soriana's, CCC, Ley and City Club have proliferated in Baja Sur, we don't lack for anything anymore. Yeah, Office Depot and Home Depot are here now too....

I'm one of those people who could make a whole meal of appetizers. I love them and I'm always adding new ones to my collection. So the choices here range from traditional guacamole (avocado dip) and chips to fiery hot peanuts and include seafood appetizers, quesadillas and an array of other treats. Remember to enjoy yourself. It's a prerequisite to have fun while cooking - and to have even more fun while consuming! There are some new surprises in Baja Magic Dos ... more seafood appetizers from down south and Hotel Buena Vista's Killer Nachos.

At this point in the book, I think it's time to make a confession. Although I would never be so obtuse as to write a Baja cookbook without including seafood recipes - I don't eat seafood (except Leo's Coconut Shrimp and La Cola de la Sirena). Never have. Scores of folks in my life have tried to turn that one around, but so far no one has succeeded. I have several theories as to why I don't eat seafood. My current favorite is that I was a mermaid in a former life and I can't bear to eat my friends! So give all credit for the tried, true and certifiably delectable seafood recipes in this book to the many Baja chefs who've contributed their best recipes and to Nina Hazard Baldwin, my sister and cohort in culinary crime from the time she was about ten. She is a Baja chef extraordinaire in her own right.

GUACAMOLE & CHIPS

Guacamole (we call it "guac" for short) is a staple throughout Mexico. If fresh ingredients aren't available, you can find prepared guacamole in the deli and freezer sections of your supermarket.

In Baja we make it by the bucket-full. It's next to impossible to be conservative and make just a little bit of guac with all those cheap avocados around! Whenever we have a dinner party and serve Baja cuisine (imagine that?) we serve it with totopos (chips). Guacamole is a fundamental part of a Baja diet ... right up there with salsa. Get used to it!

Guac
3 - 4 ripe avocados
Juice from 2 limónes (Mexican limes) or key limes
1 large tomato, diced
½ white onion, chopped
1 tsp garlic powder or 2 garlic cloves, minced
1 tsp salt
½ tsp pepper
4 tbsp salsa verde or to taste (Salsa section)
¼ cup grated Mexican queso cacique or feta cheese
1 large black olive

Totopos (chips)
1 dozen corn tortillas
1 cup corn or canola oil
Salt to taste

To make Guacamole
Slice avocados in half and remove seed.

Scoop avocado pulp out of the skin using a spoon. Mash avocados in a medium-sized bowl. Add lime juice, diced tomatoes, onions, garlic powder, salt and pepper. Add salsa verde to taste. Stir well, but stop while it's still slightly lumpy. Refrigerate, covered until ready to use. Can be made up to three hours in advance.

To make Totopos (chips)
Slice tortillas into eight pie-shaped wedges. Heat oil in frying pan until a drop of water sizzles when dropped into the oil. Cook tortilla wedges about one to two minutes, browning on both sides. Remove from pan and drain on paper towels. Lightly salt. These can be made up to three hours in advance.

To serve, place guacamole in a bowl in the center of a round serving dish. Garnish with crumbled cheese and olive. Surround with chips. Feel free to substitute packaged tortilla chips, made from either yellow or blue corn. This recipe serves four serious munchers or eight casual snackers.

Mural in the Hotel Buena Vista Beach Resort Restaurant
painted by Jesse Valdez.

HOTEL BUENA VISTA'S WORLD FAMOUS NACHOS

I spent 33 years as a tourist in the East Cape village of Buena Vista, midway between La Paz and Cabo San Lucas on the Sea of Cortez. In 2002, Terry and I were married on the sand at the Hotel Buena Vista Beach Resort. Then in 2003 we sold everything in the States and northern Baja and moved to Buena Vista. In honor of our favorite hotel in our new home, we're sharing their most celebrated recipe. Hotel guests rave about these nachos, and eat them by the platterful. In fact, reading the recipe alone is guaranteed to give anyone who's done happy hour at the swim-up bar serious flashbacks.

Yeah ... it's about 4:00 in the afternoon and you're perched on an underwater barstool. In front of you is a piña colada, Margarita or cold cerveza. Up comes my favorite bartender, Ricardo (or my other favorite bartender, his brother Ramiro) with a huge plate of nachos. You and your three new best friends dig in. Heaven on earth! This will feed four hungry fishermen (or women).

2 - 3 cups totopos (tortilla chips)
1 can refried beans: heat on stove with 1 tbsp bacon fat and 1 tsp milk
sliced pickled jalapeños from can (to taste)
1 cup Monterey jack cheese, grated
1 cup guacamole (see previous recipe)
¾ cup salsa fresca

On serving platter, place a layer of tortilla chips. Scoop hot refried beans over chips. Put on as many sliced jalapeños as your palate can handle. Sprinkle cheese over everything. Nuke for one minute or until cheese is melted. Top with guacamole and salsa fresca.

¡Ay, yay yay!

POSADA LA POZA'S FLAUTAS DE ATÚN AHUMADO SMOKED TUNA FLAUTAS

Sometimes the honeymoon has to precede the wedding; that was Terry's and my conclusion. We got married two days after Thanksgiving. We chose the date because my family was scheduled to spend Thanksgiving at the Buena Vista Beach Resort, like we always do. We figured that it would be a small, intimate wedding. Wrong! By the time we left for Baja Sur, 28 friends had made airplane and hotel reservations. There promised to be great revelry, but romance and privacy? Hardly!

We headed over to the Pacific coast to Todos Santos. We'd heard about an amazing new resort there and wanted to check it out. You've heard me say before that in Baja the worst roads lead to the best places. There should be a deserted beach involved. Privacy, beauty and ample wildlife are essential. Camping is the order of the day, because rarely is there a world-class, boutique hotel at the end of one of these awful roads. There are a few scattered up and down the peninsula, but not many. The road leading from Todos Santos to Posada La Poza proved to be very bad. We bumped and twisted, dodging rocks and mud puddles in our low-slung Neon, praying all the while that we wouldn't get a flat tire.

Finally, we passed through a dense palm grove, and brilliant gold, ochre and orange buildings sprang up in front of us. We parked and walked through the gate. Lush cacti and flower-filled gardens embraced us. There was a saltwater pool next to a lagoon that fronted a magnificently deserted stretch of beach. The owner, former Swiss banker Juerg Wiesendanger and his Czech artist wife, Libusche welcomed us personally and gave us a tour of the grounds.

With only seven rooms, this place is all about privacy and romance. For the three days we were there, we were the sole occupants of two chaise lounges under a palapa, nestled between the pool and lagoon. Our major activity was bird watching. Pelicans soared by, riding the warm air currents. Occasionally they dive bombed, scooping fish out of the water. Frigate birds glided along the surface, touching down like prehistoric seaplanes, snatching up shrimp, fish or crabs and sailing off. Lease terns, cranes and ducks shared the waters with them. The cries of the birds blended with the pounding of the surf, the steady splash of the pool's waterfall and the hum of dragonfly wings. Terry told Juerg he'd never seen me so relaxed.

Whenever we were hungry or thirsty, the bar and restaurant were only steps away, and Juerg was always willing to make us whatever we wanted. Having trained under a famous Swiss chef, Juerg doesn't just cook. He prepares gourmet cuisine. When we got tired of bird watching, eating and drinking, we walked in the gardens trying to identify the different flowers, trees and cacti. We hiked through the jungle to the beach and interrupted a beachside pelican convention. We could've borrowed mountain bikes and explored nearby beaches, but we were too lazy. We did spend an afternoon wandering through town, exploring the numerous galleries and checking out the restaurants. At sunset, we made the mandatory climb up to the Whale Deck and counted whale spouts as the sun sank - pink-orange, red and purple - into the Pacific.

This is one of Juerg's amazing creations. Serves eight.

12 jalapeño chiles
1½ pounds smoked tuna
3 medium sized shallots
6 cloves garlic, minced
12 leaves fresh basil
¾ cup chopped Italian parsley
1 bunch cilantro, stems removed and finely chopped
Celery salt and freshly ground black pepper to taste
1 tbsp olive oil
Salad garnish
2 cups corn or canola oil
20 corn tortillas or 16 flour tortillas
Toothpicks

To make the filling
Buy one larger piece of smoked tuna as the small pieces tend to be dry. Instead of cutting the meat, tear the fiber apart in small pieces with two forks. Place in a bowl.

If you have a gas stove, lay the jalapeños over the open flame and char skins well, turning with tongs frequently until they're uniformly blackened and stop snapping. The more charred they are, the easier it is to remove the skins. If you have an electric stove, place chiles in a large skillet on high heat. Turn frequently as above. Remove chiles to plastic bag, close it and let stand for 10 minutes. Remove from bag, place in ice-cold water and remove the stems, skins, veins and seeds. Chop and add to tuna.

Chop the shallots and put them for one minute in hot water. Rinse then with cold water and put it in the bowl, together with the chopped garlic. Add basil, parsley and cilantro. Season with celery salt and olive oil. Mix well. Add to tuna-jalapeño mixture.

To make the flautas
For the presentation, prepare either a big plate to be put in the center of the table or prepare individual plates with some salad garnishment leaving sufficient space (half the plate) for the flautas.

Heat the oil in a large skillet. Warm up the tortillas on stove or in microwave for about half a minute, so they are flexible to roll. Put the filling in a line of 1½ inch on the tortilla and roll it. Fix with a tooth stick. Put all the rolls on a plate.

Prepare some paper towels in a basket to soak up excess oil after frying. Fry four tortillas at the same time until they become golden on all sides. Do not overdo frying. The tortilla has to be crispy, but still a little flexible. Put the fried ones in vertical position in a basket to let the oil drip. Keep them warm until the last one is fried.

Cut each fried tortilla roll into even sized pieces (2 pieces for corn tortillas, 3 for flour) and put them on prepared plate(s).

CHAMPANCHA - THE KING OF SEAFOOD COCKTAILS

Ensenada's fish market is the most famous in all of Baja. Located on the north end of town, adjacent to the fish docks, it serves up whatever's fresh, plus the staples: Baja fish tacos, ceviche and every kind of seafood cocktail imaginable. Every vendor has his/her own specialty and their own unique method of preparation, so it can be fun to eat around. Champancha is a mixture of shrimp, clams and scallops in a spicy cold broth and served in a parfait glass. Depending on which vendor you visit, you may also be served pulpo (octopus) or the fish catch of the day in your cocktail. Be creative! Experiment with this recipe and use it to make different seafood cocktails, just by varying the ingredients. This recipe makes enough to satisfy four hungry people.

1 cup fresh shrimp
1 cup fresh scallops
1 cup fresh clams
1 cup fresh calamari rings
2 medium tomatoes, finely diced
1 medium cucumber, peeled and finely diced
1 medium white onion, peeled and finely diced
4 jalapeño chiles, finely diced (remove seeds if a less spicy cocktail desired)
1 bunch cilantro, stems removed and finely chopped

3 cups Clamato juice
Tabasco sauce to taste
Worcestershire sauce to taste
Juice of 4 limónes (Mexican limes) or key limes
Celery salt and pepper to taste

Steam the seafood in a double boiler or steamer for five minutes, or until done. In a medium bowl, mix all vegetables. In a quart size pitcher, mix together Clamato juice, lime juice, Tabasco and Worcestershire sauces. In four parfait glasses, scoop in a quarter of the mixed vegetables, then a cup of mixed seafood. Pour Clamato juice mixture over the top and season with celery salt and pepper.

EL CHILAR ESQUITES CALLOS DE ALMEJA CORN KERNELS AND SCALLLOPS WITH CHILE MAYONNAISE

El Chilar is one of the most happening restaurants in San Jose del Cabo. Located just across from the telephone company, it is on the cutting edge of Nuevo Mexican cuisine. Each of the three owners, Ulises Méndez, Armando Montaño and Mónica Martínez de Montaño is especially talented in his/her own way. Ulises is the general manager and a wine connoisseur. He has built El Chilar's wine list into the largest and most moderately priced in all of Los Cabos with 94 wines as of 2005. He specializes in the wines of Mexico (See Baja's Boutique Wineries in the Bar section) and

EL CHILAR
mexican cuisine

Armando Montaño
CHEF
CO-OWNER

Mónica is a public relations whiz. Her warm, friendly personality makes diners feel immediately welcome and special. She is decorating an epicurean corner of the restaurant with contemporary exhibitions of fine Mexican art and art crafts so people can enjoy and learn more about Mexican artists, culture and traditions. Dining at El Chilar is an amazing experience and one not to be missed on any visit to San Jose. In summer 2005 the trio opened a wine bar next door to their restaurant, where people can enjoy a glass of wine or cocktail while waiting for their table in comfort.

Armando told me this recipe reminds him of the corn and scallop cocktails served right after church on Sundays in plazas all over Mexico. It's made with mayonnaise, so Ulises suggests enjoying it with a Pinot Grigio or a Monte Xanic Sauvignon Blanc. Serves four.

Latin America and offers an unprecedented 21 by the glass. All foods are paired with a particular wine and all wait staff are trained to know which wine to recommend with each dish.

The menu changes monthly. El Chilar is the name of the chile bush, so it's understandable that every entrée features chile. Chef Armando wants clients to understand that because chile is used in a dish, it doesn't automatically mean that it will blow your head off. On the contrary, if used subtly, chiles enhance the flavor of the food. Armando takes traditional Mexican recipes and fuses them with Asian and European ingredients, giving his cuisine a contemporary Mexican flare. His use of local organic produce makes it even more interesting.

2 cups fresh corn kernels
2 tbsp butter
2 tbsp chopped garlic
1 tbsp chopped epazote
1 tsp olive oil
1 tsp butter
1 lb small scallops
2 cups mayonnaise
Chile piquin powder to taste
Salt and pepper to taste
2 limónes (Mexican limes) or key limes
Queso cotija (can use feta) to use as garnish

In skillet, sauté corn in butter. Add garlic and epazote and a little water to make it slightly juicy. In another skillet, melt butter and olive oil. Sear the scallops over high heat for a minute on each side. Add to corn and then add in mayonnaise, chile powder, salt and pepper. Serve in shrimp cocktail glasses and garnish each serving with a halved lime and a sprinkling of cheese.

CHILE CON QUESO FAMOSO

This is one of my mother's old recipes. She served it often as an appetizer at her Mexican fiestas, and on our Baja camping trips, so I practically grew up on it. It's not very authentic, but it is really good! And now that we can find Velveeta cheese in Baja, it's much more feasible to make it! This is one of those easy camping recipes that are so great when you don't have a lot of fresh ingredients on hand. Makes four cups.

1 pound Velveeta cheese, cubed
1 cup salsa verde (Salsa section)
1 - 7 ounce can diced green chiles
1 - 3½ ounce can sliced jalapeños (optional)
2 large tomatoes, diced
½ red onion, diced
2 tbsp garlic powder
½ tsp oregano
¼ tsp paprika
1 - 2 tsp chili powder
Totopos (tortilla chips)

In top of a double boiler, cook cheese, stirring constantly until half melted. Add salsa verde, green chiles, jalapeños, onion, tomatoes, garlic powder, oregano, paprika and chili powder. Cook slowly, stirring constantly until cheese is completely melted and all ingredients are blended.

Serve immediately with chips, keeping mixture hot in a chafing dish or crock-pot. Check on it and give it a stir from time to time.

SHRIMP IN AVOCADO BOATS

My family was first served this appetizer almost 40 years ago at the old Hotel Oceano on the malecón (ocean-front promenade) in Puerto Vallarta. We munched on these (mine were sans shrimp) as we sipped frosty Cokes and people-watched at sunset. Once he figured out how to make them, my dad would whip 'em up on our camping trips to San Felipe over Easter break, using fresh shrimp just hauled in by shrimp boats right off the coast. For those (like me) who don't eat shrimp, the avocado and sauce are perfectly awesome by themselves. Makes me salivate to even think about 'em! This recipe serves eight.

4 avocados, cut in half and seeded (do not remove skin)
1 cup red seafood cocktail sauce
Juice from 1 limón (Mexican lime) or key lime
1 tbsp American chili powder
2 cups small shrimp, cooked, skinned and deveined
Place avocado halves on small plates. In

small bowl mix cocktail sauce, lime juice and chili powder. Fill the hollow left by the seed with cocktail sauce. Heap shrimp over the top and serve.

* * *

CEVICHE GONZAGA BAY STYLE

Gonzaga Bay is a good day's drive south of Mexicali - along several miles of what has historically been washboard road below San Felipe. It's on the east coast of Baja - the desert side of the peninsula, where rains are sparse and the cacti march right on down to the shores of the Sea of Cortez. The climate is warmer than on the Pacific side; the water is warmer and the sunrises over the sea are worth climbing out of bed for. Ceviche originated in places like Gonzaga - places where seafood was plentiful but refrigeration rare. This appetizer is light, low in calories and has become popular all over California, Baja and mainland Mexico because of its subtle but spicy taste. Initially, I used the avocado as a garnish. However, once I accidentally mixed it into the ceviche and people preferred it that way. So I modified the recipe. Serves six to eight, depending on their appetites.

2 pounds cubed white fish or bay scallops, raw
2 cups juice from limónes (Mexican limes) or key limes
(bottled lime juice will do)
5 - 10 fresh serrano or jalapeño chiles (hot), diced (remove seeds if you prefer it less spicy)
1 red bell pepper, diced
1 green bell pepper, diced
1 onion, diced
3 ripe tomatoes, diced
2 cloves garlic, minced
1 bunch cilantro, with stems removed, finely chopped
1 tsp brown sugar
Salt and pepper to taste
2 avocados, diced
Totopos (tortilla chips) or saltine crackers

In a bowl, cover the cubed fish with lime juice. Cover and refrigerate for two to three hours, stirring occasionally. Fish should become quite white and scallops will lose translucent appearance. (Once this happens, you will know that the lime juice has "cooked" them and they are okay to eat.)

Transfer to a larger bowl, and mix with all other ingredients except avocado. Immediately prior to serving, add diced avocados and remaining cilantro. Serve in a bowl surrounded with chips or saltine crackers.

CONFETTI DIP CARNAVAL

My mom first came up with the idea for this dip when she, my dad, Aunt Hope and Uncle George were on a month-long camping trip together in Baja and mainland Mexico, right after the highway was finished in 1973. The four of them drove all the way to La Paz and got there just in time for Carnaval (Mexico's version of Mardi Gras). They hung around a week or so, camping at various pristine beaches, then caught the ferry over to Mazatlán (a 17 hour trip) on the mainland and drove home on the opposite side of the Sea of Cortez. Mom and Hope came home with all kinds of new recipes they'd concocted together that trip, and this was one of the first my mom tried on me and Nina. It was obviously named in honor of Carnaval and its wonderful array of flavors and colors truly does remind me of confetti. We loved it then and we love it now!

You can make it spicy or mild, depending on whether you include or omit the jalapeños. At parties, I make a bowl of each and put a little red flag on the "hot" bowl to warn those people who can't take the jalapeños' fire. It's festive, camper friendly and it's an original too. Makes about two cups.

2 large tomatoes, chopped
1 - 3½ ounce can sliced black olives
1 - 3½ ounce can diced green chiles, rinsed
¼ to ½ cup sliced pickled jalapeños from can (optional)
6 green onions, chopped with tops
½ cup grated cheddar cheese
2 tbsp red wine vinegar
3 tbsp olive oil
1 tsp garlic salt
¼ tsp pepper
Totopos (tortilla chips)

Mix all ingredients except chips in medium sized bowl. Cover and refrigerate at least an hour. This can be made ahead and chilled for up to eight hours. Place in serving bowl on large round platter surrounded by tortilla chips. Then sit back and wait. The compliments will astound you.

RED HOT FLAMING PEANUTS

I was first introduced to these fiery little peanuts on an Easter vacation camping trip to the Meling Ranch, which is a real cattle ranch (that caters to tourists on the side) in the mountains southeast of Ensenada. We caravanned down with four other families and one of the moms turned me onto these nuts. At 15, I was already hooked on hot and I loved to show off my cast-iron palate, so you can imagine how many of these I ate. Believe me, they can be addictive. And dangerous too, as I learned when my mouth (and later my stomach) began to burn like a three alarm fire! Makes about a cup.

1 tsp corn or canola oil
1 cup raw, unsalted, skinless peanuts
1 tsp garlic powder
1½ tsp each New Mexico chile powder and cayenne pepper (hot!)
Salt to taste

In small frying pan, heat oil until a drop of water sizzles when dropped into it. Add peanuts and garlic powder. Fry for about two minutes, turning constantly. Reduce heat, add chile powder and salt and cook for a minute longer, stirring constantly to ensure that chile powder doesn't burn. Cool before serving.

SEVEN LAYER DIP

Twenty minutes north of the Tijuana - San Diego Border is where those of us who are die-hard Charger fans have always flocked every fall to watch them play football. A real local's favorite, this Seven Layer Dip (which, of course, was imported from Baja) can be found at nearly every San Diego Chargers' tailgate party. Just waltz around the parking lot some Sunday afternoon and check out the picnic scene. You'll see! Because this variation uses a layer of shredded lettuce instead of the usual meat, dipping into it is like scooping up a bite of spicy salad. It's lightening-bolt good and easy to whip up in an RV. Makes one large platterful.

2 - 16 ounce cans refried beans (jazzed up with hot pepper sauce if desired)

1 cup crema media ácida or sour cream
¼ to ½ cup sliced pickled jalapeños from can
1 cup salsa fresca (Salsa section or use bottled)
2 cups shredded lettuce
2 cups guacamole
2 cups grated cheddar cheese
Sliced black olives and green onions for garnish
Totopos (tortilla chips)

On a large serving plate, layer first the refried beans, then crema or sour cream and jalapeños. Next spread a layer of salsa fresca and a layer of lettuce. Add guacamole. Top with cheddar cheese and garnishes. Place it next to a basket of tortilla chips and watch it disappear!

JICAMA FRESCA

Jicama (HEE-kuh-muh) is a crisp, white root vegetable that is sold as a snack by vendors all over Baja and mainland Mexico. Its flavor is light, zesty and unusual, and it makes a great low calorie appetizer sprinkled with lime and chili powder. Ask for it in the produce section of your supermarket and be prepared to be pleasantly surprised! While I use it in lots of recipes, this is your basic Baja version. Clean, simple and sold on street corners in clear plastic cups so you can munch and crunch as you window shop. Serves four to six.

1 - 2 tbsp salt
½ - 1 tsp American chili powder
1 - 2 pounds jicama, peeled
6 limónes (Mexican limes) or key
limes, cut in wedges

Blend salt with chili powder in a small serving bowl. Slice jicama into ¼ inch by two inch sticks. Arrange on serving tray with lime wedges and bowl of chili salt. To eat: Squeeze lime over jicama and dip into salt.

JALAPEÑO JELLY WITH CREAM CHEESE

This tasty and colorful dip makes an excellent Christmas party appetizer because of its intense green glaze. Or sell yourself as an Irish Mexican (I've been known to do that every so often) and serve it up on Saint Patty's Day. The rest of the year, your guests will applaud your creativity as a gourmet chef if you spoon jalapeño jelly over broiled fish. It's as good as it is green - honest! Makes two pints.

5 poblano chiles, seeded and chopped
or 1 - 7 ounce can diced green chiles
½ cup whole pickled jalapeños, seeded
and chopped
1½ cups cider vinegar
6 cups sugar
6 ounces Certo or pectin
3 - 4 drops green food coloring
2 pint jars with lids
1 - 8 ounce package cream cheese
Wheat Thins

Purée chiles and jalapeños in food processor with ½ cup vinegar. Pour mixture into Dutch oven. Rinse food processor with remaining vinegar and pour into pan. Stir in sugar and bring to a rolling boil. Boil one minute. Remove from heat and cool. Skim off any foam. Stir in pectin, food coloring and chiles. Boil the jars and lids in water for 15 minutes. Remove and cool. Pour jelly into pint jars. Keeps up to a month in refrigerator. To serve, scoop three to four tablespoons over softened cream cheese. Serve as a spread with wheat thins.

LOS CABOS CHILI CHIPS

Serve these spicy chips with ice-cold Mexican beer (Try Pacifico, Bohemia, Tecate or Corona) and you will swear that you're sitting in a swanky outdoor cafe across from the world-class marina in Cabo San Lucas. As you watch the parade of incoming fishing boats, check out the game fish flags that are flying from their masts. You'll see navy blue marlin flags, (with a red triangular flag flying if the fish was released) yellow dorado (mahi mahi) flags, white tuna flags and others too. Take in the incredible array of upscale yachts anchored in front of you. Then look out toward Land's End, at the dramatic rock formations that mark the merging of the Pacific Ocean into the Sea of Cortez. Keep your eyes open, so you don't miss that cruise ship as it slides out of the harbor and heads south.

If you strike up a conversation with a couple

of locals, they might tell you what the town of Cabo San Lucas, which boasts close to 175,000 people these days (that's including the tourists who account for nearly half the bodies in town on any given day) was like just 15 or so years ago. It was a sleepy little fishing village with a handful of hotels and no nightlife. San Jose del Cabo, a half hour to the north of Land's End, has been around for over 275 years and is a major commercial, agricultural and cattle ranching community. It's grown up a lot in the last decade, offering up the best in Mexican art, jewelry, handcrafts, along with world-class dining. It's also home to one of the earliest California missions. The entire area between San Jose del Cabo and Cabo San Lucas is now called "Los Cabos."

Now that you've had your daily lesson in Baja history, how about trying those Los Cabos Chili Chips? They're great - as an appetizer or on the side with a spicy chicken or fish entrée. Makes two cups.

½ cup corn or canola oil
2 cups tortilla wedges
1 tbsp chili powder
1 tsp cayenne pepper (optional)
1 tsp salt

Heat oil to smoking point in skillet. Fry tortilla wedges, turning constantly until crisp. Drain off excess oil, reduce heat and add chili powder and salt. Cook, stirring constantly for a minute more. Drain and cool on paper towels.

CHILI CHEESE DIP

This is another one of my mom and Aunt Hope's camping-on-the-beach-in Baja-concoctions. It's easy to make and because it doesn't require a lot of fresh ingredients, it's very camping friendly! You might not believe this until you make this recipe for yourself, but people go crazy over it. For more years than I care to count, I was asked to bring this dip to every single party I was invited to. Eventually, in self-defense I brought copies of the recipe with me so my friends could make the dip themselves. No matter how much you make, it never lasts more than half an hour. Ever. Honest. You can also make it with leftover homemade chili. Makes one 9 x 13 pan.

2 - 16 ounce packages of cream cheese, softened
2 - 12 ounce cans chili con carne without beans
½ cup sliced pickled jalapeños from can (spicy) or diced green chiles (mild)
2 cups grated cheddar cheese
Sliced olives and green onions for garnish
Totopos (tortilla chips)

On the bottom of a 9 x 13 pan, spread the cream cheese. Layer the chili on top of it. Next, place sliced jalapeños on top of the chili. If you don't want the zap of jalapeños, use diced green chiles or a mixture of both. Top with grated cheese.

You can make this ahead and refrigerate overnight. Before serving, place in a 350° oven and bake for 40 to 45 minutes.

During the last five minutes of baking, add garnishes and return to oven. Serve immediately with a basket of chips and try to hide your smile as you watch it disappear.

SASHIMI

In Buena Vista, anglers eat freshly caught sashimi as an appetizer after a day of fishing. According to my sources there, the key to perfect sashimi is the proper cleaning and cutting of the fresh yellow fin tuna. If you catch it on a fishing boat in Baja Sur, your deckhand will do this for you, so if you freeze it and bring it back to the States, it will be ready whenever you are. If you catch your own, it needs to be killed quickly and then bled out and placed in a mixture of ice and saltwater. When it's cleaned, it should be cut with a very sharp knife, dipped in ice water after each slice is made. First, the bones, bloodlines and skin are removed and the tuna cut into large chunks. If you buy your tuna at a grocery store, make sure it is red or dark pink. Otherwise, it is not "sashimi" grade. This recipe will serve 10 to 12.

3 large blocks of fresh yellow fin tuna, about 2 pounds
1 cup soy sauce
½ to 1 cup Wasabe
Toothpicks

Take a large chunk of tuna and cut it into a thin strip, about 1/3 inch thick. Slice at a right angle slightly across the grain using a very sharp knife, so that your slices are no more than 2 inches long. Rinse the knife in ice water after each slice. Arrange sliced fish on a platter with a bowl of Wasabe and another of soy sauce. Serve with toothpicks for easy dunking.

SEARED AHI

An angler friend of ours named Leigh gave me his famous recipe for seared ahi. Served very, very rare, it's important that the fish is prepped as in the Sashimi recipe above. The addition of the seared asparagus spears and the ginger-sesame crust on the fish makes this dish unique and the Wasabe cream sauce will get you serious raves. Serves four as appetizers or two for dinner.

16 asparagus spears
½ cup water
4 - 3 ounce appetizer portions of Sashimi grade (see above) yellowfin tuna cut to resemble a small brick
Salt and cracked black pepper to taste
3 tbsp olive oil
½ cup toasted sesame seeds
1 tsp fresh ginger root, grated
1 tbsp fresh basil, crushed
1 tbsp butter
1 tbsp olive oil
1 tbsp powdered Wasabe mixed with ¾ cup heavy cream

Blanch asparagus in boiling water for one

minute. Remove. Season tuna with salt and cracked pepper. In medium bowl, mix sesame seeds, ginger and basil. Roll each piece of tuna in this mixture, coating lightly.

Heat a heavy skillet until very hot. Pour in olive oil and immediately add each piece fish. Sear each piece for about 45 seconds to a minute on each side, depending on thickness. At the same time, put butter and remaining olive oil into a second skillet and heat until very hot. Place asparagus spears into hot skillet and sear for about a minute.

Remove both ahi and asparagus and serve immediately on a platter with four spears arranged around a portion of seared tuna. Add a big scoop of jasmine rice if desired.

ROLLED TAQUITOS WITH GUACAMOLE

Taquitos, or rolled tacos have been a staple in my diet since I was a toddler. My kids used to love them cold in their sack lunches. They can be served as an appetizer or as a light lunch. Garnished with guacamole and shredded cheese and offered with salsa on the side, this recipe serves three for lunch or six for snacks. (Short cut: If you're short on time, you can probably find rolled tacos - or taquitos - in the freezer section of your supermarket.)

1 dozen corn tortillas

½ cup corn or canola oil
1 cup beef, chicken or turkey filling
(Tacos, Burritos & Tostadas section)
1 cup salsa fresca (Salsa section)
1 cup guacamole (Appetizer section)
1 cup shredded lettuce
1 cup crumbled queso cacique or feta cheese
12 wooden toothpicks

In a small frying pan heat oil until a drop of water sizzles when dropped in it. Put a tortilla in, frying lightly on both sides. Make sure the tortilla is still pliable (not crisp) when you remove it from the oil. Place on a paper towel and blot off excess oil.

Put a small amount of filling on one end of the tortilla. Roll up the tortilla and hold together using a toothpick. Place in metal baking dish and put in oven on low. Repeat process until all 12 rolled tacos are in the oven. Bake at 325° for about 10 minutes.

Serve on a bed of shredded lettuce. Top with guacamole and cheese. Serve salsa on the side.

CAFFÉ TODOS SANTOS CHICKEN FLAUTAS

An hour's drive north of Cabo San Lucas, on the Pacific side of the penin-sula will land you in Todos Santos. Founded in 1724, the town sort of crept along as a remote outpost until the late 1800s when a vast supply of under-ground water was discovered. Virtually overnight it became a booming agricul-tural community. Today, in addition to a flourishing cattle ranching business, all kinds of tropical fruits and vegetables are grown in and around Todos Santos.

The most surprising thing of all about the area is the gringo population. It has become a renowned artist colony, thanks to the former Taos, New Mexico resident, Charles Stewart, who became its first expatriate artist back in 1986. These days there are more than 800 American and Canadian creative types who make Todos Santos their home, and a recent influx of Mexican and European artists as well. Why have they come here? Is it because of the Pacific breezes, the climate, its Baja-ness? Partly. But the most-often discussed reason I've heard is that the artists love the light. They say it rivals Santa Fe. Carmel. Or the Bermuda Triangle. I wandered around town not too long ago contemplating the light. The locals are right. The light in all of Southern Baja is luminous. The colors are deeper, brighter. The air is clearer. Softer. The ambience is somehow pure. Lively. Real. Just bursting with Baja Magic!

There are several gourmet restaurants in town - and - get this - there's the Hotel California. For years it was rumored that it was "The" Hotel California, the one the Eagles sang about in the early '70s. Well, Don Henley squashed that urban legend, but the Hotel California lives on, with a newly renovated, spectacularly sexy new look. And the food rocks.

Our friend, Marc Spahr owns the Caffé Todos Santos and has since 1993. A gringo and a self-taught chef, his culinary creations are nothing short of awesome. Everything I have ever eaten at his restau-rant is original and delicious! And the por-tions are more than generous. These flau-tas differ from their cousins, the taquitos in that these use flour (not corn) tortillas. He marinates them in coconut milk with a hint of curry - and oh man - are they ever good! Serves four.

4 boneless, skinless chicken breasts
12 flour tortillas
2 cups fresh (if possible) coconut milk
1/8 tsp curry powder
1 cup corn or canola oil
1 head Romaine lettuce, shredded
1 cup Cheddar cheese, shredded
1 cup tomatoes, chopped
1 cup guacamole
1 cup crema media ácida or sour cream
¼ cup Parmesan cheese, grated
Salt and pepper to taste
Marc's mango salsa tropical (Salsa section)

Simmer chicken in coconut milk until cooked through. Set aside to cool and mar-inate for about an hour. Then shred chicken and place in bowl with curry and just enough coconut milk to wet. Mix well, adding salt and pepper to taste. Roll chicken in tortilla tightly and fasten shut with a toothpick. Fry in oil just until tortilla is golden brown. Drain on paper towels.

Place three flautas on each plate and cover each serving with shredded Romaine, tomatoes and cheese. Add guacamole and sour cream sauce. Sprinkle with Parmesan cheese and serve with Marc's mango salsa tropical.

MARINATED HOT CARROTS & JALAPEÑOS

These traditional Mexican snacks are not recommended for people with dainty palates! For those of us who can take the heat, they're low in calories and tantalizing. If you're not sure about your aptitude as a chile-eater, try them anyway - just avoid the jalapeños if they start getting to you!

10 carrots, peeled and sliced in rounds
8 - 10 sliced pickled jalapeños from can
¾ cup cider vinegar
½ cup water
1/3 cup olive oil
1 onion, sliced thinly
1 tbsp oregano
1 bay leaf

Blanch carrots in boiling water for about a minute, or until only slightly crisp. In medium bowl combine carrots, jalapeños, vinegar, water, olive oil, onion, oregano and bay leaf. Set aside in refrigerator for at least eight hours. Will keep up to a week.

ZESTY RELLENO BITES

An old friend of mine from La Bufadora, Vee, gave me the original recipe for these relleno bites. It's one of those recipes everyone took turns tinkering with, so it just kept on evolving. It even continued to evolve after Baja Magic came out. This is my current favorite version! Beware, however. It's one of those super yummy appetizers that tend to disappear before the chef even has a chance to have one single bite! Makes a 9 x 13 pan.

4 cups shredded cheddar cheese (set aside ½ cup for topping)
4 cups shredded Chihuahua or jack cheese (set aside ½ cup for topping)
12 fresh poblano or 12 fresh Anaheim chiles, blistered and peeled
or 3 - 7 ounce cans diced green chiles (mild)
5 eggs, well beaten
5 tbsp flour
1 - 10 ounce can evaporated milk (not sweetened!)
1½ cups salsa verde (Salsa section)

Using fresh chiles
If you have a gas stove, lay the chiles over the open flame and char skins well, turning with tongs frequently until they're

uniformly blackened and stop snapping. The more charred they are, the easier it is to remove the skins. If you have an electric stove, place chiles in a large skillet on high heat. Turn frequently as above. Remove chiles to plastic bag, close it and let stand for 10 minutes. Remove from bag, place in ice-cold water and remove the stems, skins, veins and seeds.

Using canned chiles
Simply spread on a paper towel and pat dry.

Dice the chiles. Grease a 9 x 13 inch pan. Layer half the chiles and half the remaining cheese. Repeat for a total of two layers. (Sometimes I make this in two skinny pans and only do one layer.

That way I can make twice as many squares using the same ingredients. They seem to last longer this way!) Add flour and milk to eggs. Blend well. Pour over chiles and cheese. At this point, the dish can be refrigerated up to 24 hours. Bake at 350° for an hour. Remove from oven, top with salsa verde and remaining cheese and bake an additional 15 minutes. Cool until warm, cut into one-inch squares, serve and watch them disappear! (Reheated leftovers are great for breakfast.)

BEACHCOMBER COCONUT SHRIMP

Christine went to high school with Nina in La Jolla, CA. Then they lost touch for

nearly 30 years until we ran into each other in Buena Vista in 2001. Christine and her husband, Leo had just bought a house here. Now they're not only our good friends, but our neighbors too! When we visited them in Florence, Oregon a few summers ago they took us to their restaurant/tavern in Old Town Florence, the Beachcomber. There was a Baja specialty, coconut shrimp on their menu, so of course Terry ordered it. And lo and behold ... I loved it! So here it is. Make sure those shrimp are nice and crispy and be brave and leave the seeds in the jalapeños! As Christine says, "Mo hottah, mo bettah!" They have since sold the restaurant, but the recipe lives on. Serves four to six.

Leo's Coconut Shrimp
2 lb jumbo shrimp
1 cup flour
1 cup cold beer or ice water
½ tsp sugar
½ tsp salt
2 tbsp olive oil
1 egg
1 cup shredded coconut
1 cup corn or canola oil

Peel, devein and butterfly shrimp, leaving tail on. Rinse and drain. In mixing bowl, combine flour, beer, sugar, salt, olive oil and egg. Slightly chop coconut in food processor and pour onto plate for rolling.

Heat oil in deep fryer or deep skillet to medium high heat. Dip shrimp in batter and roll in coconut. Cook in oil until golden brown and crispy on each side.

Drain on paper towel.

Christine's Dipping Sauce
1 cup orange marmalade, mango or pineapple preserves
2 fresh jalepeños, minced
For spicier sauce, do not remove seeds.

Mix with marmalade and leave in refrigerator for an hour to give flavors a chance to blend. Arrange shrimp on a platter with dipping sauce in a bowl in the middle and serve.

AVOCADO-CRAB COCKTAIL

According to Nina and everyone else who's tried it, this recipe is a real winner! It's delicately spiced and elegant. If you close your eyes as you pop the first bite into your mouth, it may even make you believe you're basking poolside at a five star resort in Cabo San Lucas or, really anywhere along the Los Cabos strip. If you choose, you can use reduced or non-fat mayonnaise and then sit back and smile as you watch those fat grams shrink. (This part really helps the image of oneself at poolside!) Serves eight.

Cocktail
1 pound crab meat
1 tsp hot pepper sauce
½ cup celery, minced

 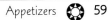

1/3 cup mayonnaise
1 tbsp lemon juice
1 tbsp seasoned salt
Pepper to taste
4 avocados, cut in half and seeds removed
1 head iceberg lettuce, shredded
8 hard cooked eggs, chopped
8 strips pimento
2 lemons, quartered
2 tomatoes cut in 8 wedges
8 black olives

Herbed Mayo Dressing
2 cups mayonnaise
1 tsp tarragon
2 tbsp chopped chives
6 tbsp tomato purée

Flake crabmeat and combine with hot pepper sauce, celery, mayonnaise, lemon juice, seasoned salt and pepper in large bowl. Place avocado halves on shredded lettuce. Fill with crab mixture and sprinkle generously with chopped eggs. Garnish with pimento strips, lemon and tomato wedges and olives.

To make herbed mayo dressing, combine mayonnaise, tarragon and chives in bowl. Add just enough tomato purée to make dressing easy to pour. Serve on the side.

SPECIAL QUESADILLAS MEXICALI STYLE

These quesadillas are absolutely the best. I've loved them and yearned for them for over 30 years, but the only place I've ever seen them on a restaurant menu is in the Imperial Valley and its sister community Mexicali - right over the border in Baja California. Local legend has it that they were created in the early part of the twentieth century by the Mexican nationals who farmed on both sides of the dotted line.

Because the raw tortilla dough is deep fried, the resulting quesadillas puff up with air like huge cheese-filled pastries. They're indescribably delicious when smothered in salsa fresca, or just plain if you're salsaphobic. Nowadays I am able to find uncooked flour tortillas in markets on both sides of the border, so I don't make my own tortillas. Either way, they rock. Makes a dozen.

3 cups self-rising flour
1 tsp salt
2 tbsp solid vegetable shortening (or lard if you're into authenticity)
1 - 1/8 cups water
12 slices Chihuahua or jack cheese
2 cups corn or canola oil
2 cups salsa fresca (Salsa section)

To make the tortillas, cut shortening into flour. Add salt. Stir in water slowly with a fork until a ball of dough is formed. Cover and let sit 20 minutes.

Grease hands with oil. Form dough into 12 balls the size of eggs. Using a tortilla press or a rolling pin, Roll or pat out until relatively thin (about eight inches in diameter). If you're using store-bought tortillas, proceed from here. Place a slice of jack cheese on one side of each "tortilla." Fold in half and flute edges to seal tightly. Seal with a wet fork.

Heat oil in deep skillet or deep fryer until a drop of water sizzles when dropped in oil. Deep fry quesadillas until golden. They will puff up like turnovers. Drain on paper towels and serve immediately with buckets of salsa.

BLUE CORN QUESADILLAS

This upscale Baja specialty can be modified to be as sophisticated as you like. Use Muenster, Brie or chevre instead of the Chihuahua or jack, add some chopped fresh basil (I grow my own here in Baja as do most of my amigos.) and even your most affluent guests will be impressed. Serves eight. Try with a variety of salsas as an accompaniment.

Cooking oil spray
8 blue corn or regular corn tortillas
½ pound Chihuahua or jack cheese, sliced or any other fancy cheese as noted above
½ pound Mexican queso cacique or feta cheese, crumbled or any other fancy cheese
Salsa medley

In small skillet, spray cooking oil. Heat until skillet is medium-hot. Place a tortilla in pan and cook about 30 seconds. Turn over. Place a slice of each type of cheese on one side of the tortilla, fold

and continue cooking, turning frequently until cheese is melted. Serve on heated platter and garnish with your favorite herbs. Serve with various salsas on the side.

HOT CHAPOTOS

Beach side eateries in Southern California and northern Baja offer deep-fried jalapeño rellenos (usually called jalapeño poppers) like these on their appetizer menus. Lately, they've become so popular that grocery stores and Costco stock heat'n serve stuffed jalapeños.

This is my version, which I named Hot Chapotos after two wild and crazy guys I worked with on a construction project back in the '70s. They ate the most and the hottest chiles (and drank equivalent quantities of beer) of any people I've ever run into in my life. We had a crew of over 75 guys on that job. I was one of two females on the jobsite, which was heavenly! On Friday afternoons at 3:30, someone would make a beer run. Almost on cue, the dynamic duo, Joe and Joe would entertain us with their chile-eating and beer-drinking talents. (Who won? Why - Joe of course!) Later on, some of the other guys would get into contests to see who could hammer a ten-penny nail into a two-by-four the fastest, but I was more impressed with the chile-eating. I still don't know how they did it. These are hot, so I don't recommend them for those of you who are fire-sensitive. Serves four.

12 whole pickled jalapeños from can (seeds in for hot, seeds out for not-so-hot)
12 - ½ x ¼ inch chunks of Chihuahua or jack cheese
3 eggs, lightly beaten
1 tsp baking powder
½ cup flour
¼ cup corn flake crumbs
1 cup corn or canola oil

Make an incision in each jalapeño and stuff it with a chunk of cheese. Beat together the eggs, baking powder, flour and corn flake crumbs. Heat the oil in a skillet until a drop of water sizzles when dropped into it. Dip each jalapeño into the egg batter then roll in corn flake crumb-flour mixture. Fry for two min-utes on each side in the hot oil. Drain on paper towels and serve hot with lots of iced tea, frosty Coca Cola or cold cerveza.

LA NUEVA COLA DE LA SIRENA THE NEW MERMAID'S TAIL

One of the most picturesque beaches in all of Baja is Tecolote Beach, 20 minutes northeast of the city of La Paz on the Sea of Cortez. When Nina and I were kids, we often picnicked there - but in those days the beach was only accessible by boat. Now the paved road goes as far as Tecolote and then stops, dropping you off at a huge stretch of sand populated only

by a few palapa-style restaurants, (a palapa, in case you don't know - is an open-air structure with a thatched palm roof - usually right on the edge of the sea) the odd camper or two and an abundance of birds, churning fish and other sea life.

One trip several years back, Nina and I cut short our stay in Los Cabos by a day so we could get back to Tecolote Beach, park ourselves under the palapa and just bask in the beauty of it all. It drew us like a magnet. A blast from our long-ago (try 35 years - then!) past. A place still cut off from the hubbub of life, still spilling over with Baja Magic.

The waiter, Marcelo remembered us from a prior visit. A super-friendly guy who loved to brag about his mixed (1/3 Italian, 1/3 African and 1/3 Mexican) ancestry, he couldn't wait to offer us his favorite recipe. He chose this one, he explained, because, after watching us swim, he knew we had both been mermaids in a previous incarnation! He also told us that the mermaids shadow the gray whales on their trek from the Arctic to their birthing grounds in Baja - those same whales who sneak into the bay of La Paz periodically. The mermaids and whales communicate by singing, and they dance together, flipping their tales in unison in the late night, under the watching eyes of the moon and stars.

When I visited the Palapa Azul a few months later, Marcelo was gone and so was his recipe. In early 2005 I found

him again, however. Since early 1998, he's owned a popular restaurant on 5 de Febrero in La Paz called Mr. Azucar's (Mr. Sugar's) and you can find La Cola de la Sirena on the menu there. When Terry and I hooked up with Marcelo, he made us a plate of this appetizer and informed me that he's changed it dramatically from his days at Palapa Azul. The first recipe used sardines and tomato juice; the new one uses smoked white tuna and is even better. Marcelo told us that people from all over La Paz stop in and buy it para llevar (to go). Mr. Azucar's is laid back. It has a sand floor, a wooden dance floor showcasing local talent on the weekends and a diverse, creative and super affordable menu. Stop in the next time you're in La Paz. You won't be disappointed! Rumor has it he may be coming to Los Barriles. Oh yeah....

I still love it that he created La Cola de la Sirena at Tecolote, because just the name alone makes me feel like taking a running dive into the 83°, lighter-than-aquamarine-green water offshore. It makes me want to swim on and on and on, unable to force myself back to land, because I too have become a creature of the sea. A mermaid. Serves eight. Make extra para llevar.

4 cups smoked albacore
(or canned in water)
4 hard-boiled eggs, finely diced
1 large white onion, finely diced
2 - 4 (depending on desired spiciness) pickled jalapenos from can, finely diced
Freshly ground pepper, to taste
Salt, to taste
1 cup mayonnaise (non-fat is okay)

Saladitas (saltines) or totopos (tortilla chips) for dipping
2 limónes (Mexican limes) or key limes, quartered
1 bottle Salsa Huichol

Combine tuna, eggs, onion and jalapeños in small bowl. Add pepper, salt and mayonnaise. Stir gently until all ingredients are thoroughly but lightly coated in mayonnaise. Add a little extra if the dip appears too dry. Chill well. Serve scooped onto saltine crackers or tortilla chips, garnished with a squirt of limón and a shot of salsa.

DRUNK SHRIMP

In Spanish, Drunk Shrimp translates to Camarones Borrachos. This easy-to-prepare shrimp appetizer is lightly spiced with herbs and beer. Its name alone makes for great party chatter and the flavors are guaranteed to live up to the name. My dad and his friend, (and camping buddy) Ben invented it in a very basic form on one of family treks to Kilometer 181 - a deserted (back then - in the '60s) stretch of rugged, spectacular coast accessible only by twelve miles of gnarly washboard, washed-out-in-places road, just south of Ensenada. Like many of my recipes, it's been jazzed up over the years. Serve this family specialty as a mid-after-noon snack or with cocktails in the evening - and be sure to tell everyone what it's called! Serves six to eight.

4 - 12 ounce cans beer
1 large onion, quartered
1 cup lemon juice
2 tsp celery salt
2 sprigs cilantro
2 tsp salt
2 bay leaves
1 tsp thyme
1 tsp basil
6 whole cloves
Dash ground pepper
Dash ground cumin
2 pounds shrimp, unshelled
1 cup seafood cocktail sauce -or- ¾ cup melted butter
Toothpicks for use in dipping

Combine beer, onion, lemon juice and spices in large saucepan. Bring to boil. Reduce heat and simmer, covered for ten minutes. Drop shrimp into stock and bring to boil. Reduce heat again and sim-mer three to five minutes, or until shrimp are pink. Remove shrimp from stock and allow to cool briefly.

To eat shrimp, hot or chilled, simply shell, stab with a toothpick and dip in cocktail sauce or melted butter as desired.

EMPANADAS ESPECIALES

This traditional Latin American specialty makes a terrific finger food. The little turnovers fit easily in the palm of your hand and they're stuffed with a variety of delectable ingredients. They're as yummy as they are appealing to the eye. My longtime Baja buddy, Sue, who donated this pastry recipe, has revamped it for Baja Magic Dos. In addition to telling you it's a much more authentic pastry, Sue has another message for you. She says, "Ladies, put on a colorful skirt, wide belt and peasant blouse, put a hibiscus blossom in your hair (men - try baggy pants and a peasant shirt - no flowers, please) and serve these empanadas on a lettuce-lined platter with salsa on the side. Oh, and be sure to lose your shoes. Then you'll feel and look like a genuine Mexican. All you'll need now is a battered but roadworthy troque!" Sue should know. She's lived fulltime in Baja for a decade. Recipe yields about three dozen.

Filling
3 onions, finely chopped
2 tbsp corn or canola oil
1 pound ground beef
½ cup beef broth
1 cup raisins
1 tsp ground cumin
1 tsp oregano
20 pitted green olives, chopped
Salt and cayenne pepper to taste
2 hard-cooked eggs, chopped
Salsa medley

Sue's Famous Pastry
2¼ cups unbleached flour
½ tsp salt
1½ tbsp solid vegetable shortening
¼ cup water
1 cup corn or canola oil for frying

Cook onions in oil in skillet until translucent. Add beef and brown lightly. Add beef broth, raisins, cumin, oregano and olives. Simmer 30 minutes. Season to taste with salt and cayenne pepper. Remove from heat and stir in eggs. Cool.

Put flour in a glass bowl. Add salt and vegetable shortening. Knead by hand until the mixture has a gritty texture. Add water a little at a time, and knead dough until it forms an elastic and shiny ball. If it is too greasy, add a little more flour and water. Set dough aside, covered with a cloth, for 30 minutes. Roll pastry on floured surface to ¼ inch in thickness. Cut into 2-inch rounds. Place one tablespoon filling on each, fold over and flute edges to seal. Pierce tops with fork.

In large skillet or deep fryer, add oil to at least ½ inch deep. Heat until almost smoking. Fry no more than three or four empanadas at a time so the oil stays hot and they bubble. Serve hot or cold, with a variety of salsas.

SHRIMP DIP SAN FELIPE

The Colorado River dead-ends where the Sea of Cortez begins. About an hour south of the delta is San Felipe, where the low tides are so low you can walk out half a mile across sand that was underwater just a few hours earlier. Imagine yourself, swinging lazily from a hammock strung up under a palapa at Pete's Camp, which is where we parked our campers back in the '60s. It's still there, too. Put your book down, gaze out to sea and watch as the tide slithers in toward you. Baitfish jump and pelicans swoop across the warm ocean, alerting the fleet of panga fishermen patrolling offshore to the whereabouts of their family's dinner. You sigh, close your eyes and drift off to dream land. This is perfection.

One of my favorite recollections from our Easter vacations at Pete's Camp was when Nina and I were in high school. Feeling a little restless, and more than a little bit ready to stir up some action, we decided to take the family dog, Victoria for a stroll. It was that magical, mystical time of day right before sunset, when the light is pure gold. As we wandered around camp, we suddenly heard the roar of an approaching aircraft. Soon enough, a single engine plane swooped down out of the sky and roared to a stop on the dirt road right next to us. Mouths hanging wide open, we stared in disbelief as the door to the plane unhinged and out popped a single dad named Steve, his teenage son and daughter. We brought them over to our campsite and they became instant friends with everyone in our group.

The shrimp caught here on the northeast coast of Baja are among the finest anywhere. From San Felipe to Gonzaga Bay, the shrimp boats patrol regularly, scooping up these delectable morsels in their nets. Drive to the dock at the breakwater any afternoon in your dune buggy (or "sand rail" as the Arizona folks call them) and you can buy them fresh off the boats - just like my parents, Nina and I did over 30 years ago during our Easter vacations. And be sure to check out Pete's Camp. I don't know if gringos are landing their planes on the dirt roads anymore - but you never know, do you? Not in Baja! Serves four.

1 - 8 ounce package cream cheese
1 cup small cooked shrimp
1½ cups salsa verde (Salsa section)
1 tsp Worcestershire sauce
½ tsp garlic salt
1 tbsp hot pepper sauce
Paprika as garnish
Totopos (tortilla chips)

Mix all ingredients in small ovenproof dish. Garnish with a sprinkle of paprika. Bake at 350° for 15 minutes or until heated thoroughly. Serve hot with tortilla chips.

Baja Swirl by Gayle Hazard

SOUPS

 Both chilled and steaming-hot soups can be found in this section. Gazpacho Rojo, a chilled vegetable soup that originates in Spain is definitely worth serving for lunch or dinner on a hot summer evening. For a different twist, you can try Gazpacho Blanco, its lighter, white Baja California cousin. A new favorite of Terry's and mine is Celery Soup with Jalapeños and Cilantro. We created it last summer on a very sticky Baja night and served it cold. It's great in the winter as a hot soup. We also love the Sopa de Chiles en Nogadas that we created sort of by accident recently. Many traditional, wonderful Mexican soups are included here, as well as some cool, tropical soups and one of my new favorites, Tío Pablo's Green Chile. Sopa Rompe Catra or Broken Cot Soup is also new and guaranteed to be much loved. The story that goes with it is pure Marcelo, owner of Mr. Azucar in La Paz, and it will make you laugh your socks off. Don't miss the Lobster Pozole with Crab from El Chilar in San Jose.

You'll enjoy the variety of soups presented here throughout the year. The frosty-cold soups are perfect for summer, while the heartier, hot soups will warm you up on the inside when it's cold outside. Be brave and try making one or two of these soups - I especially recommend trying the recipes that sound a little iffy to you. I swear to you that your adventurous spirit will be rewarded and you (and those for whom you cook) will not be disappointed. So get busy. Pretty soon you'll be acquainted with the renegade who's hiding out somewhere inside your soul!

Does this mean that if you make Lentil Soup Borracho - by next Thursday you will have sold everything you own, bought a grungy old pick-up truck (troque) and disappeared into the deepest recesses of Baja with only a bottle of tequila to keep you warm at night? Or, worse yet - if you try your hand at Cantaloupe Soup Acapulco, does that mean you'll run off to the rain forest the week after - never to be seen or heard from again?

Beats me. Your guess is a whole lot better than mine! Whip up a pot of soup and see what happens! And be sure to send a postcard if you are transformed into an instant expatriate!

GAZPACHO ROJO

Gazpacho Rojo has been a favorite of mine since my mother turned me onto it in Madrid, Spain in 1967. We ate it at least every other day and between the two of us, I'm sure we drove every waiter assigned to us nuts as we batted our eyelashes and begged ever-so-sweetly for a copy of the recipe. Our perseverance paid off. Eventually. Here is what we came up with once we got home and did a little experimenting. Served chilled, it's a delightful and healthy accompaniment to a summer luncheon or outdoor barbecue. And it is served in Baja in this new millennium, at some of Los Cabos' trendier restaurants. Best yet, you don't need to turn on the stove on those hot summer nights! No cooking required! Makes about six cups.

Soup
1 large onion, quartered
4 cloves garlic, minced
2 bell peppers, quartered
8 medium tomatoes, quartered
1 large cucumber, peeled and chopped
½ cup green onions with stems
½ cup lemon juice
2 cups tomato juice
1/3 cup olive oil
2 tsp salt
½ tsp pepper
1 cup inexpensive white wine

Garnishes
3 hard boiled eggs, diced
1 cup croutons
1 bell pepper, diced

½ cucumber, diced
½ cup chives

Purée first eight ingredients in blender. Remove from blender and put in very large bowl. Mix remaining ingredients in the blender. Combine with first ingredients in bowl and stir well.

Empty into quart jars and refrigerate at least two hours. This can be kept in the refrigerator for several days. The flavor actually improves with age!

To serve, pour a cup of chilled gazpacho in each of six bowls. In separate small serving bowls, place the diced egg, croutons, diced bell pepper, cucumber and chives. Watch your guests serve themselves, spooning a bit of each condiment onto the top of their gazpacho. Then sit back and smile politely as they rave about your culinary expertise!

GAZPACHO BLANCO

Gazpacho Blanco is a less robust version of the original. I first tasted it in a restaurant in San Jose del Cabo the year before my daughter, Gayle was born. True to my genealogical legacy, I begged the recipe off the waiter. It's every bit as good as the original red gazpacho - just different. Try it with seafood or chicken dishes, or serve with any light summer meal. This should make about six cups of compliment-worthy gazpacho. And it is guaranteed to make you feel somewhere between down home barefootin' it in blue jeans and evening dress sophisticated - depending on which direction your mood leads you!

Soup
1 large cucumber, peeled and chopped
2 cloves garlic, minced
1½ cups chicken broth
1 cup sour cream
½ cup plain yogurt
1 cup dry white wine
Salt and pepper to taste

Garnishes
2 medium tomatoes, peeled and diced
½ cup diced green onions (white part only)
½ cup chopped parsley or cilantro
½ cup slivered toasted almonds

Purée cucumber, garlic and one cup of chicken broth in blender. Remove from blender and place in large bowl. Purée remaining broth, sour cream, yogurt, wine, salt and pepper. Mix thoroughly with other ingredients in bowl.

Empty into quart jars and refrigerate at least two hours. This can be kept in the refrigerator for several days. The flavor actually improves with age!

To serve, place a cup of chilled gazpacho in each of six bowls. In separate small serving bowls, place the diced tomatoes, green onions, parsley and slivered almonds. Just as you did with the original Gazpacho Rojo, watch your guests serve themselves, spooning a bit of each condiment onto the top of their soup. Then sit back (one more time)

and grin up a storm as they applaud your culinary expertise!

JALAPEÑO-CILANTRO-CELERY SOUP

Last summer on a really hot, sticky Baja Sur day I looked into my refrigerator and saw a big bunch of celery and the rest of the ingredients listed below staring out at me. I went online and looked up celery soup - cold celery soup - and printed out four different recipes. I played around with them and using what was on hand, came up with this recipe. Terry and I thought it was a winner. It's refreshing and light, but filling. It's also great hot, as we discovered later on! Serves eight.

1 large bunch celery, chopped with stems
1 large white onion, chopped
1 yellow bell pepper, chopped
6 - 8 cloves garlic, minced
3 seeded jalapeños, minced
2 tbsp olive oil
6 cups vegetable or chicken broth
1 potato, peeled and grated
1 bunch cilantro, chopped
Salt and pepper to taste
½ cup crema media ácida or sour cream
Sprigs of celery leaf and cilantro for garnish

Sauté celery, onion, garlic, bell pepper, garlic and jalapeño in olive oil over medium heat until softened. Stir in broth and bring to boil. Grate in potato, reduce heat and simmer for 45 minutes. Stir in cilantro.

Puree soup in blender or food processor. Return to pan and stir in crema or sour cream. Season to taste with salt and pepper.

Garnish hot soup with a sprig of celery leaf and cilantro. For cold soup, chill and garnish.

AVOCADO SOUP

This rich and delicious soup combines the traditional with the unexpected. It is an easy-to-make chilled soup that looks (and tastes) wonderful served in glass bowls on a hot summer night. Originally inspired by a cruise my cousin took down the Mexican Riviera, I've tinkered with it over the years and recreated it into something a little less exotic and a little more down-to-earth. (Read that a little more authentically Baja!) This soup can be dinner party fare, beach picnic fare or just good eating in the backyard. Serves eight.

4 avocados, peeled and diced
4 cups chicken broth
Pepper to taste
4 cups crema media ácida or whipping cream
4 tbsp cognac
4 tbsp sherry

Purée avocado in food processor with

chicken bouillon. Season with pepper. Gradually stir in crema or whipping cream, retaining about 1/3 cup. Chill. Add cognac and sherry immediately prior to serving. Serve in glass bowls with a dollop of crema on top.

FIDEO TECATE

A border town, Tecate is world-famous for its beer, its health spa, Rancho La Puerta and its scenic plaza. On holiday weekends, rather than sit through nightmarish lines at the border crossings in Tijuana, I often chose the longer, but infinitely more scenic route from Ensenada to Tecate and crossed there. A lesser-known fact about that ride through the Guadalupe Valley along Mexico 3 is that it has become the premier wine-producing area in Mexico, the most well known of its vineyards being the Domeq and the L.A. Cetto Wineries, both of which conduct tours. Over a dozen small, boutique wineries have sprung up in the last decade. In winter and spring, I highly recommend making this drive. Recent rains will have made the hillsides lush and green. The mountains are strewn with spectacular rock formations and top out at 4,200 feet. Every August and September there are wine harvest festivals to check out.

One of my friends brought this recipe back to me after a camping trip in the mountains outside Tecate. Seems she had pilfered it off a waiter in town at some cute little outdoor café where she and her husband had stopped in for lunch. Fideo is vermicelli in tomato broth and can be best described as a Mexican or Latin American "spaghetti soup." Offered in place of rice and beans in parts of Baja, mainland Mexico and the Southwest, it's lightly spiced and quite flavorful. Serves six.

3 tbsp corn or canola oil
4 ounces very fine vermicelli
5 very ripe tomatoes
2 cloves garlic, minced
½ onion, chopped
3 cups chicken broth
4 cups water
Cilantro sprigs for garnish

In skillet, heat the oil until smoking. Fry vermicelli in bundles without breaking them up until they're a deep golden brown, stirring constantly. Drain off excess oil, leaving about one tablespoon in pan. Purée tomatoes with garlic and onion until smooth. Add to fried vermicelli and continue cooking over high heat, stirring constantly until mixture is almost dry. Add bouillon, water and bring to a boil. Lower heat and simmer until pasta is soft, about 20 minutes. Garnish with cilantro when serving.

CANTALOUPE SOUP BAHÍA CONCEPCIÓN

Just southeast of the steamy subtropical jungle of Mulege, almost two-thirds of the way down the penin-sula, is the incomparably lovely Bahía Concepción. It is one of the most-pho-tographed spots in all of Baja, and justly so. Its pristine white crescent sand beach-es surround an equally pristine, breath-takingly beautiful aquamarine bay. From one of our camping trips to the area comes this simple but distinctive chilled soup. The combination of cantaloupe and potato gives it a wonderfully rich flavor and texture. Serve it outdoors in the spring or summer and you'll be able to imagine yourself dining al fresco - under a palapa - on the shore of Bahía Concepción at Santispac Beach. Even if you can't be there, you're still guaranteed to get a flock of compliments. Serves six.

½ cup media crema or half and half
1 cup milk
½ cup water
1 cup potato, cooked, peeled and diced
3 cups cantaloupe, peeled and diced
¼ cup sherry
Salt to taste
Nutmeg and lime slices for garnish

Place the crema or half and half, milk, water, potato and cantaloupe in blender. Purée. Stir in sherry and season to taste with salt. Serve chilled in glass bowls, gar-nished with nutmeg and lime slices.

SOPA ROMPE CATRE - BROKEN COT SOUP

Next time you're in La Paz, you have to visit Marcelo, the owner of Mr. Azucar's

(Mr. Sugar's) Restaurant and Bar on 5 de Febrero, about four blocks off the malecón. He is an imaginative, competent chef whose story-telling abilities are legendary. His menu is extensive and his prices very good. So is the weekend musical entertainment. When I met him in 1997, he gave me the recipe for La Cola de la Sirena and it came with a story as delicious as the dip itself. This Broken Cot Soup is no different. He explained to me that when it's really hot and sticky in Mexico, people sleep on canvas and wood cots under a fan or outdoors. The married folks tend to get a little rowdy sometimes and have been known to break their cots and end up on the hard ground. He claims that this soup will induce such behavior because the catfish in it is an aphrodisiac! I can't vouch for the story, but if you try it and you break your cot, please let me know! This recipe serves about eight and the broth is wonderful with meat and nopales soup too!

2 pounds catfish fillet (no bones) cut into large chunks
1 pound crabmeat, cut into chunks
1 pound shrimp, skinned and deveined but with head attached
8 large tomatoes
2 tbsp vegetable oil
5 cups water
4 guajillo chiles, lightly toasted
20 chiles de arbol, lightly toasted
2 ancho chiles, slightly toasted
6 epazote leaves
2 medium white onions, puréed
10 cloves garlic, puréed
3 tbsp cider vinegar

¼ cup caldo de camarón o pollo (shrimp or chicken bouillon powder)
Salt and pepper to taste
8 large chunks queso fresco or feta cheese

In a large skillet, sauté tomatoes in oil until blackened and softened. Mix in bowl with one cup water, guajillo, arbol and ancho chiles. Add epazote, onion, garlic, vinegar and shrimp bouillon. Purée in food processor until completely liquefied.

In Dutch oven, place puréed chile mixture. Add remaining water, catfish, crab and shrimp. Bring to boil and simmer for three to four hours. Serve immediately with a chunk of queso fresco on the side. Now, prepare to play "crash the cot" tonight!

CHEESE AND ZUCCHINI SOUP

Have you ever planted a vegetable garden in your back yard, hoping to have a variety of fresh delicacies for your table - on the order of lettuce, cucumbers, tomatoes, maybe eggplant, watermelon and a few zucchinis? Was your garden like mine? By that I mean - did you end up with bushel after prolific bushel of zucchini and precious little else? Well, this recipe is from one of those summers in my life. I played around with an old recipe of my mom's from Ensenada for cheddar cheese soup and added a few other Mexican delicacies - and a whole lot of zucchini! It makes a perfect light meal served with hot buttered tortillas. Serves eight.

2 cans Campbell's cheddar cheese soup
2 large zucchini, cut into chunks
1 cup fresh corn off the cob
2 tomatoes, cored and cut into chunks
3 poblano chiles, blistered and peeled or 1 - 3½ ounce can diced green chiles
1 cup chicken broth
½ bunch cilantro, stems removed and chopped
1 bay leaf
1 tsp oregano
1 tsp basil
Salt and pepper to taste

If you have a gas stove, lay the chiles over the open flame and char skins well, turning with tongs frequently until they're uniformly blackened and stop snapping. The more charred they are, the easier it is to remove the skins. If you have an electric stove, place chiles in a large skillet on high heat. Turn frequently as above. Remove chiles to plastic bag, close it and let stand for 10 minutes. Remove from bag, place in ice-cold water and remove the stems, skins, veins and seeds.

Chop chiles and combine with all other ingredients in Dutch oven. Bring to boil, then reduce heat and simmer for at least one hour. Serve immediately.

EL CHILAR LOBSTER POPZOLE WITH CRAB

This is one of Armando Montaño's most famous creations. It illustrates how he takes a traditional Mexican dish like pozole and recreates it into a Nuevo Mexican extravaganza by using lobster, crab, chiles and spices. Ulises suggests that you serve this soup with a Santa Julia Torontes white wine. This grape grows in Argentina and has an aromatic flavor with hints of flowers and tropical fruits. Serves four.

Soup
4 cups white hominy (Armando suggests that you use canned)
2 lb lobster
2 quarts water
2 chiles guajillo, lightly toasted
2 chiles ancho, lightly toasted
1 tbsp corn or canola oil

---

2 bay leaves
1 tbsp oregano
Chile piquin powder to taste
2 cloves garlic, minced
1 onion, chopped
Salt and pepper to taste
1 lb crab, cleaned
1 tbsp olive oil
Juice of ½ limón (Mexican lime)
or key lime

Garnishes
¼ onion, chopped
½ cup lettuce, shredded
8 radishes, very thinly sliced
Tostadas (fried flat corn tortillas)
1 cup crema media ácida or ½ cup sour
cream and ½ cup whipping cream
Salt

In Dutch oven, place hominy, whole lobsters and water. Boil for five minutes, them remove lobster tails and leave heads and bodies to create stock. Cook over medium high heat for one hour. Remove and discard lobster shells.

In skillet, fry chiles in oil. Crumble bay leaves and oregano into chiles. Remove to blender or food processor and purée with ½ onion and garlic, adding a little broth so that the mixture becomes a thick paste. Add to stock. Add salt and pepper and cook an additional 30 minutes. Serve and garnish with the lettuce, onion and radishes and on the side place the tostadas with cream on top.

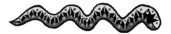

ALBONDIGAS SOUP

Albondigas, or Mexican Meatball Soup is a robust, tasty soup that can be served alone as a meal or as a first course. It's delicious and as typically Mexican as tortillas and beans. This recipe came from my mother's collection. In the late '60s, as my dad was finishing up construction on our family's "dream house," she flew off to Guadalajara, San Miguel de Allende and Mexico City with my Aunt Joan. The purpose of their trip was to decorate the new house. They had a major blast together, traipsing all over the place hunting up beautiful, finely crafted furniture, ordering custom handmade rugs and ferreting out folk art from all the different regions of Mexico. My mom's main goal was to find a hand-carved front door from the mission era. She found one, all right. In San Miguel de Allende. And she had it shipped home, along with the rest of her purchases. My parents don't own that dream house anymore, but I do know that the Mexican door still graces the house where I spent my teenage years. And ... guess who ended up with the best of the folk art?

My mom claimed that she combined a hastily scribbled list of ingredients (in Spanish of course) given her and Joan by a waiter in the El Presidente Hotel dining room in Mexico City on that trip with a recipe she conned from a waiter at Caesar's in Tijuana to come up with this soup. If she was telling the truth, then this soup is a hybrid from two internationally famous, historic Mexican restaurants. She modified it some herself, so that it's easier to make. Try it. You're guaranteed to love it! So will everyone else. Serves eight.

2 quarts beef broth
1 - 1 pound 12 ounce can tomato purée
2 medium onions, chopped
2 cloves garlic, minced
2 tbsp oregano
1 tbsp basil
2 bay leaves
1 cup salsa fresca (Salsa section)
1 lb ground beef
1 cup cooked white rice
1 tsp seasoned salt
½ tsp pepper
6 corn tortillas, cut in thin strips and fried

In Dutch oven, place beef broth, puréed tomatoes, half the onion and garlic, spices and salsa. Heat to boiling on high, then cover and reduce heat to low.

In large bowl, mix ground beef with cooked rice, the remaining onion and garlic, salt and pepper. Form into one inch round meatballs. Fry in a skillet until done. Drain. Add meatballs to broth and simmer for no more than one hour. Add the fried tortilla strips to garnish each bowl of soup. This soup may be kept in the refrigerator several days or part of it may be frozen for later use.

LENTIL SOUP BORRACHO

Uh Oh. Here it is. The concoction that just may transform you into an instant expatriate. Drunken Lentil Soup - now that's a name that really heats up the imagination! Seriously, though - I've never really heard of anyone running off into the wild blue yonder of Baja after indulging in this soup! In fact, it's superb in cold weather and has been one of Nina and my favorites forever. (We're still present and accounted for too - but not in San Diego. I went south to Baja and she went north ... to Washington.) The flavor of the beer greatly enhances this usually very sedate, traditional Mexican soup. Serves eight. So come on. Be brave. Try it! I dare you....

1 pound lentils, rinsed
3 - 12 ounce cans beer
4 cups chicken broth
1 cup celery, chopped
1 white onion, chopped
6 cloves garlic, minced
1 large tomato, finely diced
Juice from 5 limónes (Mexican limes) or key limes
4 fresh jalapeño or serrano chiles, thinly sliced with stems and seeds removed
2 dried ancho chiles, stems removed and chopped
1 tsp oregano
1 tbsp dried basil or 12 fresh leaves basil, finely chopped
Salt and pepper to taste
Cilantro sprigs and lime slices for garnish

Combine lentils, beer and broth in Dutch oven. Bring to boil, reduce heat and simmer. Add celery, onion, garlic, tomato, lime juice, chiles and spices to soup. Cook for four to six hours, until lentils begin to disintegrate and soup becomes creamy. Assist this process if you'd like with a potato masher! Garnish with cilantro sprigs and lime slices. Then serve and enjoy!

PANCHO'S TORTILLA SOUP

This delectable variation of an old Mexican favorite comes to you straight from Restaurant Pancho's in Cabo San Lucas. When I was asking the owner, Mary Bragg, what she was most famous for, she didn't hesitate one second before telling me, "Why our Tortilla Soup. Of course." Nina promptly ordered some, and since both of us are connoisseurs of tortilla soup, we were curious to see if Mary's would prove to be as memorable as she said.

She was right on. This soup is pure Baja Magic. While most versions I've run across use only one kind of broth, this one uses two ... one pot of chicken broth and another of Mary's salsa ranchera. Over the years (and after making this many times) I have combined the salsa recipe into the soup recipe for ease of preparation. It is incomparable served over crunchy, just fried tortilla strips and garnished with Mexican crema, fresh avocado chunks and cilantro!

This is a true culinary delight. And if you ever get to Cabo, be sure and visit Pancho's. We stop in for drinks or a meal whenever we're in town (which is often). The Mexican staff is entertaining, courteous and professional. Not only is the food delicious, but the restaurant's half palapa and half open air ambience is vintage Baja. And the decor - well, it's as festive as it comes with colorful handmade tablecloths, murals on the walls and papel picado (colored paper cutouts) streaming across the naked sky. Their in-house mariachis play those all-time Mexican favorites like "Cielito Lindo," "Rancho Grande," "La Bamba" and "Cuando Calienta el Sol." And, you know what else? You will fall in love with Mary's twinkling eyes and effervescent disposition. She started the premier wedding consultant in Los Cabos - so if you're in the mood for a Southern Baja wedding - Weddings in Paradise is who to call. As a host, John's no slouch either. He boasts the most extensive tequila collection in all of Mexico, with over 500 bottles! Check him out in the "From the Bar" Section of this book.
Serves eight to ten.

Soup
1 whole chicken
3 quarts water
4 tbsp powdered chicken bouillon
(Mary uses Knorr Suiza)
1 tbsp dried oregano

4 bay leaves
Salt and pepper to taste
5 poblano chiles, thinly sliced
8 large, ripe tomatoes, thinly sliced
2 large, white onions, thinly sliced
3 cloves garlic, minced

Garnishes
12 corn tortillas, cut into strips about ½ inch wide
½ cup corn or canola oil
2 avocados cut into chunks
1½ cup Chihuahua or jack cheese, grated
1 cup crema media ácida or sour cream
Fresh cilantro, in sprigs

Cook chicken in water and bouillon for one hour. Remove chicken, debone and cut into chunks. Return to pan, add seasonings and cover.

Place chiles, onion, tomatoes and garlic in large skillet with oil (this may take 2 skillets) and sauté until cooked, about 15 minutes.

About 20 minutes prior to serving, combine the chicken and stock with the vegetables and heat thoroughly.

Deep fry the tortilla strips and drain on paper towels. Divide each among eight to 10 large soup bowls. Fill almost to top with the soup. Then garnish with a few chunks avocado, some grated cheese, a float of crema and a sprig of cilantro. Serve immediately and prepare to gloat. Leftovers are great the next day too.

POZOLE

"No. I can't put menudo in my cookbook! I just can't do it. I know, I know. It's traditional. Everyone in Baja eats it. But it grosses me out! I can't bear the thought of eating tripe - or even looking at those slices of white stomach lining floating around loose in my soup bowl. Yuck!"

I couldn't do it. So I improvised and have included instead a bang-up, kick your tail feathers and take names pozole that I've had tons of fun experimenting with over the years. I like it so hot that only my bravest friends (and Nina of course) can stand it if I make it my way. So I don't let myself go crazy like that very often. I just add lots and lots of salsa on the side. This is truly a Baja favorite. If you want menudo, just sub-stitute tripe for the pork. I promise you that you will love it.

This is a January or February soup. One that will warm your innards on a rainy evening - and leave you feeling full and satisfied, even if you're in Akron, Ohio and not a deserted, windy bluff on the edge of the Pacific Ocean watching the sun sink into the cobalt sea as the last visible pod of gray whales for the day makes their way south in the fading light.... Ah yes. Enjoy this one. I sure do! Serves eight to ten.

Soup
2 lb lean pork roast, cut into bite-sized chunks (if you really want menudo, use tripe instead)
2 medium onions, chopped
6 cloves garlic, minced
2 - 4 tbsp American chili powder
3 whole cloves
2 tbsp oregano
6 cups water
4 tbsp chicken bouillon powder (or more, to taste)
2 - 16-ounce cans white hominy
Salt and pepper to taste

Garnishes
1 onion, chopped
¼ cup oregano
1 cup cilantro, chopped
1 cup fresh serrano chiles, finely diced (seeds and stems removed)
A sampler of salsas

In a large Dutch oven or crock-pot, place first eight ingredients. Heat to boiling and then cover and simmer for four to six hours. Add hominy and salt and pepper to taste. Cover and cook an additional hour.

To serve, place each garnish in a little bowl and let guests add whatever they want to their bowls of pozole. Sit down and chow down! Leftovers rock here too.

TÍO PABLO'S GREEN CHILE

Tío Pablos in Los Barriles is our neighborhood restaurant and a local landmark. It started as a taco shack back in 1989 selling hot dogs, ice cream and tacos. By 1994 Paul (Tío Pablo himself) had built a real restaurant with a store in the lobby. He says it gave Los Barriles credibility as being more than just a lonely Baja outpost with a few rustic fishing hotels. The menu is huge and offers up everything an expatriate could possibly get a craving for, plus it's open 365 days a year, even during hurricanes. Go in on a weekday afternoon and you'll be amazed by all the resident gringas hanging out in the shade, sipping iced tea and munching on nachos (they're humongous and ever-so-good!) while playing Mah Jong. Really!

Pablo is famous around town for his green chile, and since his recipe is superior to mine, I switched them this time around. It's really more a stew than a soup because it's so substantial. It's simple to prepare and the combination of flavors, after simmering together on your stove and filling your house with their aroma, will tantalize you with their magical taste. Serves ten to twelve.

1½ pounds very lean pork, cut in large chunks
2 tbsp corn or canola oil
2 large white onions, chopped
8 cloves garlic, minced
1 - 16 ounce can puréed tomatoes
½ gallon pork stock
3 jalapeños, chopped
1 - 27 ounce can whole green chiles, chopped
2 tbsp chicken bouillon powder
2 tbsp oregano
1 tbsp basil
2 bay leaves
1 tsp Worcestershire sauce
1 tsp seasoned salt
½ tsp pepper

In large Dutch oven sauté pork, onions and garlic in oil. Stir in tomatoes, pork stock and all other ingredients. Cook over medium high heat until boiling. Cover, reduce heat and simmer for two to three hours. This soup may be kept in the refrigerator several days or part of it may be frozen for later use.

SOPA DE CHILES EN NOGADA

I have a great friend who lives in Todos Santos named Suzanne. We met her and her husband Chuck camping on the beach at Cabo Pulmo in May and we instantly hit it off, snorkeling our brains out for days! Her house is adjacent to a chile field where poblanos are grown every year. After the chiles have been harvested in early June, she's invited to pick any leftover chiles for herself and her friends. Terry and I visited in mid-June and she made us this amazing creation for dinner. There were no pasas (raisins) anywhere in town, so we bought a box of Raisin Bran and fished out enough raisins to make this famous Mexican dish. The next morning she took me out and we filled giant grocery bags with fresh chiles. I went home and went on a poblano binge! I modified Suzanne's recipe and made a soup out it. I served it to my friends Kimberly and Jeff and they demanded the recipe. I gave it to them; now here it is for you. It serves four.

8 poblano chiles
4 tbsp butter
2 white onions, finely chopped
1½ tbsp flour
½ tsp white pepper
½ tsp nutmeg
6 cups chicken broth
1/3 cup raisins
1 green apple, peeled and cut in chunks
½ cup mango, peeled and cut in chunks
½ cup pineapple, peeled and cut in chunks
1¼ cup crema media ácida or sour cream
6 cups cubed cooked chicken
1½ cups chopped walnuts blanched in boiling water for 2 minutes

If you have a gas stove, lay the chiles over the open flame and char skins well, turning with tongs frequently until they're uniformly blackened and stop snapping. The more charred they are, the easier it is to remove the skins. If you have an electric stove, place chiles in a large skillet on high heat. Turn frequently as above. Remove chiles to plastic bag, close it and let stand for 10 minutes. Remove from bag, place in ice-cold water and remove the stems, skins, veins and seeds.

Melt butter in frying pan at medium heat. Add onions and cook until limp. Stir in flour, pepper and nutmeg and stir until bubbling. Add chicken broth, raisins and apples. Cook, stirring until softened. Add mango and pineapple. Gradually stir in crema or sour cream. Add chicken, chiles and gradually add more water and chicken broth until you reach desired consistency and flavor. Garnish each bowl of soup with a dollop of crema and some walnuts. It's awesome.

# SALADS

Customarily, Mexican food has always been served with refried beans and Mexican rice. While I love them, I prefer salad. In fact, I'm a serious salad-eater from way back. My love of fresh, crisp greens is hereditary, I'm certain of it.

There is a story about my grandfather that illustrates this. When he was in his mid-80s he went on a camping trip across Northern Baja with his octogenarian buddy Erle Stanley Gardner, which was chronicled in the book, **Mexico's Magic Square.** Now Mr. Gardner was one of the original Baja Aficionados. He was also a well known author and Hollywood celebrity. (In case you're too young to remember, he was the creator of the "Perry Mason" TV series.) He and Pappy were, after all, kindred spirits. In this book he explains his astonishment as Pappy (everyone called him Pappy - even Erle) broke open the first of several cases of lettuce on the first night in camp. He emphatically did not want to be caught out in the wilderness without his evening salad. Sure enough, the old guys enjoyed huge salads with their dinners every night.

A decade or so later, my parents went on a month-long camping trip down the west coast of mainland Mexico with my Aunt Hope and Uncle George. My mom came home shaking her head. She couldn't believe that my dad's kooky sister had stashed two cases of lettuce and one of cabbage in her motor home so that she wouldn't be without her salad in the evening! Didn't she know, my mom wondered, that they grew lettuce and cabbage in Mexico? Maybe not. Or maybe she was merely helpless to change the imprinting in her genes! She was Pappy's daughter, after all.

My goal in this section is to provide you with a variety of salads to enhance your menus, so that you can try a different one with each main course you prepare. In honor of our lean times, all salads use reduced amounts of oil, and in some cases, no oil what-soever. One ingredient I specify often that you may be unfamiliar with is jicama (hee-KUH-muh). It's a lightly sweet and crispy root vegetable that you should be able to locate if you ask the produce manager of your local grocery store. Most recipes have been improved and there are several new treats in here for you!

So get creative. Maybe - just maybe if you decide to rent yourself a motor home and travel Baja, you'll have become so addicted to eating salads with your Mexican food that you too will bring along your own cases of fresh lettuce and cabbage! But then, maybe not.... You know there are plenty of places to buy fresh greens along the way. Besides, you're not related to Pappy or Hope, are you?

Mexico's Magic Square was written by Erle Stanley Gardner and published by William Morrow & Company, Inc., New York, 1968. Other Baja travel books he wrote in the '60s are: **Off The Beaten Track in Baja**, **The Hidden Heart of Baja**, **Hovering Over Baja** and **Hunting The Desert Whale**. For a real treat and a tried-and-true taste of Baja back then, look for them in your local public library.

Pueblo Bonito Sunset Beach

PUEBLO BONITO CHILE FRUIT SALAD

There are four Pueblo Bonito resorts in Cabo San Lucas. Terry and I have had the pleasure of staying at three of them: Los Cabos, Rosé and Sunset Beach, which is our favorite. Located on the Pacific side of Cabo, light years (and seven minutes by free shuttle) away from everything, this hotel is on a private piece of coastline that seems to go on forever. It's terraced down a hillside and the grounds are breath-takingly beautiful and in total harmony with the environment. The views are expansive, the rooms luxurious but comfy-casual. Each has marble floors, a private oceanfront patio, TV with all the channels anyone could ever want, oversized shower and mini-bar.

Guests can walk or hitch a ride on a golf cart down the winding path that leads to the beach, pool and swim-up bar. The pool meanders along the beachfront, its waterfalls and bridges giving it the feel and look of a tropical lagoon. The swim-up bar and restaurant - instead of just offering underwater barstools - actually has booths, with tile tables above the water and underwater seating. This complex and delightful salad is indicative of the creative cuisine served at the Pueblo Bonitos. It is wonderful served with their special Baja Enchiladas (Enchilada section). Serves four.

½ cup each of diced pear, mango, papaya and apple
1 cup plantain banana, sliced and fried
8 strips of guajillo chile, fried and diced
1 tsp chives
Two pinches mint
Two pinches chopped basil
Juice of four limónes (Mexican limes) or key limes
Salt and pepper to taste

In salad bowl, combine diced fruit and guajillo chile. Add herbs and season with lime juice, salt and pepper. Serve and enjoy!

JICAMA PICO DE GALLO

Pico de Gallo (GUY-yoh) is half salsa and half salad. What makes my recipe unique is the jicama. Served on a bed of lettuce, this side dish is great with fajitas or most chicken and fish entrées. It's a Baja traveler's dream because all the ingredients can be purchased fresh at any roadside frutería. Serves eight.

Salad
3 cups jicama, peeled and diced
1 green bell pepper, seeded and slivered

1 red bell pepper, seeded and slivered
10 radishes, sliced
1 medium onion, thinly sliced
1 cucumber, peeled and diced
1 head iceberg lettuce

Dressing
¼ cup olive oil
¼ cup red wine vinegar
1 tsp oregano
Salt and freshly ground pepper to taste.

Combine jicama, peppers, radishes, onion and cucumber. Mix together oil, vinegar and oregano. Pour over vegetables and mix lightly. Add salt and pepper. Toss gently and serve on chilled plates over a bed of lettuce.

WILTED CABBAGE SALAD

I love Wilted Cabbage Salad. Nina and I created this recipe through trial and error copy-catting from our favorite Mexican restaurants in North San Diego County and a couple in northern Baja, which all serve some variation of cabbage salad with their meals. This recipe has evolved over the years, so it's not the same as in my first book. I guarantee that you too will love it even more! It's delicious, it's light and it's real change of pace from beans and rice. Serves eight.

Salad
1 head each purple and white cabbage, shredded

1 cup chopped celery
3 tomatoes, finely diced
12 radishes, finely diced
1 cup shredded carrots
6 cloves garlic, finely diced

Dressing

¼ cup cider vinegar
¼ cup rice vinegar
½ cup corn or canola oil
4 leaves fresh basil, finely chopped
or ½ tsp dried ground basil
¼ tsp finely ground oregano
Salt and freshly ground pepper to taste

In a large bowl, toss together shredded cabbage, celery, tomatoes, radishes, shredded carrots and garlic. Refrigerate for up to three hours. Just prior to serving, mix vinegar, oil and spices in a small bowl. Heat for 45 - 60 seconds in a small saucepan or in the microwave, until very hot. Pour over cabbage salad, toss and serve immediately.

AVOCADO - TOMATO SALAD

I created this recipe on a camping trip to Bay of L.A. with my kids and some friends because I'd forgotten to pack any vegetable or olive oil in our motor home. Since we'd shopped in Ensenada on our way south, I did have plenty of avocados, so I decided to let the natural oils inherent in the avocados act as my salad oil. It worked! They blended with the other ingredients to make create a

remarkable and delicate salad. For a dish that started out as a semi-accident, this turned out to be really, really good. It serves eight.

Salad
4 large ripe avocados
8 tomatoes, diced
2 onions, diced
1 green bell pepper, diced
1 red bell pepper, diced
6 large radishes, diced
4 cloves garlic, minced
1 large bunch cilantro with stems removed and diced
1 large head romaine lettuce (to line plates)

Dressing
½ cup cup limón (Mexican lime) or key lime juice
1½ tsp seasoned salt
Freshly ground pepper

Cut avocados in half. Remove seed and peel each half. Cut into one-inch chunks. Place in medium sized bowl with tomatoes, onion, red and green bell peppers, radishes, garlic and cilantro. Sprinkle with lime juice, salt and pepper.

Toss gently. Refrigerate, covered up to three hours. Line chilled salad plates with romaine leaves. Spoon avocado-tomato mixture on top.

SPANISH RICE SALAD SANTIAGO

This is an unexpected and original way to serve rice. We were served it at the Hotel Palomar, Santiago's renowned outdoor restaurant after a trip to the Santiago Zoo when my kids were really little. Not only does Santiago have the only zoo in all of Baja, but it's also a lovely farming community situated on a pair of hills separated by a wide, shallow, palm-laden huerta (valley). It's located just north of the Tropic of Cancer, just off Highway 1 and a bit northwest of Cabo Pulmo. Nearby is also the longest waterfall in Baja Sur: La Cola de la Zorra. Hike up there sometime and dive off the rocks into the cool, clear mountain water. Amazing. Then stop for lunch at the Hotel Palomar.

Salad
4 cups chilled, cooked white rice
1 cup chilled, thinly sliced cooked carrots
1 cup chilled, cooked cauliflowerettes
1 large tomato, chopped
½ bunch green onions, sliced white part only

Dressing
½ cup corn or canola oil
1 tsp onion juice

¼ cup wine vinegar
2 tsp celery seeds
1 tsp dry mustard
1 tsp sugar
Salt and freshly ground pepper to taste
1 - 3½ ounce can sliced black olives, drained as garnish

Combine rice, carrots, cauliflowerettes, tomato and green onions in large salad bowl. Combine oil, vinegar and onion juice, vinegar, and all spices in small jar. Shake well. Pour over salad and toss lightly. Garnish with black olives.

TOMATILLO - TOMATO - PANELA SALAD

Panela is a mild Mexican cheese that is similar in texture and flavor to mozzarella. This elegant, subtly flavored salad will delight and amaze guests at even the most upscale dinner party, yet it's quick and easy to make. Served on colorful Mexican plates, it is a work of art in red, green and white - the national colors of Mexico! Serves four.

½ pound tomatillos
¼ cup orange juice
¼ cup limón (Mexican lime)
or key lime juice
¼ tsp salt
¼ tsp pepper
¾ cup olive oil
4 large tomatoes

¾ pound panela (or mozzarella) cheese
Cilantro sprigs for garnish

Peel and wash tomatillos. Slice very thinly and place in marinade of orange and lime juice, salt, pepper and olive oil. Cover and marinade for two to four hours in refrigerator.

Slice tomatoes thinly and arrange in circular pattern on four salad plates. Place a smaller circle of thin slices of cheese on top of the tomatoes. On top, place an even smaller circle of marinated tomatillos and sprinkle extra marinade/dressing over entire salad. Garnish with cilantro sprigs.

AUNT HOPE'S FIRST-NIGHT-IN-CAMP COLE SLAW

I used to love going camping with Aunt Hope and Uncle George. Why? Hope made the best salads around (it was genetic, remember?) and George used to sneak out in the bushes with me and we'd smoke cigarettes and gossip like buddies together. Neither Hope or George are around anymore, but I can still make Aunt Hope's Cole Slaw and be instantly transported three or four decades back in time to some deserted Baja beach at the end of a dusty day of driving. She'd make it before we left home and serve it with a casserole my mom had made ahead of time. It didn't matter what she served it with. It was a tradition and it is still the best cole slaw I've ever tasted!

The original dressing was made of half mayonnaise and half Durkee's sauce, but I changed it because I had countless frustrated people writing to tell me they couldn't find it in their grocery store. We found it the other day at Arramburo's in San Jose del Cabo!

Try it and you will be amazed - even if you can't abide cole slaw. Hers is unique and guaranteed to disappear in record time. Whenever I serve it to a group, it never lasts long enough for second servings. Try it with just about anything - whatever you're in the mood for. Just be sure you have plenty of ice cold beverages on hand to wash the road dust from the back of your tongue! Serves eight, más o menos.

Cole Slaw
1 extra large or 2 medium heads, cabbage, shredded (but not too finely)
1 - 2 bunches green onions, sliced all the way to the ends
2 - 8 ounce packages of slivered almonds, toasted until lightly browned

Dressing
1 cup mayonnaise
1/3 cup Dijon mustard
1 tbsp cider vinegar
Coarsely ground pepper to taste

In small bowl, mix together mayonnaise, mustard and vinegar. Set aside. In very large bowl, place cabbage, onions, almonds and dressing. Wash your hands and use them to thoroughly mix everything. Move to serving bowl and top with pepper. Refrigerate from two to 24 hours. It will keep for up to three days in the refrigerator. Watch out! You'll catch people eating the leftovers for breakfast. I do!

ENSALADA CHILENO BAY

Nina maintains that the best beach in all of Los Cabos is at the Hotel Cabo San Lucas. It's called Chileno Bay and it's famous for its underwater rock formations and awesome diving. Although I don't scuba dive, I do snorkel and I can vouch for Chileno Bay being jam-packed with wildly colored tropical fish.

This salad was inspired by a trip our family took to Cabo when I was seven months pregnant with Derek. We stayed at the Hotel Cabo San Lucas and swam in Chileno Bay every day for nearly a week. The water was heavenly, especially to someone as awkward, overloaded and overheated as I was! Only underwater did I feel graceful, buoyant and cool!

In hot weather like we have in Cabo during the summer months, a crunchy, cooling tropical salad like this one is a real delight. Anytime of year it's an ideal companion to hot, spicy dishes. The medley of tangy fruits and vegetables will not only surprise and delight your palate, but it may even get you started believing you've just come in from spending a day snorkeling Chileno Bay. Or perhaps you've just gotten back from a long day of fishing off the coast of Los Cabos. As you take your first bite of this salad, you'll look across the patio of the outdoor restaurant of the Hotel Cabo San Lucas and marvel at the dimming colors of the sunset. You'll relive the day's events, seeing again in your mind the crystal clear aquamarine water teeming with abundant, colorful undersea life. And you will smile. It doesn't get any better than this! Serves eight.

Salad
2 heads iceberg, butter or romaine lettuce (or combination)
1½ cups jicama, sliced in strips
1 red onion, sliced
1 grapefruit
2 oranges
½ pound cherry tomatoes, halved

Cumin Dressing
3 tbsp cider vinegar
2 tbsp juice from limónes (Mexican limes) or key limes
6 tbsp olive oil
2 cloves garlic, minced
½ tsp ground cumin
¼ tsp crushed red pepper
Salt and freshly ground pepper to taste
1 large avocado as garnish

Mix lettuce and jicama in large salad bowl. Arrange onion rings on top. Peel grapefruit and oranges, removing all white membrane from sections. Arrange with tomatoes on top of onions. Cover and chill for one to two hours.

To make Cumin Dressing, combine vinegar, lime juice, oil, garlic and spices in food processor. Whirl until blended.

Pour on dressing and toss gently. Serve immediately with sliced avocado as garnish.

MOLDED GAZPACHO SALAD

This recipe was a favorite of my mother's. It's an exotic salad with a Spanish heritage. It's simple to prepare, but delectable - and elegant enough to grace the table any ladies' luncheon. Or perhaps, like me, you'd rather be sitting on the terrace of a remote Baja resort like Punta Pescadero on the East Cape between La Paz and Los Cabos watching the iguanas playing and sunbathing on the rocks leading down to the beach. Either way, you will enjoy this exquisite salad. It serves eight.

1 envelope plain gelatin
1½ cups tomato juice
½ cup red wine
1 large tomato, chopped
1 cucumber, peeled and chopped
1 green bell pepper, seeded and chopped
2 tbsp diced green chiles
¼ cup green onions, sliced
2 cloves garlic, minced
Salt and freshly ground pepper to taste
Romaine leaves, rinsed and dried

Soften gelatin in ¼ cup warmed tomato juice. Heat remaining juice until almost boiling. Add gelatin mixture and stir until dissolved. Add wine, vegetables and seasoning. Pour into a one-quart mold. Chill overnight. Unmold on a platter lined with romaine leaves.

of pace. If you prefer a lighter dressing, try adding an eight-ounce container of non-fat fruit yogurt instead. Serves ten.

Salad
1 large watermelon, well chilled
1 honeydew melon and/or cantaloupe, scooped into balls
1 cup seedless grapes
1 cup peaches and/or mangoes, diced
1 cup strawberries, halved
1 apple, diced
1 cup sliced bananas, sprinkled with lemon juice
½ cup chopped walnuts

Dressing
1 cup whipping cream
2 tbsp powdered sugar
½ tsp salt
2 avocados, halved, seeded, peeled and mashed
½ cup pineapple juice
1 tsp finely chopped candied ginger

Trace a zigzag pattern horizontally around the top third of the watermelon. Cut through melon with sharp knife, removing top. Scoop out all the watermelon flesh except a shell one inch thick. Scoop removed watermelon into balls.

Combine all fruit and walnuts in the watermelon bowl. Chill until ready to serve. To make dressing, whip cream until it has stiff peaks. Add powdered sugar and salt. Blend avocados, pineapple juice and candied ginger until thick and creamy. Fold into whipped cream mixture. Pour over salad and toss gently. Serve.

WATERMELON FRUIT SALAD

In summer and fall, whenever you're driving through Baja, it's not uncommon to spot a truck (oh, I mean troque) parked every mile or two along the side of the road, its tailgate down and its bed over-flowing with sandías, or in English, watermelons. The fruit is just-picked, it's cheap and it's a treat and a half. My family loves watermelon. In fact, it's difficult for me to imagine a summer bar-becue (on either side of the border) without a scooped-out watermelon filled with fruit. The avocado dressing sug-gested here is a rich, Baja-style change

MARINATED VEGETABLE SALAD

Marinated Vegetable Salad is a crowd pleaser any time of the year. Healthy and easy to prepare, it gets an unexpected Baja flavor boost from the tangy salsa verde. Serves eight.

Salad
1 zucchini, thinly sliced
1 cucumber, thinly sliced
1 green bell pepper, seeded and slivered
1 onion, thinly sliced
2 tomatoes cut into thin wedges
1 - 7 ounce can black olives

Dressing
¼ cup olive oil
¼ cup lemon juice
1 tsp garlic powder
½ to 1 cup salsa verde (Salsa section)
Salt and freshly ground pepper to taste

Combine vegetables together in salad bowl. Prepare dressing by combining oil, lemon juice, salsa verde, garlic powder, salt and pepper in jar. Shake well. Drizzle dressing over salad. Toss gently. Cover and chill one hour before serving to blend flavors.

TEAQUE SLAW

My friend Leslie was raised in New Mexico and then in El Centro, just a few miles from the Mexican border town of Mexicali. A wife of one of the bruseros (farm hands) who worked for her dad passed this recipe on to Leslie's mom a number of years ago. The first time she made it for me, Leslie explained that it's better the second day - and my birthday was the next day - so she made it the day ahead. The problem was, by the next morning it was long gone! There were five of us staying in our La Bufadora house, and even though she made a double batch, between us, we annihilated it! While nothing like Wilted Cabbage Salad or Aunt Hope's First Night in Camp Coleslaw, this slaw (pronounced Tay-AH-kay) is every bit as good. And just as simple to make too. This serves six, but obviously not six of us!

Slaw
1 large head cabbage, shredded
1 lb Chihuahua or jack cheese, grated
2 large tomatoes, chopped
1 large white onion, chopped
2 - 3 fresh jalapeños, chopped
¼ cup cilantro, chopped

Dressing
¼ cup olive oil
¼ cup red wine vinegar
1 tsp oregano
Salt and freshly ground pepper to taste.

Combine all ingredients and chill overnight (if you're lucky) in the refrigerator.

THE ORIGINAL ENSALADA CÉSAR

Did you know that the Caesar Salad originated in Tijuana? Yes. It did. At Restaurante César on Avenida Revolución, the main drag in TJ. Two Italian brothers named Alex and César Cardini owned the restaurant and created the salad in the late 1920s. Over the years, the spelling has changed, but the salad remains the same and has become famous the world over. All over Baja and mainland Mexico, white-jacketed waiters slide carts alongside diners' tables and whip these salads together exactly the way the Cardini brothers did. My mother swore this is their original recipe. I've had Ensalada César a number of times at Restaurante César, and it tastes like the same recipe I have here. It is an edible art form in Mexico and one you should go out of your way to try in your travels south of the border.

A few words about Tijuana ... did you know it boasts the busiest border in the entire world? It's also the largest city in Baja, with a population estimated (read that guess-timated) at over two and a half million. It hit its stride as a border city in that interesting span of time from 1920 -1933 when Prohibition eliminated legal partying in the US. All of a sudden cantinas (bars) and casinos sprang up all over the place as the gringos flocked to Tijuana to play. When Prohibition was repealed, the government made Tijuana into a duty free port and it quickly became a destination for world-class shoppers. These days you can buy Cuban cigars - legally there as Aeromexico flies to Havana from Tijuana daily. Do the gringos buy them? You bet they do!

Back to the salad ... nowadays anybody can buy bottled Caesar dressing and whip together a Caesar Salad in just a few minutes. No big deal. But - if you want the "real deal," try this recipe. Trust me, it's more than worth the effort, even if you make it in the kitchen and not tableside! Serves six.

Salad
1 large or 2 small heads romaine lettuce
Croutons
6 slices sour dough bread
1 stick butter, melted
1 tbsp parsley
1 tbsp garlic powder

Dressing
1 - 2 tsp anchovy paste
1/3 cup lemon juice (fresh if possible)
½ cup olive oil
1 tsp Worcestershire sauce
2/3 cup grated Parmesan cheese (fresh if possible)
2 cloves garlic, minced
Salt and freshly ground pepper to taste
1 coddled (boiled 1 minute) egg

To make croutons, preheat oven to 325°. Cut bread into half-inch chunks. Melt butter with parsley and garlic. Toss with bread until evenly coated. Place on baking sheet and bake until crisp and lightly browned, approximately 20 minutes, turning when half-cooked. Cool on paper towels.

To make dressing, combine anchovy paste, lemon juice, olive oil, Worcestershire sauce, Parmesan cheese, minced garlic, salt and pepper in jar. Shake well until mixed. Refrigerate at least an hour.

To make salad, rinse romaine leaves and tear into bite-sized pieces. Place in chilled salad bowl. When croutons have completely cooled, add them to salad. Immediately before serving, break coddled egg into dressing, pour over greens and toss gently. Serve immediately.

CHOPPED MEXICAN MEDLEY SALAD

This tangy, crunchy salad is "to die for." Its combination of northern and southern Baja flavors makes it perfect with spring and summer meals. It's a one-of-a-kind subtropical treat, no doubt about it! Where did it come from? Me! I made it up one creative afternoon in my La Buf house when I was wondering how to use up the overabundance of fresh produce Nina and I had alternately purchased at Calimax! We had a big fiesta that night and everyone there swore it was a true Baja-lovers delight! Serves eight.

Salad
1½ heads romaine lettuce, chopped
1½ pounds jicama, peeled and finely diced

6 seedless oranges, peeled and chopped into squares
2 red onions, finely diced
1 medium bunch cilantro, stems removed and finely diced
4 stalks celery, finely diced
1 large bell pepper, finely diced

Dressing
1/3 cup olive oil
1/3 cup juice from limónes (Mexican limes) or key limes
3 tbsp red wine vinegar
3 tbsp orange marmalade
¼ cup salsa verde
1 tsp garlic powder
Salt and freshly ground pepper to taste

Combine all salad ingredients in a large bowl. Chill in refrigerator up to four hours. Right before serving, add salad dressing ingredients, one at a time to the salad. Toss lightly and serve.

CELIA'S SUMMER NOPALES SALAD

Celia owns one of the restaurants in La Bufadora.
Let me tell you - not only does the lady know how to cook, but also she is a veritable fount of information on how to get along in Baja. She understands the culture, she knows the rules, and if she likes you, she may even give you a pointer or two on how to play the game.

You can pick the nopales (tender, young prickly pear shoots) yourself in spring and early summer if you live in Baja or the southwest. If you do, be sure to wear gardening gloves to avoid being pricked by the thorns. Or, if you have a Latino market near your home, you can buy fresh nopales already cut and cleaned in the produce section. They're also sold in jars. Indigenous to Mexico, nopalitos have long been recognized as having healing powers. They help lower cholesterol and control diabetes. If you don't try this at home, then visit La Bufadora and try it at Celia's. Be sure to order a giant Margarita and some of her killer nachos to go with it. Serves eight.

Salad
2 pounds of nopales (tender, young prickly pear shoots)
1 tbsp salt
1 tsp pepper
1 tbsp garlic powder
½ onion

2 quarts water
2 onions, chopped
4 stalks celery, chopped
½ bunch cilantro, chopped
3 large tomatoes, diced
Salt and pepper to taste
2 cups shredded mozzarella cheese
½ cup Parmesan cheese

Dressing
½ cup olive oil
½ cup red wine vinegar
1 tsp oregano
Salt and freshly ground pepper to taste.

If using freshly picked nopales, soak in water until thorns are soft, then remove with the point of a knife. Rinse well under cold water. Cut into strips one inch long. Place in Dutch oven and add water, salt, pepper, garlic powder and onion. Heat to boiling and simmer 20 minutes. Drain and wash them, discarding all excess liquid.

(Note: Canned nopales are pre-cooked. Fresh nopales from the grocery store come cleaned but must be cooked.)

Put nopales in salad bowl with chopped onion, celery, cilantro and tomatoes. Toss with salad dressing and mozzarella cheese. Add salt and pepper to taste and chill. Immediately before serving, top with Parmesan cheese.

SALADS THAT MAKE A MEAL

I confess - I like few things better than going out to lunch. It has something to do, I believe, with my genetically inherited salad addiction! Give me an innovative lettuce-based creation, a bottomless glass of iced tea and a good friend - and I am one happy lady.

My sister Nina loves to go out to lunch as much as I do. Not only did she inherit Pappy and Hope's salad addiction, but she and I also inherited (from whom we're not entirely sure because no one from the older generation would ever admit it) a serious salsa addiction. And, in differing levels of intensity, we both inherited from our mom the passion for visiting a restaurant, ordering different, but equally luscious-sounding salads, sharing bites and analyzing the ingredients while drinking copious amounts of iced tea (or Diet Coke in her case).

While eating, we indulge in what our father calls the "wandering fork" syndrome. This means we feel free to dive into each other's food without making any big fuss about it! We share and then we compare notes. If we're especially impressed by one of the salads we ordered, we check out the ingredients with our server. Then one or both of us will go home and experiment with the recipe - always changing a few things so we can indulge our creativity and at the same time avoid getting ourselves in trouble.

While most of these recipes in this section are derived from genuine Mexican dishes, two or three came from our forays into Southern California Restaurant-Land. (Will I let you know which ones? Maybe - but you can't expect me to divulge all our secrets now, can you?) There are three especially delicious new additions - the Tenth Anniversary Salad from Caffé Todos Santos, Tropicana Camarrón y Callo Salad and Scallop and Shrimp Ceviche Salad. Most recipes have been altered and improved too.

Fix one of these salads for your best friend, your mate, your entire family or for a crowd. They're all suitable for either lunch or dinner, depending on your appetite and prefer-ence. For the utmost in dining pleasure - pick a warm day and dine outdoors with a vase of fresh flowers on the table. Take off your shoes so you can wiggle your toes in the grass. Put on some mariachi or flamenco guitar music. Or something soothing and mystical from the Andes of Perú. As you dip your fork into your salad, picture yourself on a tiled terrace high above the sea. Listen to those waves as they break on the rocks below you. Inhale the aroma of Mexico. Look up to the skies and imagine a formation of pelicans banking around the corner of the bay below you. Sigh deeply and relish that first bite as the magic of Baja flows through your veins.

CAFFÉ TODOS SANTOS TENTH ANNIVERSARY SALAD

When I tell my friends who've been to (or live in) Todos Santos recently that Marc Spahr gave me the recipe for his Tenth Anniversary Salad for Baja Magic Dos, their eyes light up and then start to glaze over. This salad is famous in Baja Sur and it is amazing. While Marc created it in 2003 to commemorate his ten years in business, he didn't get around to having his tenth anniversary party until February 2005. Sounds like Baja, huh? Oh ... and he asked me to let everyone know that he finally attended a professional cooking school for two weeks - in Paris during the summer of 2004! This recipe will feed four people and it's guaranteed to totally blow your mind (and your taste buds) in a thoroughly wonderful way!

1 cup Thai peanut sauce
1½ cups coconut milk
1/8 cup Thai curry paste
½ tsp yellow Indian curry powder
2 boneless, skinless chicken breasts cut in strips
¼ package Juto-Naga Udon noodles (about 1 cup Thai rice noodles) cooked and cooled
3 cups exotic leaf lettuce (mixed baby field greens)
½ cup dried cranberries
½ cup pistachios
½ cup dried mango, cut into ¼ inch strips
¼ cup toasted sunflower seeds
½ cup jicama, cut into ¼ inch strips
2 tangerines, peeled and sectioned
1 cup dried chow mein noodles
½ cup crumbled feta cheese

In large skillet, combine Thai peanut sauce, coconut milk and curries. Add chicken strips and dried mango strips and cook until chicken is done. Remove chicken strips and grill over barbecue until golden brown to give them a smoky taste. Set the mango strips aside to cool.

Pour the coconut milk-curry-peanut sauce mix into a bowl and cool by placing another bowl of ice underneath it. (This will now become the salad dressing.)

In large salad bowl, place a layer of Thai noodles. Add lettuce, nuts, feta cheese, tangerines, cranberry, mango, jicama, chicken strips and Chow mein noodles. Toss lightly with dressing and serve immediately.

TACO SALAD

No, this is not a replica of the taco salad that arrives in a greasy bowl made from a deep-fried flour tortilla and contains more calories than most adult women are supposed to consume in a 24 hour period! This recipe is lighter and more authentically Baja. It makes an outrageous lunch or light dinner for two hungry people. It can be made with beef, chicken or turkey, the recipes for which can be found in the Tacos, Burritos and Tostadas section of this cookbook. Vary the salsas (use either ready-made or a recipe from this book) to suit the meat and your mood both.

Salad
½ pound shredded beef, chicken or turkey
½ cup pinto beans from can, rinsed and drained
1 head iceberg lettuce, torn into bite sized pieces
1 - 3½ ounce can sliced olives, drained
½ bunch green onions, chopped
1 large tomato, diced

Dressing
¼ cup salsa of your choice
½ cup Italian salad dressing
Salt and freshly ground pepper to taste

Garnish
1 avocado, peeled and sliced
1 cup Mexican cacique, feta or cheddar cheese, grated
1½ cups tortilla chips

On the bottom of a large salad bowl, layer shredded meat, pinto beans and lettuce. Top with olives, green onions and tomatoes. Refrigerate up to one hour.

In a small bowl mix salsa and salad dressing. Just prior to serving, Add avocado, grated cheese and tortilla chips as top layer. Toss salad gently with dressing and serve immediately.

TROPICANA ENSALDA DE CAMARON Y CALLO- SHRIMP & SCALLOP SALAD

San Jose del Cabo has evolved into an art, artesano and culinary mecca to rival San Miguel de Allende on the mainland. I was stunned on a recent visit. Having lived an hour north of there for a year and a half, our forays into town were always errand-oriented. We never spent the night and just cruised around. Well, Nina and I did in March 2005 and stayed at the Tropicana Inn, Bar and Grill right on the main drag in the heart of town. Boy, have things changed in San Jose! This hotel is one of the loveliest in Mexico, if you're into colonial architecture and furnishings, fountains, lush gardens, beautiful art, top notch service and incredible food. They offer up live music, including reggae, tropical Latino and mariachi, every night but Tuesday. From the hotel it's a short walk to the galleries, artesano and jewelry shops and of course, the restaurants.

I will say ... in my opinion ... San Jose's restaurants are the best in Baja. And the overall feel of the town is classy, friendly, colorful and oh so Mexico! Jorge Hijar, the manager of the Tropicana, gave us this recipe. It was the special of the day when we were there, and Nina said it was incredible. Serves four.

Salad
1 lb cocktail size shrimp
1 lb bay scallops

2 tbsp butter
Salt to taste
2 cloves garlic, minced
1 tbsp Cajun seasoning
1 tbsp yellow curry powder
1 large head romaine, torn into bite sized pieces
1 head escarole, torn into bite sized pieces
1 carrot, shredded
½ lb jicama, cut into very thin strips
16 cherry tomatoes, halved
1 cucumber, peeled and sliced
Paprika and 4 tbsp mango chutney for garnish

Dressing
¾ cup mayonnaise
1 clove garlic, minced
4 tbsp yellow curry powder

In large skillet, sauté the shrimp in butter for five minutes. Add scallops and sauté an additional two to three minutes. Add garlic, salt, Cajun spice and curry. Remove from stove and keep warm.

Mix all other salad ingredients, except tomatoes and cucumber in large bowl. Place a serving of salad on each of four chilled plates. Arrange tomatoes and cucumbers around the edges, then place seafood on top of salad and drizzle the dressing over it. Add a dollop of mango chutney to each plate and lightly sprinkle the edges with paprika.

HOT CARNITAS SALAD CHAPALA

This is not my original recipe for Carnitas Salad. In the summer of 2004, Terry and I went on a three-month road trip in our camper. We visited Nina and John in their new home in northern Washington, toured Vancouver Island and then headed over to Idaho to visit some old and new friends. We were all set up to camp at Ponderosa State Forest for a week or so. Then the rain started. It lasted a week. After two days, I told Terry, "Not only am I not cut out to be a fulltime road warrior, but there is no way I can live in a 10-foot box with two dogs when it's pouring rain and there's mud everywhere!" We moved to a hotel. Within three days we'd bought a small cabin in the forest. We now have a summer casita in McCall, Idaho. It has a small-town, laid back and friendly attitude that reminds us of Baja. It's just as beautiful, in an entirely different way. You'll find us there every summer.

There is a top notch, authentic Mexican restaurant (actually run by Mexicans) right on Lake Payette in McCall. It's called Chapala. The view and ambience are as good as the food and their carnitas salad is even better than mine was, so I have made a few changes to my recipe to add a bit of Chapala pizzazz. The recipe for carnitas is in the carnitas, Fajitas and Carne Asada Barbecues section of this cookbook. Serves two hungry people for lunch or a light dinner.

Salad
½ pound carnitas

½ pound queso Chihuahua or jack cheese, grated
½ small can sliced black olives
½ bunch green onions, chopped
6 radishes, sliced
1 tomato, diced
1 avocado, peeled and sliced
¼ cup salsa verde
1 head iceberg lettuce, chopped

Dressing
½ cup crema media ácida or sour cream
¼ cup juice from limónes (Mexican limes) or key limes
2 tbsp olive oil
2 tsp garlic powder
1 tsp basil
Salt and freshly ground pepper to taste

Use hot, freshly made carnitas or heat leftover carnitas in saucepan or microwave until steaming. Remove and divide between two plates. Top each with grated cheese.

On the bottom of a large salad bowl, layer olives, green onions, radishes and tomatoes. Add avocado, salsa verde and lettuce as top layer.

Put salad plates with carnitas and cheese into microwave and nuke until cheese is melted and bubbling.

  In small bowl mix together crema or sour cream, lime juice, olive oil, garlic powder, basil, salt and pepper. Pour dressing over lettuce mixture, toss gen-

tly and heap on top of carnitas and cheese. Serve immediately.

CARNE ASADA SALAD

This salad is another winner. The carne asada (marinated flank or skirt steak) is superb, low in fat and this salad is a perfect way to enjoy the subtle flavor of the meat. The recipe for carne asada is in the Carnitas, Fajitas and Carne Asada Barbecues section of this cookbook. Serves two hungry people for lunch or a light dinner.

Salad
½ pound carne asada, chilled
½ bunch green onions, chopped
¼ cup salsa fresca (Salsa section)
1 tomato, diced
1 cup queso cacique, feta or cheddar cheese, grated
1 head romaine or iceberg lettuce, torn into bite sized pieces
1½ cups tortilla chips

Dressing
1/3 cup Italian salad dressing
Salt and freshly ground pepper to taste

Garnish
½ cup guacamole
¼ cup crema media ácida or sour cream
2 whole black olives

On the bottom of a large salad bowl, layer carne asada, green onions, salsa, and tomatoes. Add grated cheese and lettuce as top layer. Refrigerate up to one hour.

Prior to serving, add salad dressing, salt and pepper. Toss gently. Line two salad plates with tortilla chips. Serve salad onto the plates. Top each serving with half the guacamole mixture and half the crema or sour cream. Place an olive on top of each salad and serve immediately.

GRILLED FAJITAS SALAD
Chicken, Beef or Shrimp

Now here's a salad with real Baja Magic flair. Grilled Fajitas Salad combines the unique flavors of jicama and Mexican pepitas (toasted pumpkin seeds) that are totally Mexican with hickory-smoked chicken and a few other eclectic treats. The dressing is a not-overwhelmingly spicy chile vinaigrette that will surprise and delight you.

Nina, another woman friend and I came up with this one. We mixed ingredients from our favorite salads at two different, but equally celebrated restaurants. One is in San Diego. The other is in Cabo San Lucas. Should you wish to tantalize your taste buds by experimenting with ingredients yourself, try using hickory-smoked beef or even broiled shrimp instead of chicken. It will be a highly unforgettable experience no matter

which way you prepare it. Just do me one favor. If it's a beautiful, warm day - eat outdoors. Barefoot ... with Latino music playing in the background. Serves two hungry people.

Fajitas
2 boneless, skinless chicken breasts or ½ pound round steak or
½ pound deveined shrimp marinated in
½ cup hickory marinade

Salad
½ red bell pepper, very thinly sliced and lightly sautéed
½ red onion, very thinly sliced and sautéed until wilted
½ head romaine, torn into bite size pieces
2 cups field greens (endive, radicchio and other red leaf lettuces)
¼ cup very thinly sliced red cabbage
½ cup jicama, sliced into thin strips
1 tomato, diced
½ cucumber, peeled and diced
¼ cup roasted pepitas (pumpkin seeds) or sunflower seeds (if unavailable)
½ cup queso cacique or feta cheese, crumbled
1 avocado, diced

Dressing
2 tbsp diced jalapeños
¼ cup balsamic vinegar
¼ cup olive oil
Juice of one limón (Mexican lime) or key lime
2 tsp garlic powder
1 tsp basil
Salt and freshly ground pepper to taste

Marinade chicken, beef or shrimp in hickory

marinade for one half hour. Grill, either under the broiler or on the barbecue until done. Slice chicken or beef (not shrimp) into thin strips and chill.

Sauté red bell peppers in skillet. Remove and drain. Sauté onions. Remove and drain. Place at bottom of large salad bowl. Layer with all other salad ingredients. Chill for up to thirty minutes.

In small bowl, stir together all dressing ingredients. Pour over salad and toss, adding chicken, beef or shrimp last. Serve immediately on chilled plates.

CAESAR SALAD
Chicken, Prime Rib or Shrimp

It seems that every trendy restaurant in Southern California (or Alta California, if you're from Baja) and even lots of places down here have added a Caesar Salad with either prime rib, chicken or shrimp to their luncheon menu. I have sampled them all over the place and came up with my own, easy-to-make variation. The dressing for this salad is lighter than the traditional Tijuana Ensalada César and its cheesy, garlicky taste is guaranteed to please you and everyone else you serve it to. It's really good and it's really easy. Serves two for lunch or a light dinner. (Don't forget the breath mints for dessert!)

Salad
1 head romaine, rinsed and torn into bite-size pieces

2 boneless, skinless pieces of chicken breast, baked 20 minutes and chilled
or
1 cup sliced, chilled pieces of left-over prime rib or steak
or
1 cup shelled, deveined cooked, chilled shrimp
¾ cup prepared Caesar style croutons
Garlic powder to taste
Fresh grated Parmesan cheese to taste

Dressing
1 lemon, halved
Your favorite bottled Caesar salad dressing to taste
Freshly ground pepper to taste

In large salad bowl, arrange romaine lettuce. Top with chicken, prime rib or shrimp and croutons. Sprinkle with garlic powder and Parmesan cheese. Refrigerate up to one hour.

When ready to serve, add croutons. Squeeze lemon over top of salad. Pour on desired amount of bottled Caesar dressing and toss gently. Serve immediately with garlic bread or hot, buttered tortillas.

ENSALADA PUERTO DE ILUSIÓN

The locals call La Paz "the port of illusion." On a recent visit there, my friend Debbie asked our waiter where the odd nickname came from. In Spanish he explained it to me and I translated it. Basically, when Sir Francis Drake and his compadres were chasing down the Spanish galleons in the 1500s, they found La Paz Bay an ideal place to hide out. The opening to the bay is almost completely hidden and gives the illusion that it doesn't exist, so no one would chase them in there. They'd just scratch their heads and wonder how the pirates disappeared without a trace!

La Paz is almost more Europe than Mexico to me. It has an understated, adventurous elegance to it - but with just a hint of naughtiness - of that renegade adventurous spirit. Maybe that's because of those pirates. Also, some of the battles of the Mexican-American War were fought in its streets. These days, it's the capital city of Baja California Sur; it boasts a population of nearly half a million. In case you didn't know, Baja Sur is the fastest growing state in all of Mexico. La Paz is a must-see. It's not only magically beautiful, but it's clean, it's cosmopolitan and its economy - which is not based on tourism - is flourishing. It was where Nina and I first discovered Baja Magic back in 1961.

Nina created this recipe after dining bayside on the malecón in La Paz back in 1997. I modified it after Debbie's 2005 visit. This salad is pure Puerto de Illusión. Pure La Paz. It's a seafood lover's delight, and the moment you take your first bite, you'll be convinced that you're sitting on the malecón at the edge of La Paz Bay watching the pelicans cruise back and forth, bathed in the pale glow of the street lights. Be a little bold and serve chilled Pacifico or Corona Beer with this one. Sip it and a balmy, desert breeze will immediately waft its way through your dining room or back yard. You'll hear strains of Mexican music in the distance and whatever stress you've been experiencing will mysteriously vanish. This incredible salad serves two hungry people for lunch or a light dinner.

Salad
½ pound cooked, deveined shrimp, chilled
¼ cup chilled cooked, flaked crab
½ bunch green onions, chopped
½ cup shredded carrots
1 tomato, diced
½ cup fresh Parmesan cheese, finely grated
½ cup shredded queso cacique or feta cheese
1 head Romaine, torn into bite sized pieces

Dressing
1/3 cup olive oil
¼ cup wine vinegar
1 tsp garlic powder
¼ tsp tarragon
Salt and freshly ground pepper to taste

On the bottom of a large salad bowl, layer shrimp, crab, green onions, carrots and tomatoes. Add grated Parmesan and cacique cheese and lettuce as top layer. Refrigerate up to one hour.

Prior to serving, prepare salad dressing by mixing together salad dressing in small jar. Shake well, pour over salad and toss gently. Serve on chilled plates.

CRAB SALAD LORETO

Quick, easy and dyn-o-mite, this salad is guaranteed to transport you right to a palapa on the beach, where you're eating barefoot, with your feet digging aimlessly in the grainy sand, sand that's still warm from the leftover heat of the just-set-sun. Can you hear the waves quietly lapping against the shore in front of you as the new moon cuts a silver sliver in the early evening sky? Ah yes. Here comes the first star.

You are in Loreto, the oldest permanent settlement in all of Baja. Yes. It's true. Located nearly three quarters of the way down the peninsula, on the Sea of Cortez side, Loreto was founded by Padre Juan María Salvatierra, a Jesuit priest on October 25, 1697. The Misión de Nuestra Señora de Loreto (Our Lady of Loreto) is located in the center of town. It was the first of 20 missions founded by Jesuit priests in Baja before they were expelled in 1767. Loreto was the capital of Baja until it was destroyed by a hurricane in 1829 - at which time the capital was moved to La Paz.

So, how are things in Loreto these days? Well, it's growing really fast and gaining rather than losing charm in the process. It has a lovely malecón, a walkway that runs right along the sea, a new marina and some pretty swanky resorts that offer tennis, golf, fishing and diving. It has daily air service from L.A. and both Aeromexico and Alaska Airlines fly in from San Diego.

So you're ready to go? Me too. Until such time as we get those plane tickets, or have the car packed and ready to roll, we can feed our Baja hunger by cooking up a storm! You'll find the medley of flavors in this tangy crab salad both scrumptious and fame inspiring. Serves two as a meal.

Salad
2 avocados, peeled, seeded and diced
1 cup Chihuahua or jack cheese, shredded
1 - 3½ ounce can sliced black olives
2 tomatoes, diced
Juice of 1 limón (Mexican lime)
or key lime
8 - 10 romaine leaves, rinsed and dried
1 pound cooked crab, diced and chilled
1½ cups tortilla chips

Dressing
2 tbsp olive oil
Juice from 2 limónes (Mexican limes)
or key limes
1 tsp garlic powder
2 cups salsa fresca

Two to four hours before serving, combine avocados, cheese, olives and tomatoes. Squeeze lime juice over it and refrigerate, covered.

At mealtime, arrange crab mixture on top of lettuce in a salad bowl. Garnish with chips. Mix together ingredients for dressing in small bowl. Pour over salad, toss gently and serve.

WILD WEST BARBECUE SALAD

My friend Kathy is from Oklahoma. Since she lived by the beach in San Diego and hung out with me for over a decade, she's now officially almost a native. What that means is that she's part cowgirl, part Baja Aficionada and part pure artist - just like this salad. It makes for an interesting and delectable combo, let me assure you! One night when we were in La Bufadora, she was the designated chef for the evening. She made this salad for me and a bunch of other folks. She used a dry marinade to blacken the chicken, but informed me that London broil or pork can be spiced up and tenderized with it just as easily. It's easy to do and awesome to eat.

She gave me the recipe, of course. This is a yummy salad that will make you so notorious you'll want to write Kathy a thank you note! Serves two or three as a meal.

Salad
1 large head romaine, rinsed and torn into pieces
1 cup feta cheese, crumbled
2 small Roma tomatoes, diced
1 avocado, sliced
1 cup white corn (you can use frozen)
2 breasts chicken, sliced in narrow strips
1 tbsp corn or canola oil
Blue corn tortilla chips

Dry marinade
1/3 cup American chili powder
1/3 cup sugar
2 tbsp salt

Dressing
¼ cup olive oil
¼ cup red wine vinegar
1 tsp oregano
Salt and freshly ground pepper to taste.

Layer romaine, cheese, tomatoes, avocado and white corn in a large salad bowl. Place in refrigerator and chill thoroughly.

Mix chili powder, sugar and salt together in bowl. Coat the strips of chicken with mixture and fry until done (about 10 minutes) in canola oil. For those of you who want to forego the oil, the chicken breasts can be barbecued before they're sliced instead. After cooking, drain chicken on paper towels and cool slightly.

Add dressing, chicken and blue corn tortilla chips to salad vegetables and toss gently. Serve immediately.

SCALLOP & SHRIMP CEVICHE SALAD

This new recipe came to me courtesy of my Baja neighbor and good friend, Christine. Whether she created it herself or plagiarized it, she won't say. It really doesn't matter because it's become one of her signature dishes and people beg for it as much as they do her husband Leo's

---

Beachcomber Coconut Shrimp! (Find it in the Appetizer section.) This serves four.

1 quart water
½ lb bay scallops
½ lb peeled, deveined shrimp
¼ lb tomatillos
Juice from 2 limónes
(Mexican limes) or key limes
1 bunch cilantro, rinsed, stems removed and chopped
½ cup minced red onion
1 cup chopped yellow bell pepper
2 cups cooked white rice, chilled
Salt to taste
Hot pepper sauce to taste
½ lb mixed field greens (about one bag)

In medium saucepan, bring water to rapid boil. Add scallops and shrimp, cover pan and remove from heat. Let stand about five minutes, or until shellfish are opaque throughout. Drain and pour into a bowl and place in refrigerator.

Husk and rinse tomatillos. Coarsely chop. Place in blender or food processor with lime juice and cilantro and purée. Pour over shellfish. Add onion and bell pepper and place in refrigerator, mixing occasionally until ceviche is chilled, about 40 minutes. Add rice and season to taste with salt and hot pepper sauce.

Arrange field greens on dinner plates and top with ceviche mixture. Serve immediately.

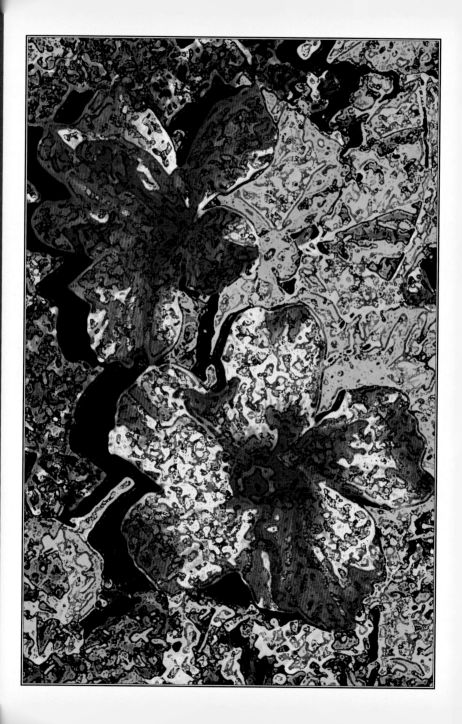

BEANS, RICE & VEGETABLE DISHES

Along with the Mexican staples, refried beans and rice, I'm offering you some new variations of these old standbys. I recommend trying Terry's and my new favorite, Frijoles Charros (Cowboy Beans) instead of regular frijoles (refried beans).

I've also kept some intriguing vegetable dishes to serve with your entrées, such as the Spa Vegetable Kabob and Zucchini with Corn and Peppers. These are zesty, light and delicious. You can alternate these dishes with the salads offered previously to keep your menus fresh and varied; or you can throw a huge fiesta and include something (or lots of things) from each section.

Either way, experimentation is fun. It will expand your horizons, enhance your perceptions and raise your consciousness. And it just may inject a little Baja Magic into your life without you even knowing it!

TRADITIONAL FRIJOLES

Refried beans, or frijoles (free-HOE-lays) have been a mainstay in the Mexican diet forever. Served with corn (as in corn tortillas), the two vegetables interact chemically in some miraculous fashion to create a complete protein. That important (to Mexicans) piece of trivia was brought to you by my mother, who swore that the increasing popularity of flour tortillas in the past few decades has wreaked havoc on the health of a nation. She refused to even go near a flour tortilla! I, on the other hand, like them just fine!

Regardless of what you eat with your refried beans, you're going to love them! My family's recipe is guaranteed to taste great even if you opt to take the high road and leave out the bacon grease. My mother tried to leave it out once and caught my dad dumping a huge lump of cold, solidified bacon grease into the bean pot when he thought she was busy folding laundry! I tend to go along with him! When we were having lunch in Cabo Pulmo at Nancy's Restaurant one Easter Sunday, I asked Nancy what made her beans so exotic-tasting. She explained that it was epazote. It took me a few months to find epazote, and when I did, it was explained to me that this Mexican herb is used in frijoles to de-gas the beans. My amigo Marcelo (who gave me a plant) further explained that epazote can be used to brew tea that rids one's intestines of impurities and bad bugs. If you can find epazote, try it. You will love the flavor. And you might not mind the de-gassing effect either!

This recipe will make enough beans to feed 16 to 20 people. I usually make a batch and freeze at least half in smaller amounts to use again and again as a side dish. Also, if you prefer your beans in a brothy sauce, try making our new Frijoles Charros.

1 lb package dried pinto beans
6 cups water
¼ cup bacon grease (optional)
3 tsp garlic powder
2 tbsp chicken bouillon powder
1 tbsp American chili powder
4 large leaves epazote, fresh or dried, chopped or crumbled

Put beans and four cups water into Dutch oven. Soak at least six hours. Pour beans into colander and rinse thoroughly. Add remaining two cups water into the Dutch oven, along with bacon grease, garlic powder, bouillon, chili powder and epazote. Bring to a boil. Cover and reduce heat, simmering for about four to six hours. Stir occasionally.

You'll know when the frijoles are done because they'll be very tender. If there seems to be too much liquid in the beans, leave the lid off for the last half hour. Stir or mash beans often when lid is off until approximately half of them are mashed and half are still whole.

FRIJOLES CHARROS - COWBOY BEANS

When we make shopping and business trips into San Jose del Cabo, we have a favorite restaurant that we love to visit. Even at 10 a.m. we can get incredible carnitas tacos, served on homemade tortillas with an array of salsas and these incredible cowboy beans! The place is called Carnitas El Michoacano and it's a very famous chain in these parts. I often stop and pick up an order on my way to do an airport pickup. My daughter, Gayle especially, always gets off the plane starving! Makes about 10 servings and will keep for a few days in the refrigerator.

1 lb pinto beans
7 cups water
2 tbsp corn or canola oil
1 large white onion, chopped
2 tomatoes, chopped
4 cloves garlic, minced
½ lb chorizo
6 strips bacon
1 - 3½ oz can jalapeño slices, pickled in escabeche
1 bunch cilantro, stems removed and chopped
2 tbsp caldo de tomate (tomato bouillon powder)

Put beans and four cups water into Dutch oven. Soak at least six hours. Pour beans into colander and rinse thoroughly.

In large skillet sauté onions, tomatoes and garlic with chorizo and bacon until tomatoes are softened and onions and garlic are translucent and meat is thoroughly cooked. Do not drain!

Add three cups remaining water into the Dutch oven, along with beans, jalapeños, and contents of the skillet. Add cilantro and bouillon. Bring to a boil. Cover and reduce heat, simmering for about four hours. Stir occasionally. When the beans are tender, remove from heat and serve. These will keep in the refrigerator for several days and can also be frozen for later use.

PAPAS FRITAS CON CHILE VERDE

These potatoes are popular with the people of Baja who do not in any way share our aversion (pretended or otherwise) for fried foods. These are cooked to nearly a crisp with strips of green chile and make an excellent companion for roasted or broiled meats, or even egg dishes at a brunch. Eight servings.

6 large poblano chiles, blistered and peeled or 2 - 7½ ounce cans whole green chiles
½ cup corn or canola oil
2 onions, thinly sliced
1½ tsp salt
2 pounds red potatoes, cooked al dente and cubed

Using fresh chiles: If you have a gas stove, lay the chiles over the open flame and char skins well, turning with tongs frequently until they're uniformly blackened and stop snapping. The more charred they are, the easier it is to remove the skins. If you have an electric stove, place chiles in a large skillet on high heat. Turn frequently as above. Remove chiles to plastic bag, close it and let stand for 10 minutes. Remove from bag, place in ice-cold water and remove the stems, skins, veins and seeds. Cut into strips.

Using canned chiles: Remove from can, rinse and pat dry. Cut into strips.

In skillet, heat oil to medium heat and fry onions until they are translucent. Add chile strips, potatoes and salt to the onions, and cook on medium high heat, stirring mixture occasionally, for about four minutes, or until potatoes are browned. Serve immediately.

CARIBBEAN FRIJOLES NEGROS

Black beans, cooked in the Caribbean style have become popular in the last couple of decades. I first had them in Florida where the Cubans introduced them. They've since made their way north and west, up the Yucatán peninsula, through mainland Mexico, across the Sea of Cortez and all the way up the Baja Peninsula. Every grocery store I've been into in Baja carries them in cans now, as do American supermarkets. What are they

like? Well, they're tangier than traditional frijoles and are really great when served with light, tropical fare like some of my eclectic salads and chicken or seafood dishes.

This recipe will make enough beans to feed 16 to 20 people. I usually make a batch and freeze at least half in smaller amounts to use again and again as a side dish. If, like Nina and me you prefer to make these without the bacon grease, we both promise you that you won't sacrifice any flavor! And, if you prefer your beans not only fat-free and in a brothy sauce, try making them ranchero style - as explained below.

In case this question is rolling around in your mind, let me answer it in advance: Will these beans instantly transport you to the tropics? You bet they will! That's Baja Magic for you - in action!

1 lb package dried black beans
4 cups water
Juice from 3 limónes (Mexican limes)
or key limes
¼ cup bacon grease (optional)
3 tsp garlic powder
2 tbsp chicken bouillon powder
1 - 2 tbsp American chili powder

Put beans and water into Dutch oven. Soak at least six hours. Pour beans into colander and rinse thoroughly. Add two cups water back into the Dutch oven, along with lime juice, bacon grease, garlic powder, bouillon and chili powder. Bring to a boil. Cover and reduce heat, simmering for about four to six hours. Stir occasionally. You'll be able to tell when the frijoles are done because they'll be very tender. If there seems to be too much liquid in the beans, leave the lid off for the last half hour. Stir or mash beans often when lid is off.

Ranchero Style
Leave out the bacon grease. Cook only until beans are barely tender and the mixture has the consistency of bean soup - about two to three hours. You can make part of your batch into refried beans and part into Ranchero style beans. It's up to you!

MEXICAN RICE

This traditional Mexican side dish is super easy to make and always tastes good. I prefer using brown rice because I like it better, but if you don't have any, you can substitute white rice easily. Serves eight.

2 cups water
1½ cups salsa fresca (Salsa section)
3 cups quick brown rice
Salt to taste

In medium sized saucepan bring two cups water and salsa to boil. Add brown rice. Stir well. Cover, reduce heat and simmer for 15 - 20 minutes until fluffy. Add salt to taste. Serve immediately.

WHITE RICE WITH VEGETABLES

This is another uncomplicated recipe that makes a colorful side dish. Light and delicious, it's perfect year-round with any Baja Magic meal. Serves eight.

3 tbsp salad oil
1 onion, chopped
2 cloves garlic, minced
1½ cups uncooked white rice
3 tsp chicken bouillon powder
¼ tsp cayenne pepper
3 cups boiling water
1 - 10 ounce package frozen or canned peas, carrots and corn
2 tomatoes, peeled, seeded and chopped

In a large skillet, heat oil over medium heat. Add onion, garlic and rice and cook, stirring constantly until onion is translucent and rice is opaque. In a separate bowl, dissolve the bouillon in boiling water. Stir cayenne into mixture in skillet. Pour bouillon and boiling water into the skillet and stir. Cover and simmer for 20 minutes or until liquid is absorbed. Add peas, carrots, corn and tomatoes. Cook over low heat, stirring until vegetables are heated through, about three minutes.

SPA VEGETABLE KABOBS

My dad has been coming to the Hotel Buena Vista Beach Resort since it opened in 1976. In the early days the resort was called "Spa Buena Vista" or just plain old "Spa" by the regulars. Locals still call it that to this day.

We first had these vegetable kabob at the Spa about 20 years and almost as many chefs ago. They're almost identical to grilled vegetables you can get state-side these days, with a couple of small, Baja differences. When you're barbecuing and in the mood for something a bit unconventional, remember these. They take next-to-no-time to make, they're are festive and serve eight.

4 medium zucchini cut in ½ inch chunks
4 yellow squash cut in ½ inch chunks
8 wooden skewers
16 medium sized fresh mushrooms
½ to 1 cup María's Salsa de Arbol
(Salsa section)
2 tbsp chopped cilantro
8 cherry tomatoes

Microwave or steam zucchini and yellow squash over boiling water for two minutes (until blanched or slightly softened). Skewer zucchini and squash chunks, alternating with mushrooms on skewers. Mix together salsa and cilantro and brush over vegetables. Broil or grill for four minutes, brushing often with salsa. Add a tomato on each skewer and grill two minutes more.

SINFUL CINNAMON RICE

This delectable (practically too-good-too-be-true) rice dish with its unexpected seasonings has its origins either in Cabo San Lucas or Todos Santos. I'm not really certain where it came from. It's just sort of a potpourri of wonderful flavors and textures that's not only pleasing to the eye but a total sensual treat to eat. The combination of long grain rice and vegetables with cinnamon and raisins has created a dramatic side dish that complements any grilled or roasted meat.

Try it and you'll either find yourself barefoot, in t-shirt and shorts under a palapa on Medano Beach in Cabo sipping a cerveza with a shot of Hornitos tequila on the side, (Hornitos is for sipping - not for shooting). Or you might end up sipping a glass of perfectly aged Merlot on your private patio at an exquisite boutique hotel in Todos Santos. Women - turquoise jewelry will drip from your ears, neck and wrists. You'll be wearing a long, colorful skirt, a white blouse and flip-flops. Men - you're outfitted in shorts, a Hawaiian shirt and flip-flops. Either way,

you will love this naughty rice! Serves eight.

4 tbsp butter or margarine
½ cup carrots, diced
½ cup celery, diced
½ onion, diced
2 cups long grain rice
½ tsp salt
1 tbsp ground cinnamon
½ cup raisins
6 cups water

Melt two tablespoons butter in deep saucepan over medium heat. Reduce heat, add carrots, celery and onion and cook, covered for ten minutes. Stir occasionally. Add rice, salt, cinnamon, raisins and water to pan and bring to boil over high heat. When the water has reduced to the level of the rice, lower heat, cover and cook 15 to 20 minutes, stirring occasionally. Just prior to serving, add remaining butter.

CHILI ONION RINGS

Chili onion rings are a renowned, spicy Baja treat that can be served harmoniously with grilled meat, fish or chicken. So simple and yet so very tasty! Oh yes! Serves six to eight.

2 large yellow onions, thinly sliced
3 cups flour
1 tbsp cayenne pepper
1 tbsp American chili powder
1 tbsp paprika
Salt and pepper to taste
5 cups corn oil

Separate onions into rings. Mix flour, cayenne, chili powder, paprika, salt and pepper in a bowl. Heat the oil in a deep fryer or heavy skillet until a drop of water sizzles when put into the oil. Dredge some of the onion rings in flour mixture and fry until golden. Drain on paper towels, keeping them warm while frying the remaining rings. Don't dredge the onions until just prior to frying or they'll give off too much moisture. Serve immediately.

ZUCCHINI WITH CORN AND PEPPERS

A colorful addition to any meal, these lightly fried red, green and yellow vegetables are delicately flavored with garlic. A long-time favorite of my mother's, their freshness and zip makes them appealing to both party crowds and family groups. And of course, they're an excellent way to use up those overflowing, overwhelming quantities of zucchini you may have gotten stuck with this summer! Serves eight.

1½ tbsp butter or margarine
2½ pounds zucchini, cut into ½ inch cubes
1½ cups corn cut from four ears
½ red bell pepper, seeded and chopped
½ green bell pepper, seeded and chopped
1 onion, chopped
3 cloves garlic, minced
Salt and pepper to taste

In large skillet, melt butter or margarine over high heat. Add zucchini, corn, bell peppers, onion and garlic. Cook, stirring frequently until most of vegetable liquid has evaporated and vegetables are tender-crisp. Serve immediately.

RAJAS EN CREMA

In the mid '90s, on a visit to the newly rechristened Hotel Buena Vista Beach Resort, then chef Carlos Leyva gave me the following recipe to include in this book. He has since moved on to become the chef at La Mar y Peña Restaurant in Cabo, but the recipe stayed with me. It's divine and goes beautifully with any chicken, beef or seafood dish. Serves four.

4 poblano chiles
4 tbsp butter
1 large onion, sliced
½ tsp salt (or to taste)
2 cups crema media ácida or sour cream
1 cup grated Chihuahua or jack cheese

If you have a gas stove, lay the chiles over the open flame and char skins well, turning with tongs frequently until they're uniformly blackened and stop snapping. The more charred they are, the easier it is to remove the skins. If you have an electric stove, place chiles in a large skillet on high heat. Turn frequently as above. Remove chiles to plastic bag, close it and let stand for 10 minutes. Remove from bag, place in ice-cold water and remove the stems, skins, veins and seeds. Cut into strips.

Melt butter in skillet. Add onion and cook until translucent. Add chiles, salt and crema or sour cream. Stir until heated clear through. Remove from heat and serve immediately, garnishing with grated cheese.

TORTILLAS & BREADS

Mexicans have traditionally used corn and flour tortillas as the starch staple in their diets, so they don't bake much bread. A trip to any panadería (pahn-ah-der-EE-yah or bakery) in Baja will show you, however, that fresh baked bolillos (boe-LEE-yoes or Mexican hard rolls) are a favorite of theirs.

When I was a kid, my mom would insist that we stop at the panadería before we got to our destination. If we got there early enough in the morning, Nina and I would sneak out back behind the bakery and watch the baker slide huge trays of hot, fresh rolls out of the rounded, Indian-style outdoor brick ovens. Out with the bolillos and in with trays of dough. Our well-rehearsed, endearing smiles were intended to net us each a roll straight from the oven. And, to our parents' chagrin, we were usually successful.

Oh, how my mouth waters at the memory of biting into a piping hot bolillo. They're still baked twice a day in Baja, first thing in the morning and during the siesta period right after the mid-day meal. Although the Mexican bakeries specialize more in sweet breads, donuts and cookies these days, bolillos can still be bought for 10 to 15 cents each. Their coarse texture comes from unbleached flour and their flavor is rich and earthy - a true peasant bread bursting with Baja Magic. And you'll rarely find them in the US. And then there are those Mexican cookies, and donuts and pastries and - all so good and so totally different than anything you'd buy in a gringo bakery. You just have to go see for yourself. There's no way around it!

My first taste of a just-made corn tortilla was at Kilometer 181, about 120 miles south of Ensenada, back in the mid-sixties. We were the only campers on a beach that went on forever. In fact, the only other people we saw all week were an old rancher and his wife, María. They invited us to their home - a tiny two room structure built entirely from scraps of plywood, tar paper and other materials scavenged from who-knows-where. Mexican ingenuity to a "T." María patted tiny balls of masa into skinny pan-cakes, tossed them onto the split oil drum that served as her stove, browned them on both sides, flipped them off the grill and handed me one filled with beans and stewed beef. Oh, was it ever good!

If you're curious about where to get the freshest tortillas in Baja nowadays, don't go looking for them in a panadería. You can buy them hot off the press (the lumps of dough are actually pressed and cooked by machine right in front of your eyes) in super-markets like Gigante or Calimax or in a specialty store known as a tortillería (tor-tee-yer-EE-uh).

To round out this section, I've included a camping favorite of my family's to the bread recipes here, Jalapeño Corn Bread. It's different from its Southern (as in south of the Mason-Dixon Line) cousin in that it's flavored with jalapeño chiles, whole kernel corn and lots of cheese. It's great when you're eating barefoot out under the Baja stars, warming your toes at the campfire - and it is just as great at home, sitting cross-legged on the living room carpet with a fire blazing in the fireplace. Its uniquely Baja flavor is truly delicious!

CORN TORTILLAS

Do you recall that corn tortillas comprise half of that complete protein my mother always bragged about? (Right - the other half is beans - very good!) Should you get hit over the head with the urge to make your own corn tortillas, here is the recipe. Most people, and I'll confess I'm one of those, find it easier to buy tortillas in the grocery store. But these are fun to make at least once, and if you have kids, they make a great project for a rainy day. Makes a dozen.

2 cups masa de harina (dehydrated masa flour)
1¼ to 1½ cups water
2 pieces cheesecloth, about 12 inches square
Wax paper

Mix masa with enough warm water to make dough hold together. Using your hands, shape dough into smooth ball. Divide into 12 equal pieces and roll into balls, flattening each slightly. Dip cheesecloth in water and wring dry, then place each ball between the cloths one at a time. Roll with light, even strokes until tortilla is about six inches in diameter. Carefully pull back cloth, trim tortilla to a round shape and place it on a square of wax paper. Repeat, stacking between pieces of wax paper.

Peel off top piece of wax paper. Turn tortilla, paper side up, onto a preheated, ungreased comal or skillet over medium high heat. As tortilla warms, peel off remaining wax paper. Cook for 1½ to 2 minutes, turning frequently until tortilla is soft but flecked with brown specks. Serve immediately, or store in refrigerator or freezer.

FLOUR TORTILLAS

Here is the ambitious, adventurous cook's recipe for flour tortillas. Makes 12 nine-inch tortillas. This recipe also forms the basis for those killer Special Quesadillas (Appetizer section).

3 cups self-rising flour
1 tsp salt
2 tbsp solid vegetable shortening (or lard if you're into authenticity)
1¼ cups water

In large bowl, cut shortening into flour using two knives. Add salt. Stir water in slowly with a fork until a large ball of dough is formed. Cover and let sit for 20 minutes. Turn out onto a board and knead until smooth. Divide into 12 pieces and shape each into a smooth ball. Flatten each ball into a four or five inch patty, then roll into a nine-inch round.

After each tortilla is rolled out, place it on a preheated, ungreased comal or skillet over medium high heat. When blisters appear on tortilla, flatten immediately with wide spatula. Turn tortilla often until blisters turn a light brown. Serve immediately or store in refrigerator or freezer.

JALAPEÑO CORN BREAD

Jalapeño chiles, real corn and lots of cheese distinguish this corn bread from the old-fashioned, all-American y'all version of corn bread. It's not too fiery, but makes an awesome side dish for roasted or grilled foods. I love it! My mom used to serve it with fresh fried chicken (fresh because the chickens were purchased - very recently alive - from rancheros we happened to come upon in our travels up and down the dusty back roads of Baja) during our summer camping trips on the Pacific side of the peninsula back when I was in high school! Mom tried to get away with only putting a couple of jalapeños in the batter, but Nina, our dad and I had a conspiracy going. As soon as she left the camper, even if the corn bread was already in the oven, we'd sneak it out and add a whole bunch more chiles! You can just imagine her shock when she took her first bite of what she thought was a subtly flavored, lightly spiced delicacy! The look on her face, the way she rushed for a soda and gulped it down - these are priceless memories! Truly they are. Serves 12.

2 - 10 jalapeño chiles, finely chopped with seeds
1 - 3½ ounce can diced green chiles
1 - 17 ounce can creamed corn
1 onion, finely diced
½ tsp baking soda
½ tsp salt
1 tbsp sugar

2 eggs
¾ cup buttermilk
1/3 cup corn or canola oil
1 cup cheddar cheese, grated
2 cups yellow corn meal

Preheat oven to 350°. Grease a 9 x 13 inch pan. In a large bowl, mix jalapeños and green chiles with corn and onion. Beat in baking soda, salt and sugar, and then add the eggs one at a time, beating well. Add buttermilk and oil, then cheese and cornmeal.

Pour batter into pan and bake for 30 to 40 minutes, or until the top is brown and a toothpick inserted in the center comes out clean. Cool in pan and serve in squares.

BOLILLOS – MEXICAN HARD ROLLS

Bolillos are different than French rolls or other hard rolls. The crust is crisp, but the roll is soft and almost crumbly inside. The texture is coarse and the flavor is uniquely Mexican. These rolls are great when toasted and served with butter and jam for breakfast. Or, split them in half and use them to make Baja style "tortas," or sandwiches, much like torpedoes. Put anything you want inside - from carne asada to carnitas to shredded beef or chicken ... even tuna salad for a truly memorable Baja Magic sandwich (or buy them at any roadside torta stand in every Baja town). And

bolillos are wonderful served piping hot at dinner. Just split them in half and load the insides up with butter or roasted garlic. Then wrap them in a cloth and place in a festive basket.

As I mentioned in the introduction to this section, in Mexican panaderías you can buy bolillos fresh twice a day, for 10 to 15 cents apiece. Today the peasant bread is losing its authenticity and becoming more Americanized as the bakers use more refined flour. If you want yours to taste really authentic, try buying unrefined flour from a health food store. Makes 12 scrumptious rolls.

2 cups water
1½ tbsp sugar
1 tbsp salt
2 tbsp butter or margarine
1 package active dry yeast
6 cups unrefined flour
1 tbsp corn oil
1 tbsp cornstarch dissolved in ½ cup water

In saucepan combine water, sugar, salt and butter. Heat over low heat, stirring until just barely boiling. Pour into large mixing bowl, add yeast and stir until dissolved. With an electric mixer, beat in five cups flour to form a dough.

Turn dough onto a board coated with about ½ cup flour and knead for 10 minutes. Dough should feel velvety. Add more flour if necessary to prevent dough from sticking to board. Form into a ball and place in an oiled bowl.

Turn dough over so that all sides are oiled. Cover with plastic wrap and let rise in a warm place until dough has doubled in size (about 1½ hours). Punch dough to release air bubbles, then turn out onto lightly floured board.

Divide into 12 equal pieces. Form each piece into a smooth ball. Shape each into an oblong by rolling it and gently pulling from the center to the ends until the ball is about four inches long and center is thicker than ends.

Place rolls about two inches apart on greased baking sheets, cover lightly with a towel and let rise for about 30 minutes or until they've doubled in size. In small saucepan, heat cornstarch and water to boiling. Cool slightly and then brush each roll with cornstarch mixture. Using a sharp knife cut a slash about ¾ inch deep and 2 inches long on top of each roll. Bake at 375° for 35 to 40 minutes, until rolls are golden brown and sound hollow when tapped. Cool and wrap tightly to store.

FULL-ON FIESTA FARE: CARNITAS, FAJITAS & CARNE ASADA BARBECUES

Welcome to Party Central. That describes this section of **Cooking With Baja Magic Dos**. Any of these recipes can serve as the focal point of a casual family dinner or a grand fiesta. Try one. Try two. Try them all! You'll be serving up "the best in good time cooking from south of the border." Guaranteed. Here is how we'll set the mood. First, make out your guest list. Next, you will want to visit your local party store and pick out some invitations and decorations from south of the border. Pick up as many plastic tablecloths as you think you'll need. Choose bright colors, like purple, turquoise, hot pink and yellow. Get some paper napkins and small appetizer or dessert-sized paper plates to match. If you want to use plastic cups, stock up on them too. Look around. Party stores stock Mexican wall decorations, papel picado (colorful paper or plastic cut outs that you string across the ceiling), paper flowers, piñatas and centerpieces. To be seriously authentic, get a dozen or two small votive candles and as many lunch sized brown paper sacks. On the day of the fiesta, fill each with some sand or soil, insert a candle and place a row of luminarios (luminaries) along the walkway to your front door.

While you're out shopping, be sure to pick up some Latino music. You can pick traditional mariachi music, contemporary Latino music like Ricky Martin, Gloria Estefan, Julio or Enrique Iglesias, Marc Antony, Carlos Santana or Luis Miguel. Throw in a Jimmy Buffet CD for good measure. With the proper mood set, you'll have everybody just oozing Baja Magic even before they pop the top off their first cerveza!

Carnitas, fajitas and carne asada are foods that have become popular north of the border in the last three decades. Before that, the only place in California where anyone had ever heard of carne asada (which is marinated strips of flank or skirt steak that are grilled to perfection over charcoal) was in the Imperial Valley, about 100 miles due east of San Diego and only a few miles north of Mexicali. That was then. This is now - and now every taco shop and Mexican restaurant serves a variation it. But it started in Baja at street stands, and carne asada street tacos are still Terry's and my favorite Mexican fast food.

Like carne asada, fajitas have become so popular in the US that even fast food chains serve them. They're made by marinating chicken, beef or shrimp with chiles and vegetables in oil, vinegar and spices and then stir frying them. Made into burritos and served with condiments, fajitas can be quite a feast. Rumor has it they really originated somewhere on the Texas - Mexico border, in the lowlands around the Rio Grande. But then I've heard other rumors from one or two restaurant owners in Rosarito Beach and Ensenada that they (or their relatives anyway) dreamed up fajitas. Who knows? For the sake of this cookbook, how about if we just go along with the second story?

Carnitas, which originated in the state of Michoacán, have become very popular as well. I don't deep-fry the pork like the Mexicans do when I make my carnitas. I buy almost the leanest pork roast I can find (the no-fat kind turns out too dry) then bake it in salsa and spices for several hours until it's fork tender. I love, love, love carnitas! So will you, even if, unlike the magazine ads, you still don't think of pork as "the other white meat," carnitas just may convert you. In fact, I'd bet money on it.

If you're feeling tentative about throwing a fiesta - hey - that's okay. Close your eyes. Take a deep breath. Smell that salty ocean breeze. Listen to the sea gulls shrieking overhead. Exhale. Breathe in again - this time inhaling some of that Baja Magic. Now you're ready to crank yourself up and get into party gear. Go for it!

Ready? Good. I see you. You're already in your car, on the way to the grocery store with your fiesta shopping list in hand and a Jimmy Buffett tune blaring out of your CD player! All right!

CARNITAS

Whenever I throw a dinner party for 20 or more people, I invariably include carnitas on the menu. Why? It requires little preparation time. I can make the beans and salsas ahead of time, and the carnitas pretty much cook themselves. This allows me the freedom to enjoy my guests and not relegate myself to the role of kitchen slave. The pork is tangy, crispy but not greasy (the way I do it) and makes a terrific fiesta dish. As a buffet, serve a platter of steaming carnitas with corn and flour tortillas, and have your guests make their own burritos filled with the succulent pork and the condiments listed below. On the side, serve frijoles charros. This recipe for carnitas serves eight to ten. And it's to die for! I have modified the condiments served with carnitas so that they're now more authentic.

Carnitas
1 - 4 to 5 pound lean boneless pork loin roast, with excess fat removed
4 cloves garlic, minced
1 tbsp seasoned salt
2 tsp pepper
1 cup salsa verde or María's salsa de arbol (or both, in Salsa section)

On the side, buffet style
2 dozen warm corn and/or flour tortillas
8 cups frijoles charros (Bean section)
2 cups white onion, chopped
1 bunch cilantro, stems removed and diced
2 bunches of whole radishes, stems removed, chopped
2 cups salsa fresca (Salsa section)
2 cups salsa verde (Salsa section)
2 cups María's salsa de arbol (Salsa section)
2 cups avocado sauce (Salsa section)

Place pork roast in 9 x 13 pan. Rub garlic into the roast. Sprinkle with salt and pepper. Cover with salsa. Loosely cover the pan with aluminum foil. Bake at 300° for four and a half hours, or until fork tender.

Remove roast from oven. Cool until you can touch the meat comfortably. Using two forks, shred the pork. Remove any excess fat from meat. When all meat is shredded, mix the pan juices thoroughly into the pork.

Return to oven. Cook, uncovered for 30 minutes or until pork is crispy on top. Remove from oven. Turn pork. Return to oven and cook another 20 minutes, until pork is crispy on top and there is almost no liquid left in the pan. Serve as suggested above with a bowl of frijoles charros for everyone.

LA CONCHA BEACH CLUB STYLE FAJITAS
Chicken, Beef or Shrimp

Fajitas have been the rage for years now. This recipe came to us courtesy of our waiter at the La Concha Beach Club, which is right to the north of the Melia Cabo Real resort in Los Cabos. It's home to a gigantic tide pool - a naturally occurring salt water formation big enough for plenty of people to swim in. We swam first and then went up the cliff to the restaurant and ate sizzling hot fajitas on the terrace under a giant palapa. And soaked up the incomparable beauty of the place! Unfortunately, at press time the restaurant was closed, but we're betting it will open again before long. It's too spectacular to stay gone for good.

Fajitas are incredibly simple to prepare, they're fun to eat and they're delicious. These make enough great eats and good times for eight people. ¡Olé! ¡Olé! ¡Olé! Mariachi or salsa music is definitely in order to set the right mood for a fajitas fiesta. And maybe barefoot would be good too....

Fajitas
3 pounds boneless chicken breasts, cut into chunks
or 3 pounds round steak, cut into chunks
or 3 pounds large shrimp, peeled and deveined
3 green bell peppers cut into chunks
3 yellow bell peppers cut into chunks
3 red bell peppers cut into chunks
1½ large onions, diced
2 tomatoes cut into chunks
¼ to ¾ cup sliced, pickled jalapeños from can
¾ cup olive oil
Juice from 6 limónes (Mexican limes) or key limes
4 tbsp wine vinegar
2 tbsp oregano
1 tsp Worcestershire Sauce
½ cup beer
3 tbsp garlic powder
Salt and pepper to taste

On the side, buffet style
2 dozen corn and/or flour tortillas
2 cups guacamole (Appetizer section)
2 cups salsa fresca (Salsa section)
1 cup crema media ácida or sour cream

In large bowl combine chicken, steak or shrimp with red and green bell peppers, onion, tomatoes, and jalapeños.

In small bowl mix together oil, lime juice, vinegar, oregano, Worcestershire, beer, garlic, salt and pepper. Pour over meat and vegetable mixture and toss gently. Cover. Marinate three hours or overnight in refrigerator. About 20 minutes before dinner is to be served, heat a large skillet or wok until very, very hot. Drain off excess marinade. Pour chicken, steak or shrimp mixture into skillet and stir-fry for six to eight minutes, or until done.

Place in serving dish. Put serving dish on plate warmer so that when it's served at the table, it stays hot. Put a bowl of guacamole,

a bowl of salsa and a bowl of crema or sour cream on the table. Wrap tortillas in foil and heat in oven, or cook in microwave until steaming. Serve in a breadbasket to keep warm. Have each guest put fajita mixture into a tortilla. Garnish with guacamole, salsa and sour cream. Roll up into a burrito.

* * *

¡CARNE ASADA!

When I lived in the Imperial Valley in the mid '70s, carne asada was unheard of anywhere else in the US. You could buy it, marinated and ready to throw on the grill at every independent, mom and pop Latino market in the valley. Everyone in the farming community of El Centro (where I lived) had their favorite "source" for the lean, flavorful flank steak. That hasn't changed. El Centro-ites still barbecue carne asada at every opportunity. But - its fame and availability has spread considerably in the last three decades.

When I moved away, I discovered that I had become quite attached (addicted perhaps?) to carne asada. I loved the whole ritual that surrounded it, from the trip to the Mexican meat market for the best meat available to the chopping of goodies for salsa together with the other women in the kitchen and the making of the guacamole to the sound of the meat sizzling on the barbecue. I loved hanging out with my friends and shooting the breeze, inhaling the aroma of the meat as our stomachs growled in time with the beat of the music. I missed the mad rush for the serving table when the meat was finally ready. To this day, I never fail to smile at the memories of the empty tortillas being transformed into bulging burritos, smothered in fresh salsa in a matter of moments. Then, silence would descend on the party (except for the music of course) while everyone practically inhaled their burritos. We would stuff ourselves until we were groaning - but no one ever seemed to stop eating until everything was gone. It was that good. Really, it was. It wasn't just a barbecue - it was an event - a celebration!

I longed to recreate that wonderful, intimate yet lively feeling I got from those carne asada barbecues in El Centro, so I decided to start with the meat. I started experimenting with marinades until I came up with my own recipe. I stuck with it for years, but I wasn't ever happy with it - it just wasn't quite right. So I cheated. I asked my friend, Leslie to help me get it right, and she did. The recipe she gave me is a hybrid between two of El Centro's most famous meat markets. At long last I have the real thing - and now - so can you!

As you prepare your own carne asada fiesta, don't forget to serve up some delectable Baja appetizers. Pass around a pitcher of Margaritas, sangría or just leave an ice chest full of (Mexican) beer out in the back yard and let people help themselves. Put on some really good mariachi or salsa music and watch as everyone starts tapping his or her feet in time with the beat. Check out their noses as they turn and inhale the awesome aroma of carne asada. Then, finally, when all is ready, send your guests over to the buffet table. Let them whip together their own tacos and burritos by filling tortillas with chunks of carne asada and the other condiments listed below. Don't forget to set a colorful table and remember that mood music! It's a must! I promise you, your backyard barbecue will take on the lively air of a full-on Baja blast. Serves six.

Carne Asada
3 pounds flank or skirt steak, tenderized and sliced very thin
Seasoned salt to taste
Pepper to taste
2 tbsp oregano
3 tbsp garlic powder
Juice from 6 limónes (Mexican limes) or key limes
Juice from 1 orange
1 large white onion, thinly sliced

On the side, buffet style
2 dozen corn and flour tortillas
1 cup frijoles (Bean section)
2 cups Chihuahua or jack cheese, grated
1 bunch green onions, diced
1 bunch cilantro, stems removed and diced
1 cup radishes, diced
1 cup salsa fresca (Salsa section)
1 cup salsa verde (Salsa section)
1 cup María's salsa de arbol (Salsa secction)
1 cup avocado sauce (Salsa section)
24 chiles toreados (Salsa section)

Place the steak in one or two 9 x 13 pans. Sprinkle the seasoned salt, pepper, oregano and garlic evenly over the meat. Pour lime and orange juice over everything. Top with sliced onions. Seal the pan with plastic wrap and leave in the refrigerator for one to two days to marinate. When ready, remove meat from marinade and cook on a very hot barbecue until cooked to desired doneness. Remove from grill, slice into thin strips and serve immediately, as suggested above.

Moon Over Mulege

TACOS, BURRITOS & TOSTADAS

Tacos, burritos and tostadas - the indispensable, traditional Mexican foods that everyone in the United States is familiar with - thanks to Taco Bell! Although I like Taco Bell (and I actually like their hot sauce), don't expect the recipes here to bear much resemblance to the food they sell. Theirs may taste good, but it's hardly authentic Baja cuisine!

Back when I lived in San Diego, the minute I crossed the border and headed south, visions of street tacos started dancing in my head. Street tacos! Are you asking yourself, "What in the world are street tacos?" Well, I'll let you in on a secret. They are the best! I could eat street tacos at least every other day. But, you ask - aren't they just loaded with those toxic amoebas? Not to the best of my knowledge.

Okay. Imagine this if you will - you're walking down the street in Baja and you smell that distinctive aroma that tells you someone nearby is barbecuing steak. Your olfactories are instantly electrified; your mouth waters and you turn your head to see where the wondrous smell is coming from. Two stores away is an outdoor counter jammed with people sitting on stools, hunched over plates of food.

You move in for a closer look. They're scarfing down plates full of tacos. The lady behind the counter tosses a few slabs of carne asada onto a grill behind the counter, cooks them, removes the meat to a wooden board and quickly chops it into tiny pieces with a meat cleaver. Meanwhile, she's heated up corn tortillas and she heaps grilled meat on top of each tortilla. She hands a plate to a salivating gringo and motions for him to add cilantro, roasted chiles, cheese, onions, tomatoes, any of several types of salsa, cabbage, huge radishes and sour cream sauce to his tacos. He reaches out and piles on the goodies. Now she's back at it, frying up fish tacos and slicing red pork for tacos al pastor off a huge roast.

You see a couple paying their bill (la cuenta). They start to get up. Before they're all the way off their stools, you and your companion have slid onto them. You're ready. Order up. And don't forget an ice cold, frosty bottle of Coca Cola or a cerveza. Hey, wait. I want to be in this picture too. Paint me in, will you? My taste buds are all revved up and ready. Let's go eat tacos....

Both Baja and Alta Californians have gotten pretty creative with our tacos, burritos and tostadas. (You can also order burritos and tostadas at these sidewalk taco bars.) You aren't limited to just carne asada, but can often order shredded beef, carnitas and turkey, lamb, fish and ceviche. As kids, we were served lobster tacos once for lunch at Bahía de Los Angeles. The recipes for all of them are here, except the carne asada, which you already have.

To start with, I've provided you instructions for how to make tacos, burritos and tostadas. Then I've given you the recipes for a variety of fillings. If you have leftover meat (like duck or lamb) and get the urge to make up your own variation of tacos, burritos or tostadas, go for it! That, my friend, shows you have caught the Baja Magic attitude. And remember, if you ever find yourself standing in front of a street taco stand - don't be a coward. Let your renegade spirit loose. Indulge yourself. Try those street tacos! You'll be hooked for life!

Mural - Rancho Buena Vista Cantina

HOW TO MAKE TACOS

It seems like tacos are everyone's first introduction to Mexican food. Initially in the US all tacos were made with ground beef. Now there are a myriad of meat, poultry and seafood fillings for tacos, all of which follow in this section.

I've also listed two ways to serve tacos: using fried tortilla shells or hot, soft tortillas. You're probably more familiar with fried tacos, but as you read on the previous page, soft tacos are served curbside all over Baja and mainland Mexico.

They taste just as good, though and are actually preferable if you're making fish, carne asada or carnitas tacos. The recipe below serves four to six.

½ cup corn or canola oil (only for fried tacos)
12 corn tortillas
2 cups shredded beef or other filling (all recipes for fillings follow)
2 cups Chihuahua or jack cheese, grated
1 tomato, diced
1 bunch green onions, chopped
½ head lettuce or cabbage, shredded
1 cup salsa fresca (Salsa section)

Fried tacos

In small frying pan, heat oil until a drop of water sizzles immediately when added to it. Fry tortilla lightly on one side. Turn and fry lightly on the other side. Before tortilla becomes crisp, bend it in half, using tongs and a fork to hold it steady and crisp the folded end. Remove from oil and drain on paper towel. Repeat with all 12 tortillas.

Heat filling until steaming. Place one to two tablespoons filling mixture inside taco shell. Add shredded lettuce, onions, tomatoes and top with cheese. Repeat for all tacos. Serve immediately.

Street tacos (soft tacos)

The difference here is that soft tacos are not fried. Heat tortillas in the oven or microwave until hot and pliable. Fold and fill in the same way as fried tacos. If your tacos seem inclined to fall apart, try using two tortillas for double the strength. Serve immediately.

Quesa-tacos (a Baja street taco extravaganza)

My all-time favorite tacos are carne asada quesa-tacos. The only difference between soft street tacos and these are that after you fill the corn tortilla with meat, you add some grated jack cheese and flip it back onto the grill (or frying pan) until the cheese is melted. Then add the rest of the goodies. It is beyond delicious!

HOW TO MAKE BURRITOS

As I described in the introduction to Carnitas, Fajitas and Carne Asada Barbecues, burritos make a wonderful do-it-yourself buffet dinner. They're like street tacos, only they're made with flour tortillas and are twice as big as corn tortillas - which means you can cram a lot more goodies into them!

The flour tortillas are put on the table in a covered dish, the meat or fish is put in another serving dish and all other fillings, such as those listed below are displayed, along with a variety of salsas. People put whatever ingredients they choose into their burrito, roll it up and eat it. It's easy for the chef and entertaining for the guests.

8 large flour tortillas
2 cups shredded beef or other filling (all filling recipes follow)
1 cup refried beans
2 cups Chihuahua or jack cheese, grated
1 white onion, chopped
1 bunch cilantro, stems removed and diced
1 cup guacamole (Appetizer section)
1 cup salsa fresca (Salsa section)
For a sauce-covered burrito: 1½ enchilada suiza sauce or 1½ cups salsa ranchera (optional, from Salsa section)

Heat tortillas in oven or microwave until hot and pliable. Heat filling and beans in small saucepans or microwave until steaming. Fill heated tortilla with meat, beans, cheese, onion, onion, guacamole and salsa fresca. Fold ends under and roll into a log-like shape. If you prefer sauce on your burrito, omit the cheese inside the burrito. Immediately prior to serving, pour heated enchilada or ranchero sauce over burritos and top with cheese. Broil until cheese is bubbling.

HOW TO MAKE TOSTADAS

Tostadas are like flat tacos that usually have a layer of frijoles on the bottom and different fillings, lettuce, guacamole, cheese and salsa on top. Tostadas are almost-salads and are perfect for a light meal. They too make great buffet fare. The recipe below serves six.

½ cup corn or canola oil
12 corn tortillas
2 cups shredded beef or other filling (all filling recipes follow)
1½ cups frijoles
1 tomato, diced
1 white onion, diced
½ head lettuce, shredded
2 cups guacamole
2 cups Chihuahua or jack cheese, grated
1 cup salsa fresca (Salsa section)

In small frying pan, heat oil until a drop of water sizzles immediately when added to it. Fry tortilla lightly on one side. Turn and fry lightly on the other side. Remove from oil and drain on paper towel. Repeat with all 12 tortillas.

Heat filling and frijoles until steaming. Place one to two tablespoons of frijoles

on top of fried tortilla. Top with another two tablespoons of filling. Add shredded lettuce, onions, tomatoes and guacamole. Top with cheese and salsa fresca. Repeat for all tostadas. Serve immediately.

SHREDDED BEEF FILLING for TACOS, BURRITOS & TOSTADAS

There are two ways to make shredded beef. The lightening-fast way uses canned roast beef, while the traditional way takes hours. Whether you're a purist and take the longer pot roast route, or if you're a hurried cook or short-cut seeking camper (like me most of the time) and opt for the quick way - your beef will end up savory, tender and delicious! And no one will ever know if you cheat (unless you confess, of course).

Super easy shredded beef
1 - 12 ounce can roast beef in gravy, rinsed
½ cup salsa fresca (Salsa section)
Salt and pepper to taste

Place rinsed and drained roast beef in medium sized bowl. Add salsa fresca, salt and pepper. Shred the beef while mixing in the other ingredients until it has a stringy texture. Heat in small saucepan on medium low heat until hot. This makes about 1½ cups shredded beef, or enough for eight tacos or tostadas, or four burritos.

Traditional shredded beef
1 - 4 to 5 pound pot roast

¼ cup flour
2 tbsp corn or canola oil
1 large white onion, chopped
3 cloves garlic, minced
1 cup water
1 - 16 ounce can puréed tomatoes
1 cup salsa fresca (Salsa section)
1 tbsp beef bouillon
1 tsp each cayenne pepper, chili powder and oregano

Dredge pot roast in flour. In a Dutch oven, heat oil until sizzling. Brown pot roast on all sides in oil. Remove roast from pot, add onion and garlic and cook until translucent. Put roast back in pot. Add water and all other ingredients. Stir well. Bring to boil. Cover and reduce heat. Simmer for at least four hours, until meat is fork tender. Remove from heat and cool until you are able to comfortably handle meat. Using two forks, shred the beef.

You have enough shredded beef for two dozen tacos or tostadas, or about fifteen to eighteen burritos. Any unused meat can be frozen for future use.

CHICKEN FILLING for TACOS, BURRITOS & TOSTADAS

Use this filling in any of the taco, tostada or burrito recipes. It's a lean, lighter way to fill your tortillas, but I guarantee you, you won't be sacrificing any flavor! You'll have enough chicken filling to make 12 tacos or tostadas, or about eight burritos.

2 pounds boneless skinless chicken breasts or 2 - 12 ounce cans white meat chicken
1 cup salsa fresca (Salsa section)
2 cloves garlic, minced
Salt and pepper to taste

Bake chicken breasts in oven for 30 minutes at 350°. Remove from oven and cool. Using two forks, shred the chicken. If you are using canned chicken, drain off excess liquid, place in bowl and shred. In a medium sized bowl, mix shredded chicken with salsa and garlic. Add salt and pepper to taste.

TURKEY FILLING for TACOS, BURRITOS & TOSTADAS

Use this filling in any of the taco, tostada or burrito recipes. It's lean and light, yet delicious. Thanks to the cumin you'll never taste anything that compares to this turkey filling. It's delectable! You'll have enough filling to make 12 tacos or tostadas, or about eight burritos.

2 pounds white turkey meat
½ cup salsa fresca
2 cloves garlic, minced
2 tsp ground cumin

Pico Pica sauce or any red pepper sauce to taste
Salt and pepper to taste

Bake turkey in oven for 30 minutes at 350°. Remove from oven and cool. Using two forks, shred the turkey. In a medium sized bowl, mix shredded turkey with salsa, garlic, cumin, Pico Pica sauce, salt and pepper. Serve.

BRISAS DEL MAR GROUND BEEF & POTATO TACOS

Beachfront resorts in Los Cabos can come with price tags from the hundreds to the thousands per night. I have found a couple hotels in downtown Cabo that charge less than $60 per night for a room, but they aren't on the beach. The best deal going is the Brisas del Mar RV Park just north of Zipper's in San Jose del Cabo. For $25 a night you can park your RV in a lovely, quiet garden-filled park. The beach is only a few steps away, and the restaurant and bar are top notch. People without rolling homes can stay in one of the super affordable rooms on the south end of the park.

When we last stayed there (it's exceedingly dog friendly, which is hard to find in Los Cabos) I had these tacos for lunch. I moaned my way through the whole meal! Makes six tacos, enough for two or three people.

1 lb ground beef
1 tsp ground cumin
1 tsp salt
¾ tsp pepper
1 medium russet potato
6 corn tortillas
1 cup corn or canola oil
2 cups shredded queso Chihuahua or jack cheese
1 head iceberg lettuce, shredded
2 tomatoes, diced
Salsa fresca (Salsa section)

In large skillet, crumble ground beef. Add cumin, salt and pepper. Peel potato and cut into small chunks. Add to beef mixture and cook, stirring occasionally until potato is tender to the bite and meat is very well browned, about 10 to 15 minutes.

In another skillet, heat oil over medium high heat. Lightly fry tortillas on each side, fold and remove to drain on paper towel.

Put two or three tacos on a plate. Stuff with filling. Cover with cheese and microwave for a minute or until cheese is melted. Garnish with shredded lettuce and tomatoes. Serve immediately with salsa on the side.

NINA'S FISH TACOS

This Baja creation has been around longer than I have. According to local legend, fish tacos originated in San Felipe where they have always been the street taco of choice. In the early '80s, they were discovered by a young Baja Aficionado who pirated the recipe from a now defunct taco vendor and bought it northwest to San Diego. He opened a tiny taco shop named Rubio's down by Mission Bay that specialized in authentic Baja-style fish tacos. At time of publication, there were Rubio's franchises in six western states! I guess I don't really need to tell you that the popularity of those fish tacos has skyrocketed.

For the best fish tacos south of the border these days, (in Nina's opinion) you have to travel to San Felipe (on the Sea of Cortez) or Ensenada (directly west on the Pacific). Her favorite tacos can be found at the fish market in Ensenada. When you first drive into town, you'll make a right turn just past the ship repair yards and immediately you'll see the outdoor fish market. There's a huge palapa on the right, at dockside, where vendors sell an incredible array of just-caught seafood, fresh shrimp cocktails and the most awesome fish tacos around.

This recipe is Nina's version of the Baja Fish Taco. Depending on their appetites, this will serve three to four people. But then again - if your friends are anything like ours - they may be so enamored with your fish tacos that you'll have to double the recipe next time around. You could have worse problems! Oh, and if you don't want to use fried fish, you can lightly season and broil or grill the fish fillets instead. You won't sacrifice either the taste or the inherent air of festivity generated by these colorful, incredible tacos.

4 fillets of white fish cut into strips of about one inch each
2 eggs, lightly beaten
½ cup corn flake crumbs
¼ cup Italian breadcrumbs
½ cup corn or canola oil
8 corn tortillas
6 radishes, minced
1 cup shredded cabbage
½ bunch cilantro, in sprigs
1 large tomato, chopped
1 cup Chihuahua or jack cheese, shredded
An array of your favorite salsas (I suggest salsa fresca, salsa verde, avocado sauce and María's salsa de arbol from Salsa section)
Fish taco sauce made from 1/3 cup mayonnaise, 5 tbsp milk and 1 tbsp lime juice

Dredge each fish fillet in beaten egg. Coat thoroughly with mixture of corn flake crumbs and Italian breadcrumbs.

In frying pan heat oil until a drop of water sizzles when dropped in the pan. Cook each fish fillet for three to four minutes on each side. Remove from pan and drain on paper towels. Place fillets in oven on warm until you are ready to serve.

In a small bowl, mix the fish taco sauce. Put a fish fillet on one half of a hot corn tortilla. Place one to two tablespoons of sauce on top of fillet as you are serving it. Garnish with your choice of condiments and your favorite salsas.

AUTHENTIC BAJA FISH TACOS

In this book, I've added a much more traditional and authentically Baja recipe, which comes from a blend of recipes sent to me. A few years back I did a survey of all my Baja amigos and asked which fish taco stand in Baja was their favorite. McLulu's Fish Tacos in Loreto came in first, followed closely by Leonelly's Fish Taco Stand in Guerrero Negro. Coming in third was Tía Maguí's Fish Tacos from Mercado Negro on the wharf in Ensenada. My friend Debbie tried all three recipes and came up with this one. According to her and my army of fish taco enthusiasts, it really allows the flavor of the fish to shine through. Feeds three to four and makes eight tacos.

4 fillets of white fish cut in strips about one inch wide each
2 limónes (Mexican limes) or key limes
2 eggs, lightly beaten
1 cup flour
1 tsp baking powder
2 cups corn or canola oil
Salt to taste
8 corn tortillas
6 radishes, minced
1 cup shredded cabbage
½ bunch cilantro, in sprigs
1 large tomato, chopped
1 cup Chihuahua or jack cheese, shredded
An array of your favorite salsas
(I suggest salsa fresca, salsa verde, avocado sauce and María's salsa de arbol

from Salsa section)
Fish taco sauce made from 1/3 cup mayonnaise, 5 tbsp milk and 1 tbsp lime juice

Squeeze the lime juice over the fish. To make the batter, gradually add flour and baking powder to lightly beaten eggs in a medium bowl. Season to taste with salt.

Pour oil to a depth of 1½ inches and heat until water sizzles when dropped in the pan.

Cook each fish fillet for three to four minutes on each side. Remove from pan and drain on paper towels. Place fillets in oven on warm until you are ready to serve.

Put a fish fillet on one half of a hot corn tortilla. Place one to two tablespoons of fish taco sauce on top of fillet as you are serving it. Garnish with shredded cabbage and serve immediately with your favorite garnishes and salsas.

BAY OF L.A. LOBSTER TACOS

The first time I ever heard of lobster tacos was at Mama Diaz' restaurant in Bahía de Los Angeles. (Bay of L.A., as we gringos call it, is a remote but spectacularly scenic fishing village on the Sea of Cortez, a third of the way down the Baja peninsula.) That trip was nearly 40 years ago, before there was even a paved road south of El Rosario.

We flew in with Francisco (Pancho) Muñoz, a World War II ace who ran Baja Airlines and was a great buddy of both my Pappy and Erle Stanley Gardner. Pancho's leaflets advertised the Bay of L.A. as, " ... the Fabulous Fishing Resort in Baja." A flight left Tijuana every Friday morning at 11:00 and returned every Saturday at 2:00 pm. Round-trip tickets went for $47.52. Flying time was a little over two hours in one of his Douglas B-18's (World War II bombers similar to DC-3s). After we'd traveled with Muñoz a few times, he and my dad (who were the same age) became great amigos in their own right. Often, over the years, when we flew with him, one of my folks would sit up in the cockpit and hang out with him. Sometimes Nina and I got to also, but our favorite jobs were when we got to serve canned drinks, sack lunches and other snacks to the passengers - which to two girls under 12 was - in today's gringo lingo - way cool.

I still think of Pancho Muñoz whenever I pass the airport in Ensenada and see a pair of old, dilapidated Douglas B-18s sitting beside the runway there, just rusting away. Every single time I wonder if those are his planes, the same planes I flew all over Baja in when I was a kid. I don't know. Muñoz has long since retired and is in his 80s now, but Nina and I will never forget him or his daredevil landings, some of which were on dirt runways barely wider than a truck.

A few years ago I went back to the Bay of L.A. Sure enough, the Casa Diaz was still there, even though Mama and Antero had both passed away. And sure enough, they still served lobster tacos, even though they weren't on the menu. Some things don't ever change and one of those facts of life is that the best things in Mexico are not always on the menu ... especially in obscure places. I like that. Lobster tacos are best served as soft tacos in fresh corn tortillas. Makes 12 tacos.

2 pounds cooked, diced lobster meat
2 cloves garlic, minced
2 serrano or jalapeño chiles, minced
Juice from 2 limónes (Mexican limes) or key limes
12 corn tortillas
6 radishes, minced
1 cup shredded cabbage
½ bunch cilantro, in sprigs
1 large tomato, chopped
1 cup Chihuahua or jack cheese, shredded
An array of your favorite salsas (I suggest salsa fresca, salsa verde, avocado sauce and María's salsa de arbol from Salsa section)
Fish taco sauce made from 1/3 cup mayonnaise, 5 tbsp milk and 1 tbsp lime juice

Heat all ingredients in medium sized saucepan. Serve on warmed corn tortillas as you would any tacos with condiments listed above.

LOS ARCOS CEVICHE TOSTADAS

At the very tip of Baja, just offshore from Cabo San Lucas, is what's called Finisterra, or Land's End. There is an exquisite beach that you can reach only by boat, whether it is a panga, yacht, kayak or Jet Ski. It's a two-sided spit of sand called Lover's Beach and it gets pretty windy out there because one side of it faces the Pacific and the other the Sea of Cortez. Just past it is the world-famous, frequently photographed, dramatic rock formations known as Los Arcos. These rocks rise ruggedly above an undersea cascade of rocks and sand, which was discovered and explored by Jacques Cousteau, a few decades back.

While the missionaries as far back as the 1500s visited Cabo San Lucas, and it was a favored hang out for pirates and whaling vessels in the 1800s, it really didn't take off as a town until the late 1960s. With the completion of Mexico's Highway 1 in late '73, which runs down the entire length of the Baja peninsula, Cabo finally began to grow. The first time I vacationed there in the early '80s it was a sleepy village with absolutely zero nightlife. These days it's a bustling tourist metropolis where there are an increasing number of (think Hollywood)"star sightings." Any night of the week you can hear young (and even some not-so-young) American tourists boogying the night away, hooting and hollering in any of the many bars and nightclubs all over town.

When you go to Cabo, try one of these delicate, spicy and healthful snacks at any of the beachfront restaurants on El Medano Beach, the main beach in town. You can wiggle your toes in the warm sand as the sun sets behind you and watch as the sky turns from golden to flaming crimson to a delicate almost-orange and then fades out into sultry opalescence. While the waves lap gently in front you, sip an iced libation and munch on ceviche tostadas just like these. This recipe makes 12 tostadas and will serve six to eight.

6 cups ceviche (Appetizer section)
12 fried flat tortillas

Spoon the chilled ceviche directly onto fried flat tortillas. Top with all tostada toppings except frijoles. Serve immediately.

MUSHROOM, CHORIZO & RAJA TOSTADAS

Oscar, the chef at Hotel Buena Vista Beach Resort, gave me this recipe. Even though it's not on the menu, it's one of Oscar's special creations and you can order it regardless as long as he's in the kitchen! For years, the young chefs at the hotel never stuck around. They sort of apprenticed there and then moved on to Los Cabos or somewhere else more trendy. Oscar, however, fell in love with Eva, the lead server at the hotel restaurant. Since she has two kids, Oscar has no plans of leaving. We are glad, because he's an excellent chef and a mean ping-pong player. Serves four.

8 corn tortillas
½ cup corn or canola oil
2 cups refried beans (Bean section or use canned)
2½ cups mushrooms, sliced
2 tbsp butter
8 ounces chorizo (Breakfast section)
2 poblano chiles, blistered
1 white onion, thinly sliced
2 chipotle chiles in adobo (from can)
1 cup crema media ácida or sour cream
2 cups grated Chihuahua or jack cheese
1 head iceberg lettuce, shredded
Salt and pepper to taste

In skillet, fry tortillas in oil until crisp on both sides. Drain on paper towels. Heat beans in saucepan. In another skillet, cook mushrooms in butter until done. Set aside in bowl. In same skillet, fry chorizo until done.

To blister chiles: If you have a gas stove, lay the chiles over the open flame and char skins well, turning with tongs frequently until they're uniformly blackened and stop snapping. The more charred they are, the easier it is to remove the skins. If you have an electric stove, place chiles in a large skillet on high heat. Turn frequently as above. Remove chiles to plastic bag, close it and let stand for 10 minutes. Remove from bag, place in ice-cold water and remove the stems, skin, veins and seeds. Cut into rajas (thin strips).

In blender or food processor, purée chipotles with crema or sour cream. To make tostadas, start with a layer of beans on top of the fried tortillas. Add chorizo, mushrooms, rajas and adobo-crema sauce. Top with shredded lettuce and cheese and serve.

ENCHILADAS & RELLENOS

Enchiladas and Chiles Rellenos (CHEE-lace Ray-YAY-nos) are two more typical Mexican dishes I grew up eating - and loving. While I remember having a choice between beef, chicken or cheese enchiladas at local Mexican restaurants when I was younger, there was only one kind of chile relleno around back then. It was a green chile stuffed with white cheese, fried in egg batter and smothered with a mild salsa. I still love it, but I have a new favorite now ... the grilled chile relleno. It's much lighter and to me the flavors really burst through. Check it out.

Enchiladas and rellenos are consistently and mystically altered by creative Baja chefs, and new versions are always showing up, so I've struggled to keep up. I've managed to come up with a few elegant variations of enchiladas and rellenos. But - to tell you the truth - I've only succeeded as much as I want to at this. Cooking With Baja Magic Dos isn't supposed to be a gourmet cookbook, full of recipes that take all day to make. However, every once in a while a restaurant chef gives me a recipes that crosses that line and ventures into serious gourmet territory. Oh well! Pueblo Bonito's Enchiladas Baja are a perfect example of this.

So, please be assured that I don't want you to be frustrated. I don't want you to plan a fiesta and be utterly exhausted by the time the guests arrive. Or worse yet, I don't want you to cancel the entire party at the last minute (or throw everything in the trash and order pizzas) because dinner didn't turn out. That isn't what Baja Magic is about! Baja Magic is about having fun. It's about going barefoot, putting a flower behind your ear and dancing around the kitchen to La Bamba de Vera Cruz as you dip your tortillas into a wonderful, smooth, tomatoey-smelling sauce and fill those soon-to-be-enchiladas with chicken, olives and onions.

 Anyway - I've offered you a combination of the old standbys and a few of the newer, snazzier versions of enchiladas and rellenos. Plus you get to take another trip with me down Memory Lane to the El Dorado Restaurant on the sand in Puerto Vallarta, where one of my mom's and my all-time favorite dishes was born. Chilaquiles. Do try that one! And, please - don't worry. As always, my recipes are simple to prepare without sacrificing flavor and excitement.

Just remember - take off your shoes before you start to cook. Barefoot is necessary. It loosens you up and lets the slightly offbeat, eccentric, playful imp inside you come out to play. And that is critical if you are to evolve into a real Baja chef!

CHICKEN ENCHILADAS SUIZAS

I first had these mild, yet flavorful enchiladas when I was eight years old and staying in La Paz for the very first time. Enchiladas were the top of the line as far as Mexican food goes, according to my mom (and her mom before her). So of course I was encouraged to try them on my first big Baja adventure. I loved them then and I love them now. In fact, the most recent time I had enchiladas suizas was at a bay-front restaurant right on the malecón in Lap Paz - for breakfast!

I couldn't believe they were really and truly on the breakfast menu, but they were. And I, preferring enchiladas to eggs most any day, promptly ordered them. Of course, this story wouldn't be complete if I didn't tell you what Nina ordered. She ordered a "Perrito Caliente," which was a huge hot dog, (although the literal translation is "warm puppy") smothered in mustard and loaded up with cheese, bacon, pineapple and avocado. For breakfast, mind you. With coffee! I didn't know yet that Mexican hot dogs are a national delicacy, usually served wrapped in bacon off a hot dog cart ... only at night. You can check out the recipe in the Poultry and Meat section.

While I haven't included this recipe in the breakfast section, I do recommend these enchiladas for breakfast, lunch or dinner. And the sauce can be spooned over eggs, meat, fish or poultry or used as a mild salsa with tacos. Makes three cups. This recipe serves four.

Enchilada Suiza Sauce

8 large tomatoes
1½ tbsp oil
6 chiles de arbol, lightly toasted
1 pasilla or guajillo chile (pasilla is milder), lightly toasted
1 large white onion, quartered
6 cloves garlic, peeled
1 cup water
1 cup crema media ácida or American sour cream
Salt and pepper to taste

In large skill, heat oil and cook tomatoes until blackened and softened, about 15 minutes. Meanwhile, soak chiles in water for 15 minutes to soften. Remove stems, seeds and membranes if desired. In food processor, blend together tomatoes, chiles, onion, garlic, water and crema or sour cream. Season to taste with salt and pepper and pour into a large saucepan. Heat thoroughly.

Enchiladas

½ cup corn or canola oil
12 corn tortillas
2 pounds boneless chicken breasts, cooked and cubed
4 cups Swiss, Chihuahua or jack cheese, grated
1 bunch green onions, chopped
1 cup crema media ácida sour cream

Garnish
1 cup lettuce, shredded
1 tomato, diced
½ cup queso fresco, crumbled (can substitute feta)

Heat oil in skillet until a drop of water sizzles when dropped in it. Fry a tortilla lightly on both sides so it's still pliable. Using tongs, remove it from the pan. Dip it into the enchilada sauce and lay it inside a 9 x 13 pan. Stuff enchilada with chicken, cheese and onions. Roll and place seam side down in the pan. Repeat for all 12 tortillas, reserving a small amount of cheese and onions.

When all enchiladas are made, place the pan in a 350° oven for about twenty minutes. Remove from oven, pour remaining enchilada sauce over enchiladas until almost covered. Cover with remaining cheese and onions. Broil for two minutes or until cheese is melted. Serve immediately, topped with media crema or sour cream and garnishes.

CHICKEN ENCHILADAS VERDES

After my son Derek was born, a friend of mine brought this dish over to us for dinner one night. I loved it and immediately called to ask her where she'd gotten the recipe. Amazingly enough, she'd had these enchiladas with a tangy green sauce at a fancy restaurant in Ensenada while on one of those three-day cruises to Baja. She, like my mother and me before her, had begged the recipe off her waiter and brought it home with her to add to her repertory. Since she shared it with me, I can now share it with you and you too can enjoy these enchiladas with a true Baja flair. Serves six.

Sour Cream-Green Chile Enchilada Sauce
1 pint crema media ácida or sour cream
2½ cups salsa verde
4 cloves garlic, minced
3 poblano chiles, blistered and peeled
or 1 - 7 ounce can diced green chiles, puréed

Enchiladas
18 corn tortillas
2 bunches green onions, chopped
4 cups Chihuahua or Jack cheese, shredded
2 pounds boneless chicken breasts cooked and cubed.
1 additional cup of salsa verde

If you have a gas stove, lay the chiles over the open flame and char skins well, turning with tongs frequently until they're uniformly blackened and stop snapping. The more charred they are, the easier it is to remove the skins. If you have an electric stove, place chiles in a large skillet on high heat. Turn frequently as above. Remove chiles to plastic bag, close it and let stand for 10 minutes. Remove from bag, place in ice-cold water and remove the stems, skins, veins and seeds. Purée.

To make sauce, combine crema or sour cream, salsa verde, minced garlic and puréed chiles in a medium saucepan and stir well. Heat over medium to low heat.

Heat oil in skillet until a drop of water sizzles when dropped in the pan. Fry a tortilla lightly on both sides so it is still pliable. Using tongs, remove it from the pan and drain on paper towels. Lay it inside a 9 x 13 pan. Place a tablespoon of sauce on each dipped tortilla. Top with chicken, cheese and onions. Roll and place seam down in pan.

When all tortillas are filled, mix leftover sauce with additional cup of salsa verde. Pour over enchiladas. Top with remaining cheese and onions. Bake at 350° for twenty minutes or until cheese is melted. Serve immediately.

Ann & Terry at Pueblo Bonito Rosé

PUEBLO BONITO ENCHILADAS BAJA

This recipe is one of the most popular served by the chain of Pueblo Bonito resorts. The Béchamel sauce is not difficult to make, but it certainly takes the taste and presentation of an enchilada to a whole new level. The combination of shrimp, crab and fish take it up yet another notch! Elegant and sophisticated, it is pure Cabo Magic! Serves six.

Béchamel Sauce
½ cup unsalted butter
½ cup all-purpose flour
4 cups milk
1 large white onion, puréed
1 bay leaf
Dash dried leaf thyme, crumbled
Salt and white pepper to taste
Nutmeg, to taste

In saucepan, melt butter over low heat. When it starts to foam, add the flour all at once and mix well. Cook over low heat for three to four minutes, stirring constantly. Remove from heat and let stand up to 15 minutes.

In a medium saucepan, scald milk (heat until just below boiling point). Return saucepan with roux (flour-butter mixture) to stove at medium-low heat. Add all of the scalded milk at once to avoid the formation of lumps. Simmer, stirring gently. Add onion, bay leaf and thyme. Cook, stirring, over low heat for another fifteen minutes, or until thickened. Strain. Add salt, white pepper and nutmeg to taste.

Enchiladas
16 ounces shrimp
12 ounces lobster meat
16 ounces fish fillet
4 tsp chopped garlic
4 tbsp chopped white onion
8 tbsp butter
1 cup white wine
Salt and pepper to taste
12 flour tortillas
1½ cups Oaxaca cheese or other easily melted white cheese

½ cup tomato, diced
Fine herbs as garnish

Peel, devein, and dice the shrimp. Dice the lobster and fish fillet. Sauté the garlic and onion in butter until translucent, add the seafood and cook thoroughly over low heat. Add the white wine, reduce it, and add the béchamel sauce. Season with salt and pepper.

Heat the tortillas, fill with the seafood mixture and roll them. Top each with 2 slices of Oaxaca cheese and melt in the oven. Sprinkle with diced tomato and fine herbs as a garnish.

CHILAQUILES VALLARTA

We used to eat chilaquiles at the El Dorado Restaurant in Puerto Vallarta when I was a kid. We sat in yellow and green chairs right on the sand and ate at low tables in our wet bathing suits. To this day, whenever I go to Puerto Vallarta, the El Dorado is one of my first stops. Even though the resort has grown astronomically and bears little resemblance to the sleepy village Nina, our dad and I remember from the '60s, the El Dorado is still there and it still serves some of the best food in Puerto Vallarta. And hey, there's no way you can beat the location!

One of my favorite memories from the El Dorado dates back to the Christmas of 1967. We had just ordered lunch. My parents were discussing the concept of the empty nest. I could tell that my dad was worried about my mom being lonely as he anticipated Nina's and my eventual departure for college. Suddenly he stood up. My eyes followed his until I spotted the cutest little black and white puppy I had ever set eyes on. It was under the pier, on a frayed rope held by one of two little Mexican girls. Within two minutes my dad had bought that dog for $4.00 USD, plus a few pesos to buy ice cream for the crying little girls. We named her Victoria, and she was my mother's shadow for the next 16 years.

Meanwhile, back on the beach, Victoria fell asleep in Nina's lap. Our lunch arrived and we dug in. A beach vendor selling silver earrings, necklaces and rings diverted Nina's attention. When she looked back down at her plate, her chilaquiles were gone. Little Victoria, barely six weeks old, had scarfed the entire meal!

Chilaquiles were, and still are, a favorite of mine. They're served all over Baja and are offered on most breakfast menus as a local alternative to eggs and such. I maintain that you can eat them for breakfast, lunch or dinner. They are that versatile! Oh, and by the way - Victoria flew home with us on Francisco Muñoz' Baja Airlines. Unlike a pet on an American airliner, she wasn't treated like a piece of luggage and relegated to the baggage department. Instead, she napped on the seat next to me and chased my dad up and down the aisle, barking gleefully as he helped hand out sack lunches. This recipe serves six and

it will make you think you're right there on the sand, within steps of that 80° ocean. Oh yeah!

3 poblano chiles, roasted and cut in strips or 1 - 7 ounce can green chiles, cut in strips
12 corn tortillas
½ cup corn oil
2 cups enchilada sauce (Pick one from this section or use canned)
1 cup crema media ácida or 1 cup sour cream
1½ lb boneless chicken breasts, cooked and cut in chunks
4 cups Chihuahua or jack cheese, grated
½ cup media crema mixed with 1 tbsp water to thin out

If you have a gas stove, lay the chiles over the open flame and char skins well, turning with tongs frequently until they're uniformly blackened and stop snapping. The more charred they are, the easier it is to remove the skins. If you have an electric stove, place chiles in a large skillet on high heat. Turn frequently as above. Remove chiles to plastic bag, close it and let stand for 10 minutes. Remove from bag, place in ice-cold water and remove the stems, skins, veins and seeds. Cut into strips.

Cut tortillas into one-inch strips and fry in oil until crisp. Drain on paper towels. Combine enchilada sauce with sour cream in saucepan. Heat thoroughly.

In a 9 x 13 pan layer the tortilla strips, chicken, chile strips, cheese and enchilada sauce. Repeat. Top with a layer of tortilla strips, sauce and lots of cheese. Bake at 350° for 25 minutes, or until cheese is melted and chilaquiles are bubbling. Drizzle thinned media crema over each serving.

STACKED CHEESE ENCHILADAS TAOS STYLE

New Mexico red chiles and cinnamon give these stacked enchiladas a flavor that is singularly Southwestern. I first tasted enchiladas prepared this way on a trip to Taos, New Mexico in 1980. I clearly remember that chilly winter evening as my boyfriend and I dined in a 400 year-old adobe building in the Old Taos Pueblo. We could have been in a museum; there were so many Native American artifacts. Navajo rugs, Hopi and Zuni kachina dolls and Pueblo pottery and baskets surrounded us. A kiva, or round stucco fireplace dominated the room. From it radiated wonderful, cozy warmth.

My stomach growled as my nose caught wind of the aromas drifting in from behind the swinging kitchen doors. There was one smell in particular that intrigued me and I asked our waiter what it was. (Can you guess?) These unusual enchiladas are still as good as they smelled that night. Even though there's nothing Baja about them, they are so incredible that I couldn't resist sneaking them into this book! They make an attractive and not-often-seen presentation, especially if you use blue corn tortillas. Overall, they're easier to make than rolled enchiladas and the fried egg on top makes for a diner's delight. Serves four.

Taos Style Enchilada Sauce
12 - 20 seeded dried red New Mexico red chiles (hot) or 4 - 6 tbsp New Mexico chile powder (hot)
or 4 - 6 tbsp American chili powder (milder)
3 cloves garlic, minced
1 medium onion, quartered
1 tsp cinnamon
1 tbsp sugar
2 - 12 ounce cans tomato sauce
Salt and pepper to taste

Making the Enchilada Sauce
Remove stems and seeds from chiles. In a medium saucepan, simmer chiles in ¾ cup water for 10 minutes or until tender. Puree in food processor with garlic, onion, cinnamon and sugar. (If you're using powdered chiles, purée all ingredients including tomato sauce and an additional ½ cup water in food processor.) Return to sauce pan. Add tomato sauce, salt and pepper. Simmer for 20 minutes to an hour. This recipe makes over three cups, so you should have leftover sauce to freeze for next time.

Making the Stacked Enchiladas
1 cup corn or canola oil
12 blue corn or regular corn tortillas
1 large onion, chopped
4 cups cheddar cheese, shredded
3 tbsp butter
4 eggs
Garnish
4 green onions, diced

1 - 3½ ounce can sliced black olives
1 cup shredded lettuce
1 fresh avocado, diced

Heat oil in small skillet. Fry each tortilla until slightly crisp. Dip each tortilla in enough enchilada sauce to lightly coat it. After you dip the first four tortillas, place them side-by-side in a greased 9 x 13 pan. Sprinkle with a tablespoon of onion and ¼ cup cheese. Fry the next tortilla, dip in sauce and lay over the first tortilla and filling. Sprinkle on more onion and cheese. Fry, dip and lay on the third and last tortilla of each stack. Sprinkle the remaining cheese on top of each stack.

Fry the eggs three minutes in butter. Lift each stack, using a wide spatula to waiting dinner plates. Top with fried egg and garnish with minced green onion, olives, shredded lettuce and diced avocado.

CRAB ENCHILADAS CALAFIA STYLE

A few minutes south of Rosarito on the free road (no tolls) is the resort, Calafia. It has been around for as long as I can remember and is famous for its rocking and rolling pirate ship, painted in an array of wild colors that hangs precariously out over a hot surf spot on the Pacific Ocean. The deejay actually plays his music from inside the ship as revelers dance the afternoons and nights away on its wooden decks or on one of the restaurant's many patios.

More sedate or hungry people can order

lunch at one of the many outdoor tables terraced down the side of the cliff, overlooking the crashing waves (and the dancers). This recipe for Crab Enchiladas was inspired by one of our escapades to Calafia. Since I don't eat seafood, Nina ordered these enchiladas and raved about them so profusely that the other people in our group began attacking her plate and nearly wiped it out before she could finish a single enchilada! In our family we've always called that the "wandering fork game" and Nina has always been our star player, as her fork can dart in and out of other people's meals faster than anyone else's. It was amusing to see the tables turned on her.

Because the waiter refused to give us the recipe, we proceeded to analyze the ingredients. After a bit of trial and error in the kitchen, this recipe was born. These crab enchiladas are delicate, unique and - as Nina will absolutely guarantee you - a real crowd pleaser. Serves four.

1 tbsp butter or margarine
1 tbsp corn or canola oil
2 garlic cloves and 1 medium onion, minced
1 tbsp chili powder
1½ pounds fresh cooked crabmeat
1/3 cup mayonnaise
½ tsp salt
1 tbsp cilantro, chopped
12 corn tortillas
3 cups enchilada sauce (Pick one from this section or use canned)
½ cup corn or canola oil (to fry tortillas)

4 cups Chihuahua or jack cheese, grated
1 bunch green onions, chopped

Melt butter and oil in a medium saucepan over low heat. Add garlic and onion and cook over medium heat until translucent. Remove from heat and add chili powder, crab, mayonnaise, salt and cilantro. Heat enchilada sauce in another saucepan.

In a skillet, heat oil until a drop of water sizzles when dropped in the pan. Fry a tortilla lightly on both sides so it is still pliable. Using tongs, remove it from the pan. Dip it into the enchilada sauce and lay it inside a 9 x 13 pan. Stuff enchilada with crab mixture, cheese and onions. Roll and place seam side down in the pan. Repeat with all tortillas. When all enchiladas are made, place the pan in a 350° oven for about twenty minutes. Remove from oven; pour remaining enchilada sauce over enchiladas until almost covered. Top with remaining cheese and onions. Broil for one to two minutes until cheese is melted. Serve immediately and await compliments.

CARNITAS ENCHILADAS

This simple enchilada dish is festive, relatively new on the Baja scene and fabulous. It's a perfect way to use up left over carnitas, which if you recall, I am quite partial to. So you can bet that I invariably find myself in a good mood whenever I'm getting ready to make Carnitas Enchiladas. I especially like the salsa verde instead of enchilada sauce in this dish, because its tart but zesty flavor complements the pork perfectly. Serves four.

1½ pounds left over carnitas (Carnitas section)
½ cup corn or canola oil
12 corn tortillas
2 - 3 cups salsa verde (Salsa section)
2 cups Chihuahua or jack cheese, grated
1 cup crema media ácida or American sour cream thinned with ¼ cup water
Paprika as garnish

Steam carnitas meat in saucepan or microwave until hot. Preheat oven to 400°. Heat oil in heavy skillet until a drop of water sizzles when dropped in pan. Using tongs, cook a tortilla until pliable. Drain on paper towels.

Heat salsa verde in saucepan. Place two tablespoons carnitas meat and some cheese inside the tortilla. Roll and place, seam side down in baking dish. Repeat. Sprinkle remaining cheese over the enchiladas and place in oven until cheese is melted. Pour salsa verde and thin sour cream sauce over the enchiladas. Garnish with paprika. Serve immediately.

CHILES RELLENOS

Sue and Jim are about my age. They're former urban professionals who ducked out of the rat race and expatri-ated themselves to Baja in the early '90s. During our decade in La Bufadora, my kids and I shared a lot of adventures with them. We went on kayaking trips, we hiked and we hung out at the beach and snorkeled.

This is Sue's incredible chiles rellenos recipe. She insisted I use it because it's far better than the one I invented back in college. I had a phobia about blistering and skinning chiles, so I used canned chiles instead of fresh in my recipe. "Naughty, naughty," said Sue, shaking her head in disbelief. She proceeded to teach me how to blister and skin those chiles, and I've never used a canned chile since! Serves three to six, depending on how many you eat!

6 large poblano chiles or 6 large Anaheim chiles
½ pound Chihuahua or jack cheese, thinly sliced
¼ cup flour
6 raw eggs, separated
½ to ¾ cup flour
2 cups salsa verde, salsa ranchera or María's salsa de arbol (Salsa section)
1½ cups corn or canola oil

If you have a gas stove, lay the chiles over the open flame and char skins well, turning with tongs frequently until they're uniformly blackened and stop snapping. The more charred they are, the easier it is to remove the skins. If you have an electric stove, place chiles in a large skillet on high heat. Turn frequently as above. Remove chiles to plastic bag, close it and let stand for 10 minutes. Remove from bag, place in ice-cold water and remove the skin. Make a small slit on the side of each chile and remove all seeds and membranes. Do not remove stem! Insert a slice of cheese into the hole.

Whip egg whites at high speed until stiff peaks have formed. At the same time, heat the oil in a deep skillet until a drop of water sizzles when dropped into the pan. (Note: the oil needs to about three inches deep to cover the chiles about 2/3 of the way.) Beat egg yolks and stir in flour until it makes a very thick paste. Mix into egg whites.

Roll chiles in flour and dip in egg batter. Place seam side down in the pan. Fry on one side until golden brown, then gently roll over. When golden brown on both sides, drain on paper towels. Meanwhile, heat salsa (either one type or some of each) and pour over chiles rellenos. Serve immediately. I can't begin to tell you how good these are!

GRILLED CHILES RELLENOS

I first tried grilled rellenos at Las Olas Restaurant in Cardiff-by-the-Sea, where Terry and I used to live. It was and is our favorite Mexican restaurant in the area. I was instantly hooked and always order them when I'm there with a double order of their cabbage salad. A very healthy, non-fatty Mexican meal, I have to say. I played around and finally figured out how to make these and now, since I only get to Las Olas a couple times a year on my visits to family and friends, I can make

them any time the craving hits me. So can you! Serves three to six.

6 large poblano chiles or 6 large Anaheim chiles
½ pound Chihuahua or jack cheese, thinly sliced
2 cups salsa verde, salsa ranchera or María's salsa de arbol (Salsa section)
Toothpicks

If you have a gas stove, lay the chiles over the open flame and char skins well, turning with tongs frequently until they're uniformly blackened and stop snapping. The more charred they are, the easier it is to remove the skins. If you have an electric stove, place chiles in a large skillet on high heat. Turn frequently as above. Remove chiles to plastic bag, close it and let stand for 10 minutes. Remove from bag, place in ice-cold water and remove the skin. Make a small slit in the side of each chile and gently remove all seeds and membranes. Do not remove the stem! Insert a slice of cheese into the hole. Secure with a toothpick if necessary.

Place chiles rellenos on a heated griddle on stove or over a very hot barbecue. Heat about five minutes on each side, until steaming and slightly charred again. Meanwhile, heat salsa (either type or some of each) and pour over chiles rellenos. Serve immediately. When I made a test batch for some Buena Vista amigos, every single person preferred these over the fried version!

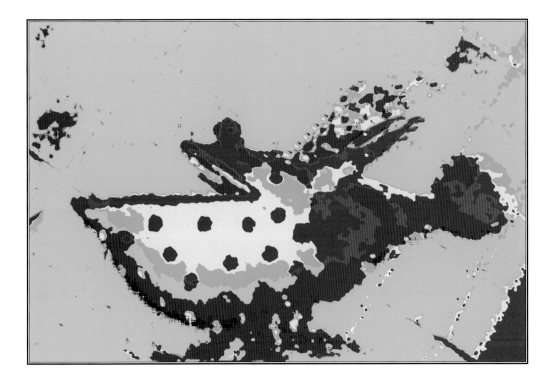

SEAFOOD ENTRÉES

California and Baja California coexist on over 3000 miles of coastline - not counting any of the zigs and zags. Off the west coast of both are the cool waters (about 55° - 70° Fahrenheit) of the Pacific. This ocean offers up lobster, abalone, tuna and halibut - to name only a few varieties of its bounty. The much warmer (about 70° - 85° Fahrenheit) Sea of Cortez is a 1000-mile ocean trench that extends between Baja on the west and the Sierra de la Madre Mountains of mainland Mexico on the east. It's home to at least 850 known species of marine creatures, (the richest abundance of undersea life anywhere on the planet) ranging from shrimp to dorado to huachinango to tiburón to the magnificent marlin and sailfish.

Some of the best big game fishing in the world is found just north of Cabo San Lucas off the east coast of southernmost Baja. I know - my dad began taking us there when I was eight. Back in the early '60s when we first visited La Paz and the East Cape area just to the south of it, the only way to get in was by boat or by air. The paved road wasn't completed for another decade. Our friend Francisco Muñoz' Baja Airlines flew in from Tijuana, along with Aeronaves de Mexico and Mexicana de Aviación. No gringo airlines did. Our friend Muñoz carried his share of rich and famous Baja Aficionados down there to fish. Guys like Chuck Connors, Desi Arnaz, Fred Astaire and my Pappy's pal, Erle Stanley Gardner. Back then the waters churned with roosterfish, the wildest fighters in all of the Sea of Cortez - said to be even more exciting to reel in than a marlin.

I caught one. Nina caught one. My mom caught several. In fact, my mother liked to say that she, Nina and I were all over-fished before I was ten. An exaggeration? Probably not. I remember the Easter vacation when I was eight. We flew into La Paz on a Saturday. Before dawn on Sunday morning we were aboard a cabin cruiser, speeding towards fertile fishing grounds. My parents were on deck fishing until lunch. Nina and I got bored by 9:30 and by 11:30 we'd tasted our way through every cold burrito and cookie and sandwich in every single sack lunch on the boat! You can imagine our parents' embarrassment when they discovered we'd sampled pieces (a la Goldilocks) of everyone's food. My dad did his best to explain the situation in his fishing boat Spanish to our captain (who of course spoke no English). Finally, with my mom's help, he got the point across. The growling stomachs on board won out over any pretense of convention and everyone agreed that eating pre-tasted food was better than eating no food at all! So they ate. We, obviously, weren't hungry! By the time they'd finished lunch, it had all become a great joke. And one we laugh about to this day.

We were, by then, anchored off Isla Espiritú Santo, that huge multi-bayed island populated only by sea birds, sand, cacti, driftwood and shells - and surrounded by see-through aquamarine water. As I peered overboard, I glimpsed bright colors flashing against the current, as school after school of tropical fish darted below us. Mom taught us how to snorkel that day. Our next time out we found another deserted cove on the same island and picnicked there. We returned to the boat with our t-shirts fashioned into sacks that overflowed with seashells. We fished four out of the five days we were there. To top off a great trip, we ran into John Wayne at the La Paz airport and Nina had her picture taken with him. We've been hooked on Baja ever since. When my dad had completely over-fished us, about five years later, he began making his annual fishing trips without us. He began going to Buena Vista on the East Cape with his brother, Bruce and a gang of their construction buddies instead. In 1970 he brought the whole family down for Thanksgiving and it became our new "place."

Only Derek has inherited his grandpa's passion for fishing. My dad spends 11 weeks a year down here, and Derek five or six. And every morning, they're up before dawn, slapping on the sunscreen, lugging their fishing poles down to the beach. Ready to fish!

This section offers up an abundance of seafood dishes. Some are spicy, some aren't. There are plenty of new ones, and many improved ones too. They come to you courtesy of Nina, the family seafood aficionada and other great Baja chefs. They're all guaranteed to transport you - south.

Mural - Rancho Buena Vista Hotel Cantina

BASIC BAJA FISH MARINADE

When my cookbook first came out, I was invited by Vagabundos del Mar (a Baja travel club) to hang out in their booth and autograph books at the Fred Hall Fishing Show in Long Beach, CA. An avid fisherman from Big Game Fishing out of Oakland came up to me,

thumbed through the book, informed me that I was lacking in seafood recipes and said he'd be right back. His name was Rich Falletti and he returned shortly with recipes for this marinade and his "famous" fish rub. Of course, I haven't seen or heard from him since, but I thank him here for this very popular addition to Baja Magic Dos. He told me it works on any kind of fresh fish ... also on chicken or pork. This makes enough for six servings.

6 fillets of fish, no more than ¾ inch thick
1 cup oil (any kind except motor)
1 cup vinegar (any kind)
1 cup soy sauce
1 cup limón (Mexican lime)
or key lime juice
2 tbsp seasoned salt
2 tbsp ground black pepper
Crushed garlic to taste (at least 2 tbsp)
Sesame seeds (optional)

Make small slits in the skin and marinate fish at least two hours. Barbecue for two to three minutes a side and serve immediately.

BIG GAME FISHING DRY RUB FOR SMOKING FISH

Thanks again to Rich from Oakland for this recipe. Everyone I know who's tried it, swears by it, especially for smoking tuna. Makes enough rub for four pounds of fish.

4 lb fish
1 lb brown sugar
1 lb white sugar
¼ cup seasoned salt
¼ cup garlic salt

Mix ingredients well in a glass bowl. Coat fish evenly on all sides and layer in a glass 9 x 13 baking dish. Sprinkle left-over rub over the top. Cover and refrigerate overnight. Remove fish from brine and wash under cold water. Pat dry and lay flat on layer of paper towels. Let glaze over before placing them in smoker.

RANCHO BUENA VISTA'S CATCH OF THE DAY

The first fishing resort on the East Cape was Rancho Buena Vista, a 10 minute walk down the beach from my house. Herb Tansey opened it in 1952 as a fly-in fishing resort with 12 rooms. It soon became a favorite hideaway for the rich and famous. Early guests included President Eisenhower, Bing Crosby, John Wayne and Chuck Connors. One year Chuck Knox brought the entire Rams football team down! In 1959, when Herb Tansey passed away, Colonel Eugene Walters bought Rancho. His grandson Mark, who is about my age, runs the resort these days and it hasn't changed much from my first visit there in 1970. Its beachfront palapa bar is one of our favorite happy hour destinations!

Mark told me that for as long as he can remember, their guests' favorite ways to have their catch of the day prepared is empanizado (breaded and fried) or al mojo de ajo (sautéed in butter and garlic), therefore I am including both of these tried and true recipes. Both recipes serve four.

Pescado Empanizado a la Plancha (Fish

Breaded and Fried on the Grill)
4 fillets of freshly caught fish (any white fish can be used)
2 eggs, beaten
1 cup corn or canola oil
1 cup flour
1 tsp salt

Dip the fish fillets into the eggs, coating thoroughly. Heat oil in large skillet to medium high heat. Dredge fish with flour and lightly salt. Fry in the skillet or on a flat grill about three minutes on each side, until crispy and fish is flaky. Serve immediately.

Pescado al Mojo de Ajo (Fish Sautéed in Garlic and Butter)
6 tbsp butter
4 fillets of freshly caught fish (any white fish or even marlin can be used)
6 cloves garlic, minced
1 tsp salt

In large skillet, heat butter at medium heat. Add minced garlic and salt. Fry fish about three minutes on each side, until cooked through and flaky. Serve immediately.

GARLIC SHRIMP ON SKEWERS

A long time ago I knew a guy who was completely hooked on garlic shrimp. On a trip to San Jose del Cabo back in 1983, he ordered it twice a day. By the fourth day we had to turn the air conditioning off in our hotel room and leave all the windows open because I couldn't breathe when we were together in a closed room! He didn't even need to open his mouth! The garlic was so overpowering it literally oozed out his pores and swirled around in circles around him, like a garlic aura!

This shrimp is skewered, saturated with garlic and cooked over hot coals. But don't eat it twice a day for four days, or you too will be too fragrant for your own good! Serves six to eight.

4 tbsp minced garlic (depending on how brave you are)
¼ cup white wine
¼ cup lemon juice
½ bunch cilantro, stems removed and finely chopped
½ cup butter or margarine, melted
3 pounds jumbo shrimp, peeled and deveined
Wooden skewers

In small bowl, combine garlic, wine, lemon juice, cilantro and melted butter or margarine. Place shrimp in 9 x 13 pan. Cover with marinade. Refrigerate up to three hours. When ready to barbecue, place the shrimp on skewers, making sure that they are well saturated with the marinade. Grill for three minutes on each side, basting frequently with marinade until done.

HOTEL CALIFORNIA SHRIMP AND SMOKED SALMON OPEN-FACED RAVIOLI

For years, day-trippers coming from Los Cabo to Todos Santos have flocked to the Hotel California, hoping to see "mirrors on the ceilings and pink champagne on ice." Don Henley burst that bubble a while back when he denied any connection between the Eagles and the hotel. That's too bad. He should stop by next time he's down here. Once he tours the grounds and samples the gourmet fare served in La Coronela Restaurant, he just might change his tune. Hotel California's new owners, John and Debbie Stewart have recreated this former eyesore into an architectural, artistic and culinary masterpiece.

For John, whose previous career was designing restaurants and office buildings, this project was the dream of a lifetime. He indulged his passion for brilliant, bold colors, colonial Mexican architecture and furniture, metal and glass sculptures, exotic plants and art. Truly a celebration of the senses, the Hotel California explodes with purples, reds, hot pinks, oranges, periwinkles, and pulsating shades of green and golden yellows. The old blends gracefully with the new, as original tile floors and 100-year-old beams merge with the best modern Mexico can offer.

The patios, pool and terraces are private and lushly landscaped. Hotel guests have a choice of 11 luxuriously appointed, wildly imaginative rooms and suites. They can sit on a balcony overlooking the town and watch the sun set in the Pacific as the choir sings in the church across the street. This is a perfect place for weddings, honeymoons or just to get away and wander along cobble stone streets, exploring Todos Santos' art galleries, restaurants and historical buildings. Venture out of town and enjoy some of the most spectacular surfing beaches on the west coast.

When you visit the hotel, make time for a leisurely lunch under the pagoda-style palapa at La Coronela Restaurant. Breathe in the fragrance of tropical flowers; listen to live Mexican music with a backdrop of softly tinkling fountains. John Stewart lured Chef Dany Lamote away from Calgary, Alberta. Born in Belgium, Dany studied culinary arts in Brussels. He immigrated to Canada in 1979 and settled in Calgary. There he was a chef and partner in many successful restaurants, from small European style bistros and cafes to fine dining establishments. Local organic ingredients influence his style of cooking. As a passionate traveler he loves to fuse the cuisines of different cultures in his recipes. For 15 years he was a culinary instructor teaching in small private schools. Here in Mexico he draws from Baja California ingredients to create a fresh, innovative seasonal menu at the Hotel California.

Chef Dany offers this explanation about this unique, popular dish: "The concept of open-faced ravioli is between lasagna and ravioli. The dish is made in a frying pan. The ingredients are stacked and assembled at serving time instead of being baked in the oven. The shrimp comes from the Sea of Cortez; the salmon is imported. We smoke the salmon in our Texas smoker, parked outside the restaurant. After having the smoker inside on the patio for ambience and smoking out our customers a few times, we decided that it was a better business practice to move the smoker outside. My preferred wood for smoking is a fruitwood." Serves four.

16 lasagna pasta sheets
1 tbsp olive oil
16 jumbo shrimp
1 cup white wine
½ lb sliced smoked salmon
1 cup whipping cream
¼ cup finely chopped cilantro
Salt and pepper to taste

Cook the lasagna sheets according to package directions. Drain and allow to cool off. Rub with olive oil to prevent sticking.

Poach the shrimp in white wine for five minutes or until they turn white. Add the cream and cilantro. Season with salt and pepper and add the pasta sheets. Bring to a boil and let the cream thicken a bit.

Stack by alternating the shrimp and pasta. Garnish with the smoked salmon.

TÍO PABLO'S CABRILLA VERACRUZANA

Seaport resorts in Baja and mainland Mexico always offer fresh cabrilla (sea bass) or red snapper (huachinango) served this way. It's a timeless classic, full of nutritious vegetables and subtly spicy. Terry swears that the best Veracruzana he has ever, ever had is at Tío Pablos's Bar & Grill in Los Barriles, about five minutes from our house. It's the best game in town. The ambiance is pure Baja and the food is consistently delicious. This meal serves four and at Tío's they serve it on a bed of fluffy rice.

¼ cup olive oil
8 cloves garlic, minced
4 white onions, sliced in half-rings
3 green bell peppers cut into strips
4 tomatoes, sliced in half-moons
2 - 8 ounce cans tomato purée
1 tsp oregano
1 tbsp salt, or to taste
1 tsp black pepper, or to taste
1 - 8 ounce can pitted green olives
2 cups water
4 tbsp butter or margarine
8 fillets cabrilla, huachinango or other delicate, firm white fish

Salsa Veracruzana
Heat the olive oil, and then add garlic and onions. Cook until onions are translucent. Add bell peppers and tomatoes, tomato purée and seasonings and cook for five to eight minutes, or until the flavors are well blended. Add the water to prevent sticking. Add olives the last three minutes.

Fish
In a large skillet, melt the butter or margarine. Sauté fish until white and flaky. Smother the fillets in the Salsa Veracruzana. Serve immediately, dig in and enjoy!

MANGO LIME SNAPPER

This new recipe is so quick and easy it will blow your mind. My Baja friend and neighbor, Kimberly, made it for dinner on a camping trip to Todos Santos for the third annual Reggae Festival. It's exotic but easy to make. The flavor of the fish is delicately enhanced by the uniquely Mexican combination of tastes, textures and spices. Your taste buds will be delighted with the sweetness of the mango and orange, the tang of tequila and lime, the crunch of the cucumber and the surprise zip the chile powder provides! Recipe serves four.

4 fillets of huachinango (red snapper) or dorado (mahi mahi)
2 tbsp olive oil
1 mango peeled and cut into ¼ inch chunks (substitute canned if unavailable)
1 ounce tequila

Juice of one orange
Juice of two limónes (Mexican limes)
or key limes
6 mint leaves, chopped
2 tsp Dijon mustard
1 cucumber, peeled, seeded and cut
into ¼ inch chunks
1 tsp chile powder (New Mexican chile
powder is better, but American will do)
Salt and pepper to taste

Preheat oven to 350°. Arrange snapper
or dorado fillets in lightly oiled baking
dish. Mix all other ingredients together
and pour over
filets. Bake for
30   minutes
and serve.

EAST CAPE DORADO
IN CILANTRO BUTTER

Picture yourself dining on a balmy
evening in February when the weather is
worse than miserable stateside - on a terrace overlooking the sea in one of the chic
multi-starred hotels that have popped up
along the Sea of Cortez between San
Jose del Cabo and Cabo San Lucas.

No? Oh. I get it. Your renegade spirit is
acting up, isn't it? You say you don't feel
like dressing up for dinner? You want simple, not swanky? Okay. Then go back to
the airport, get in a taxi and transport
yourself about an hour north, to the gulf's
fishing mecca - the East Cape. Here, in
casual-but-gorgeous, old-style hotels like
the Buena Vista Beach Resort or the

remote but breathtaking resort just down
the beach, Rancho Leonero. From there you
can catch a glimpse of the Baja California
del Sur that used to be. And still is, in our
neck of the woods.

The pace is slower on the East Cape. It
doesn't appeal to the crowds that flocks to
Cabo to sip piña coladas at the swim-up
bars by day, dine al fresco at night and
dance until the wee hours at one of the
plentiful night clubs and discos. (Although
Cabo is great if that's what you're in the
mood for.) It draws instead the fisher people, divers, windsurfers and tranquility seekers - those of us who want to escape the rat
race and get in touch with Mother Nature.
Like I said, you don't have to dress for dinner. And, women - one of the best-kept
secrets of non-resort Baja living is that after
you do it for a while, it's real likely that you'll
forget panty hose ever existed. If you stay
long enough, you won't even remember how
to put on makeup. The thought of this may
freak you out at this moment in time, but I
promise you - if you spend enough time in
Baja (especially in off-the-beaten-track
places) you will forget about things like
mascara, blush - even lipstick.... Serves six
and it is sure to please you, whether you're
into high heels or going barefoot.

6 fillets of dorado (or any other white fish)
¼ cup white wine
Juice from 6 limónes (Mexican limes) or
key limes
1 shot tequila
2 tbsp White Worcestershire sauce for
fish or chicken
¼ cup salsa verde
1 tbsp minced garlic

½ cup butter or margarine
½ bunch cilantro, stems removed and finely chopped
Salt and pepper to taste

In a 9 x 13 pan, pour wine, lime juice, tequila, Worcestershire Sauce and salsa verde over the fish. Marinate in refrigerator from one to two hours. Remove fish from marinade and grill on barbecue for four minutes on each side, or until done.

While fish is grilling, melt butter or margarine in a small saucepan with garlic, cilantro, salt and pepper. Immediately prior to serving, pour equal amounts of butter sauce over each piece of fish. Serve immediately.

FISH MEUNIERE

As the oldest city in Baja, Loreto has its share of traditional Mexican family names - Guzman, Murillo, Martinez. Through the years many English names have been added as sailors jumped ship to stay in this beautiful small paradise.

Nowadays there are Mexicans with the last names of Cunningham, Green, Drew and a gazillion who answer to Davis.

Francisco Drew was born and raised in Loreto but left as a young man for work in the hotels and restaurants of Puerto Vallarta and Cabo. After 20 years he returned and became the chef at Isla Loreto, a small restaurant along the malecón with a wonderful view of Loreto Bay. In his travels he picked up this simple and excellent recipe using fresh local fish. My friend Ray Lieberenz and his wife moved to Loreto recently. When another friend, Dick VanBree emailed me raving about this fish dish, I emailed Ray. He told me loved it too and within a week he'd emailed me this recipe complete with the above story! Amazing. Serves four.

4 - 6 oz fillets fresh pinto bass from Loreto (or substitute any sea bass)
2 cups butter
2 cups fresh parsley, chopped
1½ cups flour
3 to 4 tbsp red chile powder
2 tbsp garlic powder
Salt to taste
½ cup Controy or Grand Marnier

In saucepan, melt butter with parsley for one minute. Coat fish fillets in a mixture of flour, chile powder, garlic powder and salt. Broil fish (no butter or oil) for one minute on each side. Before serving stir orange liqueur into sauce, place fish fillets on plates and pour sauce over fish.

ISLA ESPIRTÚ SANTO PRAWNS WITH SALSA

Directly northeast of La Paz is a large island with at least 12 separate, pristine, uninhabited bays. When I saw them from the airplane on a long ago flight south, I counted. Twelve - and I only counted the big ones on the west side. This island, named after the Holy Spirit, is famous with divers all over the world. You can catch a dive ship from downtown La Paz, or at any of the local hotels. You can pick your bay. Or you can dive or snorkel with the sea lions that live just north of Espiritú Santo at Isla Partida.

Whether you're a diver, a snorkeler, an avid fisher person or just a Baja cruiser, Isla Espiritú Santo is a must-see. We visited many of its bays on our first foray into La Paz Bay when I was eight. They still offer up the amazing undersea life and equally amazing shell hunting on land that they did over 40 years ago!

This spicy, saucy dish is pure La Paz. More cosmopolitan and sophisticated than the usual Baja fare, you will find it worthy of any five star resorts. So, hey, dress up tonight and try this for a dinner party with an upscale Southern Baja flair. You'll love the unusual flavor of the shrimp. Served on a bed of rice, it's almost a full meal in itself. Serve with a chilled Chenin Blanc. Elegant! Serves six.

2 pounds jumbo shrimp
1½ cups white wine
1 cup water
4 tbsp minced garlic
Juice from 5 limónes (Mexican limes)
or key limes
2 cups María's salsa de arból (Salsa section)
8 cups hot cooked rice
Cilantro sprigs and limón wedges for garnish

In large saucepan, cover shrimp with wine and water. Bring mixture to a boil. Add garlic and lime juice. Cook three to five minutes until shrimp turn pink. Drain shrimp. Rinse well with cold water. Shell and devein shrimp. Let rest in a warm oven.

Heat salsa in small saucepan. Serve shrimp on a bed of white rice topped with heated salsa. Garnish with cilantro and lime slices.

Mural - Rancho Buena Vista Hotel Cantina

LOBSTER PUERTO NUEVO

Thirty miles south of the Tijuana border is (what used to be a fishing village) Puerto Nuevo. In recent years its size has multiplied many times over until it has reached resort proportions. Puerto Nuevo is renowned throughout Southern California for its succulent lobster. It all started back in 1954, when

Rosa María Plasencia's father came because he'd heard there were lobsters there - lots of them. There were. A year later Rosa María's mother's family came. The two young people met, fell in love, married and built a tiny house across the street from what is now the family restaurant, Puerto Nuevo II.

At that time there were only two or three families living on the cliffs overlooking the

Pacific. Every day the men went out to sea in their pangas, free diving for lobsters. Every afternoon their wives would scan the waters until they saw their husbands' boats materialize on the horizon. Once a positive sighting was made, they'd rush to heat up beans and rice, pat out some fresh tortillas and put a kettle of lard on the fire. The men always came back ravenous, and when they unloaded their catch of lobsters, they'd slice a few in half, drop them into the bubbling lard and fry them up. There was no refrigeration back then, so the now-famous meal of fresh fried lobster, beans, rice and tortillas came into being purely out of necessity. The sea provided the lobsters. Beans and rice didn't need to be refrigerated, and the tortillas could be made on the spot.

Occasionally some Americans would show up and ask the men to take them out in their pangas. When they came back in, they'd join the Mexicans in a big meal. As is typical still today at fish camps up and down Baja, no money changed hands. The principle down here has always been, "barter is better," because everyone makes out. The Americans shared soda, ham sandwiches, cookies, candy and whatever else they had to spare in return for the fine food.

In the '50s, more families migrated to the area. One built a little stand next to the bus stop, where the welcoming arches are now. They sold sodas, snacks and burritos. Next to their stand was a billboard advertising Newport cigarettes. The Americans named the village after

that sign, which, translated into Spanish, is Puerto Nuevo.

A major growth spurt occurred in Puerto Nuevo in the '70s when the Ortega family came to town and built four restaurants, which they publicized widely. The signs for all the Ortega's are easily visible from the toll road and these days, about four thousand people make the trip to Puerto Nuevo to enjoy lobster dinners each week.

Puerto Nuevo lobster is deep fried in lard, the Mexican way. If you don't want to fry your lobster, try grilling it on the barbecue or boiling it in water plus a half cup of beer for five minutes. When served with beans, rice, tortillas and an array of different salsas, the meal takes on a festive atmosphere all its own. Frosty beers or Cokes are a must with this one. Serves six.

6 large Mexican lobsters, cut in half lengthwise
2 cups lard or solid vegetable shortening (optional: see above)
1 tbsp seasoned salt
1 tsp pepper
2 cups frijoles
2 cups Spanish rice
18 corn and/or flour tortillas
Salsa medley (Salsa section)

In heavy, deep skillet heat lard over medium high heat. Fry each half lobster for five minutes on each side, until meat is crisp, tender and will pop out of the shell on your fork. Continue for all lobsters. Drain on paper towels and place on serving dish in the oven on warm until ready to serve.

Heat frijoles and rice. Place in serving dishes. Heat tortillas in microwave one to two minutes until warm. Place in covered basket. Serve lobster with frijoles, rice, tortillas, salsas. People can eat the lobster either in a burrito with beans and salsa, or solo.

The Mexicans use tortillas the way our ancestors used bread, to scoop up and mop up their beans, rice, excess pan juices and salsa. Try it out yourself.

RAY'S SHRIMP PAPAGAYOS

Thirteen miles south of Mulege, on scenic Santispac beach is Ray's Place. We first visited in 1998, and Terry and Nina both fell in love with the house specialty, Camarones Papagayos (Parrot Shrimp). They're stuffed with fresh seafood (usually crab, but it varies, depending on what's fresh) and queso Chihuahua. Then they're wrapped in bacon and grilled to a crispy perfection. If you've been to Bahía Concepción, then you know Santispac, and you've probably been to Ray's and hung out with the locals there. You also know what a treat it is to find a gourmet restaurant under a giant palapa with a sand floor in a fairly remote but spectacularly beautiful place. This recipe isn't quite Ray's. It's one of our friend Carol's works of culinary plagiarism as she helped me recreate this masterpiece. She should be an expert; she and her husband Mike lived in Mulege for a few years and this was their favorite meal. Next time you're in Santispac, don't forget to stop at Ray's. Serves four.

1 tbsp green onion
1 tbsp green bell pepper
1 tbsp celery salt
4 tbsp butter
¼ cup chicken broth
1 tsp cornstarch
1 tbsp Dijon mustard
1 tbsp red wine vinegar
1 tsp Tabasco or other hot pepper sauce
 1 tsp Worcestershire sauce
2 cups cooked, flaked crab 24 jumbo shrimp, peeled and deveined
24 - ½ x 1 inch chunks of queso Chihuahua or jack cheese
24 pieces bacon and toothpicks

Place the green onion, bell pepper and celery salt in food processor and process until well minced. In a small saucepan over medium heat, melt the butter and sauté minced vegetables for two minutes. Whisk the chicken broth and cornstarch together in a small bowl and then whisk into the vegetables. Add the mustard, vinegar, hot pepper sauce and Worcestershire sauce and whisk to combine the ingredients. Bring the sauce to a boil and cook for one minute while whisking. Remove from the fire and cool. Stir in the crabmeat and refrigerate.

Fire up the barbecue. In skillet, cook bacon until about half done, but still limp. Butterfly the shrimp and put one tsp of stuffing and a piece of cheese inside each shrimp. Close and wrap securely with bacon and secure with a toothpick. Lay the shrimp on a buttered pan and cook over very hot fire, turning occasionally, for about 10 minutes until shrimp is cooked and bacon is crispy.

✦ ⭐ ✦

CHIPOTLE CABRILLA WITH VEGETABLES

This is one of Nina's most sought-after dishes. She created it on a camping trip to Cabo Pulmo one year. If you haven't been to there, put it on your agenda for your next trip. Cabrilla is a light, white fish from the sea bass family. Fishing is illegal there, so she brought dinner with her.

In 1995 Cabo Pulmo was officially declared a Marine preserve by the Mexican Government - which means it's off limits for fishing and a perfect eco- and adventure tour destination. Located about midway between San Jose del Cabo and Buena Vista, Cabo Pulmo is off the beaten track and it's not crowd- ed. The underwater park is 11 miles long with eight different fingers of coral reefs. A Mexican fishing vessel, the Colima - sunk during a storm in 1939 - lies in 18 feet of water offshore, and offers the added bonus of a wreck dive for scuba enthusiasts. Visibility ranges from 60 to 100 feet in the water, and the water temperatures range from about 70° to 85°. It's perfect for a day trip and even better for a prolonged camping trip!

Because the cabrilla and vegetables are baked together with wine, chipotle chiles

and cilantro, the fish takes on a distinctive, mouth-watering flavor. Serves six.

2 pounds cabrilla, or 6 fillets
Salt and pepper to taste
6 tbsp minced garlic
Juice of 1 lemon
4 - 6 chipotle chiles, diced
(buy the kind that are canned in adobo)
1½ lemons, quartered
½ cup butter or margarine
1 onion, thinly sliced and slightly blanched
2 medium potatoes, peeled and very thinly sliced and blanched for 10 minutes
2 tomatoes, peeled and quartered
1 cup adobo sauce from the chipotles
1/3 cup white wine
3 tbsp chopped cilantro

Season fish on both sides with salt and pepper, garlic and lemon juice. Sprinkle diced chipotle chiles over top. Melt butter in large skillet. Brown fish on both sides.

Transfer fish and juices to a 9 x 13 inch baking pan. Arrange onion and potato slices around fish and bake at 375° for 30 minutes. Add tomatoes. Stir wine and adobo sauce together and pour over fish. Sprinkle with cilantro. Bake ten minutes, or until fish flakes easily with fork and pota- toes are done.

Arrange fish on large platter with toma- toes, potatoes and onions. Pour juices over fish and sprinkle with cilantro. Garnish with remaining lemon quarters.

✦ ⭐ ✦

BATTER FRIED SHRIMP MAZATLÁN STYLE

Mazatlán is a busy seaport and industrial city on the west coast of mainland Mexico just south of the tip of Baja. It was one of Mexico's first beach resorts back in the early '60s and is still a major stop on all Mexican Riviera cruises. We spent a few Easter vacations in Mazatlán when I was a kid, enjoying the sunny weather, warm water and friendly ambience.

The last time I was there, every night the tourists converged en masse on one of the town's premier eateries, the Shrimp Bucket. My father swears it has the best fried shrimp served anywhere. They sell it everywhere in Baja now. This is Nina's version of the dish, which she and my Mom and Dad made up together. Don't forget the cerveza! Serves six.

2 eggs, beaten
2 tbsp lemon juice
2 tbsp chopped cilantro
2 pounds jumbo shrimp, shelled and deveined
1½ cups Italian breadcrumbs
1½ cups corn or canola oil
1 - 2 tbsp garlic powder
1 tbsp seasoned salt

In small bowl, mix eggs, lemon juice and cilantro. Dip each shrimp into the egg mixture and dredge in breadcrumbs combined with garlic powder and seasoned salt.

Heat oil in skillet over medium high heat. Fry each shrimp about two to three minutes, or until crisp and golden. Drain on paper towels and place on platter in oven on warm until ready to serve.

FRIED CALAMARI STRIPS

My amiga Debbie shared her favorite calamari recipe with me on a recent visit to Buena Vista. She says the Krusteaz pancake batter (yes, we can get it in Cabo at Costco and it makes pancakes so airy they're almost like crepes) makes this indescribably delicious. And she brags that this is the only calamari recipe she knows of where the calamari doesn't have to be pounded and yet is still tender. Serves six.

6 cups water
6 calamari steaks, about ¾ inch thick
Krusteaz pancake batter to make six servings
1 cup corn or canola oil
Seasoned salt and pepper to taste
Cocktail or tartar sauce

In a Dutch oven, heat water to a rapid boil. Toss in the calamari steaks and cook until they start to curl. Immediately remove from water and set aside to cool on paper towels. Cut into two-inch strips.

Prepare Krusteaz pancake mix according to package directions. Make sure it is on the thick side and not runny. In a large skillet, heat oil until barely smoking. Dip each calamari strip into the batter and fry, turning often until crispy, about three to four minutes.

Drain on paper towels, season and serve immediately with cocktail or tartar sauce.

SHARK STEAKS SANTA ROSALÍA

Santa Rosalía, almost two thirds of the way down the Baja coast is the only place in Baja with a French heritage. It was first occupied by the French in the 1870s and for nearly 80 years flourished as a manganese mining town. Its church is still world-famous. It was designed by Gustav Effeil for the Paris World's Fair in 1898 and actually constructed by one of his fellow students. After the fair's completion, the church was dismantled and shipped in pieces to Santa Rosalía around Cape Horn. These days the town still has the best bakeries in all of Mexico, the most famous being El Boleo, named after the French Mining Company that settled it. It has a new marina and has begun to attract a few yachties that travel the Sea of Cortez in their sail and powerboats during the pleasant fall, winter and late spring months. Other than that, Santa Rosalía is pretty much off the beaten tourist path. Caravans of motor homing travelers stop in to rest and stock up on supplies. A few folks, old school Baja aficionados, the serious peace-and-quiet seekers, come to camp, fish and hang out a while. Others stop in to catch the ferry to Guaymas on the mainland.

One of our yachtie friends brought this recipe back from a trip up the Sea of Cortez a few years back. Its simplicity is authentically Baja - with just a hint of that French flair! Never eaten shark, you say? Well, most culinary experts, including - of course - our resident expert, Nina, swear it's as good as or better than swordfish. Even though it's served at all the best seafood restaurants in Baja and Southern California, our yachtie friend swears that she heard a rumor that it was a French miner, living in Santa Rosalía, who was the first one to have the courage to eat a shark. Whatever the truth may be, this quick and incredibly easy recipe for grilled shark steaks is a sure winner. It works just as well for an elegant dinner al fresco as it does for a shorts, t-shirts and bare feet affair. Choose your own array of accompaniments. Serves six.

2 pounds shark fillets or steaks
Salt and pepper to taste
Dash paprika and cayenne pepper
½ cup butter or margarine
2 tbsp limón (Mexican lime) or key lime juice
4 cloves garlic, minced
4 tbsp cilantro, chopped

Season fish fillets to taste with salt, pepper, paprika and cayenne. Melt butter in saucepan and add lime juice and garlic. Gently pour lime butter over fish. Grill on barbecue on both sides until fish flakes easily when tested with a fork. Garnish with chopped cilantro.

DORADO ISLA SAN JOSE

Just about midway between Loreto and La Paz on the Sea of Cortez is an island called Isla San Jose. Quiet and off the beaten track, it's a place visited mostly by fishermen, kayakers and other serious wildlife buffs (they call them eco-tourists these days!). My dad told me once that the biggest and widest variety of billfish once hung out in that area. Supposedly they were over-fished and pretty much disappeared from the area about 25 years ago - before tag and release programs became popular and did much to curb the wasteful slaughter of game fish in Baja.

Dorado Isla San Jose is a tangy, baked dish that takes little time, but will get you rave reviews. You can substitute bonita, cabrilla or sierra if you feel like it. And once again, you can pick and choose your side dishes. Get a little creative. Surprise yourself! Why not? You could be in Baja, anchored off this exquisite, pristine island, with only the sea, stars and sky to observe you as you dance barefooted after dinner in the moonlight on the deck of your yacht. Hey? Why not? Can I come too? Serves six.

6 fillets of dorado, sierra or cabrilla
Salt and pepper to taste
6 tbsp olive oil
1 cup sliced green onions, tops included
4 tbsp chopped cilantro
1½ limónes (Mexican limes)
or key limes, quartered
1 tomato, cut in six wedges

Sprinkle fish fillets with salt and pepper. Place in a single layer in 9 x 13 inch baking dish. Coat each steak heavily with olive oil. Sprinkle green onions over fish. Bake, uncovered at 350° for about 20 minutes, or until fish flakes easily when tested with fork. Remove to serving platter. Sprinkle with cilantro and garnish with lime and tomato wedges.

* ⭐ ✦

ISLA CERRALVO CINNAMON-CHILE SNAPPER

If you cruise northeast out of La Paz Bay, round the corner and head south, the first decent-sized island you'll come to is Isla Cerralvo. It takes longer to get to than Isla Espiritú Santo (it's at least a two hour boat ride in a double engine super panga from La Paz or from the East Cape) but the diving is spectacular.

The snapper (or huachinango, if you recall, in Spanish) is another one of those fish I caught lots of off the coast of La Paz during those Easter Vacations from ages eight to twelve. And Isla Cerralvo was one of the islands we visited back then.

This is one of my sister's all-time favorite recipes and one she pilfered from a restaurant hanging out over the edge of the Sea of Cortez near Los Barriles. According to Nina, the delicate flavor of cinnamon and chile complements the fish wonderfully in this recipe. Why do people love it so? Well - the answer to that one is probably summed up in one word - taco. Yes, the snapper is seasoned first, grilled and served in soft tacos with avocado, onion and orange. A real palate pleaser. Serves six.

1 tbsp American chili powder
1 tsp cinnamon
¼ tsp ground pepper
1½ tsp salt
½ tsp oregano
¼ tsp cayenne pepper
6 tbsp minced garlic
¼ cup orange juice
1 tbsp grapefruit juice
6 red snapper fillets, about 3 pounds
1 tbsp olive oil
12 corn tortillas
2 avocados, sliced
1 onion, minced
1 tomato, diced
1 orange, membrane removed and diced

Blend chili powder, spices and orange and grapefruit juices until a smooth paste is made. Spread paste over the fillets, top and bottom and set them aside to season overnight.

Brush the fillets with oil and barbecue for ten minutes over the grill. Serve with hot tortillas and allow guests to make soft tacos with avocado, onion, tomato and orange.

* ⭐ ✦

RESTAURANT LA BUFADORA'S ORPHAN CALAMARI

Miguel Toscano used to run the La Bufadora Restaurant back in the late '90s. When I asked him what his house specialty was, he told me, "Orphan Calamari." I didn't get it. "It's so delicious that in Spanish we say it needs no parent," he explained. I was still confused. Finally, he told me that a good translation for orphan in this sense would be, "outasite." Okay - I got it - Outasite Calamari.

After he gave me the recipe, he led me into the kitchen where his chef, Ricardo Vasquez, prepared two orders for us. As I watched, I scribbled like crazy. Afterwards, the guy I was with scarfed both of our servings down. He asked me to tell you that it's every bit as good as Miguel claimed it is. In fact, it soon became both Derek and Nina's favorite dish at La Buf Restaurant. Here it is for your dining pleasure. Like Ricardo, you can serve it with beans, rice and a light, spicy cole slaw or you can dress it up any way you like. It's not difficult to make, it serves six and it will earn you the reputation as a bona fide Baja chef.

Steaks
6 calamari steaks about ¾ inch thick
½ cup flour
2 eggs, beaten
Salt and pepper to taste
1 - 3 tsp Tabasco or other red pepper sauce
¼ cup milk
½ cup corn flake crumbs
2 tbsp butter or margarine
2 tbsp corn or canola oil
3 cloves garlic, finely minced

Ricardo's Outasite Orphan Sauce
½ cup powdered shrimp consommé or caldo de camarón with ½ cup water
1 tbsp butter or margarine
1 cup milk
2 tbsp brandy
3 tbsp parsley, finely chopped
1 red bell pepper, finely chopped
2 to 3 pinches flour, as needed to thicken sauce

Partially defrost the calamari steaks. Using a knife, peel off the membrane surrounding the flesh. Put steak in a plastic bag, lay on a cutting board and pound until almost lacy. Repeat. Dredge steaks in flour. Season eggs with salt, pepper and red pepper sauce. Add milk to egg mixture and whisk. Dip calamari into eggs, and then dredge again, in corn flake crumbs. Heat butter with oil in skillet until melted. Add garlic and calamari steaks and cook until golden on both sides. Place in oven to keep warm.

In another skillet, mix together all ingredients for sauce, stirring constantly. Add flour and thicken to desired consistency. Spoon over calamari steaks and enjoy!

PALAPA AZUL'S STUFFED CLAMS ON THE GRILL

The Palapa Azul is one of three restaurants at the end of the paved road on Tecolote Beach. To the north is an expanse of pale jade green and aquamarine water, merging with the darker blue water as one's eyes edge out toward Espiritú Santo Island. It's quiet there, unless the restaurant's generator is running so that the stereo can play Mexican country music. The restaurant is built into and around an old wooden fishing boat. The palm-thatched palapa roof leans off it and angles down toward the sea. All tables and chairs are planted right on the sand. You can take a swim and eat lunch in your wet bathing suit. You can catch a boat ride to the island and snorkel, dive or visit with the sea lions. And eat lunch when you get back. If you catch a fish while you're out, they'll cook it right up for you.

When we visited back in 1997, Nina and I swam in the 85° water. Then we ordered lunch. Nina had this dish and our waiter Ramón shared the recipe with us. We're glad he did, because she swears it's way better than the stuffed clams she's had in much fancier restaurants in other parts of Baja - places where you have to wear shoes and that sort of thing!

These clams are served inside the shell, so you'll have to find a seafood market that sells them that way. Or else visit San Quintín, a few hours south of Ensenada and go clamming yourself. Or you could go to La Paz and dig them out of the bay there. Or - the fish market! Whatever works for you! Just try it. It's a true Baja Lover's delight. Serves four.

16 chocolate or queen clams in their shells (about the size of your palm)
4 tbsp butter
6 - 12 fresh jalapeños, finely diced (with or without seeds depending on spiciness desired)
2 cups cheddar cheese, cut into small cubes
2 large white onions, finely diced
2 large tomatoes, finely diced
1 tsp garlic powder
2 limónes (Mexican limes)
or key limes, quartered
1 cup ham, finely diced
Salt and pepper to taste

Remove the clams from their shells and dice into small pieces. Mix together in bowl with jalapeños, cheese, onion, tomatoes, garlic powder, lime juice and ham. Add salt and pepper to taste and scoop back into each of the 16 clamshells. Wrap each shell in aluminum foil and place over hot coals on the grill. Cook four minutes on each side.

MARGARITA SCALLOPS

Back in our early days in La Bufadora, Nina and her husband John dove for scallops all the time. She got to playing around with some of the neighbors around cocktail hour and invented Margarita Scallops. They've been very popular with the locals ever since! Serves six.

1½ lb scallops
¾ cup tequila
Juice of 8 fresh limónes (Mexican limes) or key limes

¾ cup Controy or orange juice
crushed red pepper flakes or crushed chile de arbol
1 white onion, sliced very thin
1½ cups crema media ácida or sour cream
Salsa medley
1 can pitted black olives
12 flour tortillas

Combine all ingredients except tortillas, salsas, olives and crema in bowl. Cover and refrigerate up to 24 hours. Drain marinade off and place scallops in a broiler pan. Broil for three to five minutes on each side. Wrap in a flour tortilla and serve with salsas, olives and crema.

Back Country Fiesta by Janna Kinkade

POULTRY AND MEAT ENTRÉES

Remember the '80s? That decade not so long ago when the Baby Boomers transformed themselves from latter day hippies (many of whom had indeed inhaled) into serious, ladder-climbing yuppies? When conspicuous consumption was in and our credit card bills escalated right along with the national debt? When comparing ourselves to our neighbors and friends was epidemic? And when Corporate America was considered the only place to find our identity, security and value?

I was the consummate upwardly mobile urban professional in those days - so slick and so thirty-something! Everything and everyone had a label. My friends and I became as obsessed with labels as we did with health and fitness. We were as hooked on our images as we were on aerobics, light mayonnaise and a whole plethora of fat-reduced or fat-free foods. By the end of the decade even nine year olds could quote the number of fat grams in a granola bar.

My how time changed things. For me, the '90s were about being downsized, out placed and being a single mom. It forced me to look at myself in the mirror, rip off the labels I had thought defined me, try to figure out who I really was and just what the heck really mattered in life. I learned that riches are fleeting, that separating one's personal and professional selves is bullshit and tends to fracture one's soul, and of course I learned that beauty fades. I learned to look more deeply into people, to look for their hearts and to care about them without being concerned what they did for a living. After departing from the corporate scene, I began writing. I also went back to Baja. Not the fancy resort side of Baja that defined my yuppie years, but the simple, humble, rural Baja. It was in the hillsides of rustic, remote La Bufadora that I began to relearn things like trust, faith and love. And other things like adventure, laughter, hope and joy.

Think of this section on chicken, turkey, beef, lamb and pork entrees as the journey of rediscovery. Like all conscientious chefs, 10 or 15 years ago, I set out on a mission to formulate recipes using only the healthiest ingredients. And of course, the healthiest meats were lean, leaner and leanest. I created some of these recipes after eating a wonderful dinner in an exotic restaurant. Others I got from friends and family members. I even found a few in magazines, tried them and adapted them to my particular Baja style of cooking. Many were created on camping trips in Baja or at my house in La Bufadora. Of course, that was all before Atkins, when people stopped counting fat grams and carbs became the enemy. But these recipes are still good. I've added a few new true blue Baja specialties in here, like Birria and Chile Colorado to spice up your life, along with Tamales and Terry's Bombero (fireman) Chili. Oh yeah and Pollo con Salsa Alcaparra too. And then, of course, there's that staple of every expatriate's diet, the Baja Beach Burger. This recipe is new and it rocks, so you gotta try it! And don't forget to check out Hotel California's amazing Chevre Stuffed Chicken Breasts, their Lamb Burger, Arrachera from Posada La Poza and my new Baja Street Hot Dog recipe!

By the way, many sauces in this section specify using a blender or food processor. While I've seen RVs big and fancy enough to have garbage disposals and blenders on board, I have a hand powered salsa maker that serves as my food processor when I'm camping. I use it to make chunky fresh salsas and blended sauces. It lives with me here in Baja, it goes on the road and it summers with us in Idaho. I obviously couldn't live without it! My mother got it for me years ago at a swap meet. They also sell them at kitchen stores, county fairs and online.

HOTEL CALIFORNIA CHEVRE STUFFED CHICKEN BREAST WITH JAMAICA COULIS

Chef Dany Lamote of the Hotel California in Todos Santos asked me to explain to you that the very exceptional sauce for this dish is made with jamaica (Hah-MIKE-ah), a plant native to Baja. Often confused with the hibiscus flower, this annual has leathery flowers and a single stem without any leaves can produce a dozen flowers. It has a deep burgundy color and a bitter flavor that reminds me of cranberry juice, only better. The dried flower is not edible because of its leathery texture, but the petals of the fresh flower are quite pleasant. The flavor pairs well with chicken, turkey or pork. Serves four.

4 chicken breasts
6 ounce log chevre (soft goat cheese)
½ each yellow and red bell peppers cut in very thin strips
2 ounces almonds or pecans - slightly toasted
¼ cup olive oil
½ cup dried jamaica flowers
1 cup water
1 cup freshly squeezed orange juice
½ cup honey
½ cup sugar (do not use Splenda!)

Pinch of fennel seed
2 ounces anisette or orange liqueur (optional)
½ tsp dried dill
Salt and pepper to taste
Toothpicks

Place chicken breasts on a cutting board and pound until lacy. In small bowl, combine goat cheese, bell peppers and toasted nuts. Stuff the chicken breasts with cheese mixture and roll the breasts, securing with toothpicks.

In a skillet brown the chicken breasts in olive oil over medium high heat, about three minutes on each side. Place in a baking dish and cook at 350° for 15 minutes.

To make jamaica sauce, boil the flowers for 15 minutes in a cup of water. Strain flowers out. Add orange juice, sugar, honey, dill, fennel and liqueur and cook until it reduces to thick syrup. Lightly season with salt and pepper.

Chef Dany says that for a delectable presentation, pour some sauce on the plate, slice the chicken in half and display artfully on the sauce.

SNOWBIRD CHICKEN IN TOMATILLO SAUCE

I got this recipe from a Canadian Snowbird who was traveling in a caravan of 14 monster motor homes down Baja's Highway 1. She was a burly 60ish widow lady from Calgary who was piloting her own ship, so to speak. Feisty, hard drinking and full of raucous stories, her group camped next to ours on a previously secluded (until the Snowbirds showed up and took it over!) beach just to the south of Santa Rosalía. We cooked dinner together that night and it most certainly was a winner. Snowbird Chicken is a great dish with a true Baja flair, but it isn't spicy-hot, so you can comfortably try it on your more tentative friends. Serve with a light, white wine like a Monte Xanic Chardonnay. Serves six.

3 poblano chiles, blistered
or 1 - 3½ ounce can whole green chiles
6 boneless skinless chicken breasts
2 cups water
½ pound tomatillos
½ bunch cilantro, stems removed and chopped
1 stalk celery, chopped
1 cup green onions, chopped
1 small bunch leaf lettuce
¼ cup sunflower seeds
¼ tsp ground cumin
¼ tsp garlic powder
1 tsp butter or margarine
Salt to taste

To blister poblanos, if you have a gas stove, lay the chiles over the open flame and char skins well, turning with tongs frequently until they're uniformly blackened and stop snapping. The more charred they are, the easier it is to remove the skins. If you have an electric stove, place chiles in a large skillet on high heat. Turn frequently as above. Remove chiles to plastic bag, close it and let stand for 10 minutes.

Remove from bag, place in ice-cold water and remove the stems, skins, veins and seeds.

Boil chicken for 25 minutes in water. Drain chicken, reserving broth. Keep chicken warm. Place half of tomatillos, cilantro, celery, green onions, lettuce, sunflower seeds and chiles in blender or food processor. (Yes, the lady from Calgary had a blender in her RV!) Add ¾ cup broth and blend well. Repeat with remaining half of same ingredients plus ¾ cup broth. Blend in cumin and garlic powder.

Heat butter in large skillet. Add tomatillo mixture and simmer 15 minutes over low heat, stirring until thickened. Add more chicken broth if sauce gets too thick. Season to taste with salt and serve hot over chicken.

CHILI CHICKEN WITH CITRUS GLAZE

This incredibly yummy dish is one my mom created with her friend Helen Chadwell on one of our family camping trips to Kilometer 181, a few hours south of Ensenada. We took a lot of trips together with Ben and Helen Chadwell when I was growing up. They loved Mexico and camping as much as we did and their sons, Brandon, Brent and Bryan were all close to Nina's and my ages. We got along famously and had some amazing adventures together.

On this particular trip, the boys' paternal grandfather was along. My dad had just bought an old Scout, a four-wheel drive miniature pickup truck and we kids and the three men took off down some really bad roads in search of some really good places! We found them too. I remember a deserted beach with miles and miles of tide pools and really big waves where my dad and Ben and Ben's dad taught us how to surf fish. I remember running into a pair of young Mexican fishermen in their panga who'd beached their boat and were free-diving in the chilly water. They kept coming up, again and again, with a lobster in each hand. Big lobsters. My dad and Ben bought a whole sack full and took them home for dinner.

That wasn't the night Mom and Helen made up this dish. But it was the same trip and you can bet there was a lot of feasting done - both nights! This chicken dish has a flavor hauntingly similar to a Mexican chicken mole. But it's much easier to make (think of it as a camping dish). I wrote down the recipe that night and since then, every time I serve it I get rave reviews. Serves six.

6 boneless skinless chicken breasts
½ cup American chili powder
1 tsp seasoned salt
3 tbsp butter or margarine
½ cup corn or canola oil
3 tbsp orange marmalade
Juice from 3 limónes (Mexican limes) or key limes
2 - 3 tsp hot pepper sauce

Pound chicken breasts until tender. In

shallow dish combine chili powder and seasoned salt. Coat each chicken breast with chili mixture. Set aside.

In large skillet, heat oil and butter or margarine over medium high heat. Cook the chicken breasts about five minutes on each side until browned and done. Remove chicken to plate. To drip-pings in skillet add marmalade, lime juice and hot sauce. Heat over medium heat, stirring to loosen crispy bits from bottom of skillet.

Return chicken to skillet. Cook two to three minutes longer until heated through and coated with glaze. Serve immediately.

Mural - Rancho Buena Vista Hotel Cantina

CATAVIÑA CHICKEN ROLLS

I don't have the words in me to do justice to Cataviña. Cataviña is one of my sacred places. Midway between the Pacific and Sea of Cortez in the middle of the peninsula, a little less than a third of the way down, you can find it on a map due west of Gonzaga Bay. The Baja highway slices right through it, providing the traveler with stunning views of high country cacti found nowhere else in Baja, prehistoric rock formations and endless, endless blue sky and boulder strewn mountains. Aside from being the perfect place to stop overnight at the La Pinta Hotel on the way south, it is also a place to connect powerfully with the ancient Indian mystics who walked these hills so long ago.

I created this dish on a motor home trip back in the '80s. We were staying overnight at a lovely secluded campground just outside Cataviña on our way to the Bay of L.A. I was trying to make a Baja version of that great Russian entrée, Chicken Kiev. I made it from ingredients I had on hand in my cupboards, and we were so impressed with how it turned out that we named it after our stopping place, Cataviña. Serves six.

6 boneless skinless chicken breasts
1 - 7 ounce can diced green chiles
6 ounces jack cheese, cut in 6 strips
¾ cup cornflake crumbs
½ cup grated Parmesan cheese
2 tbsp American chili powder
¾ tsp salt
½ tsp ground cumin
½ tsp black pepper
8 tbsp melted butter or margarine

Sauce
1 - 16 ounce can stewed tomatoes, puréed
¾ tsp ground cumin
½ cup green onions, chopped
Salt, pepper and hot pepper sauce to taste

Pound chicken pieces to about ¼ inch thickness. Put about two tablespoons chiles and one strip Jack cheese in center of each chicken piece. Roll up and tuck ends under. Combine cornflake crumbs, Parmesan cheese, chili powder, salt, cumin and pepper. Dip each chicken in shallow dish of butter and roll in crumb mixture. Place chicken rolls, seam side down in 9 x 13 baking pan and drizzle with leftover butter. Cover and chill four hours or overnight. Bake uncovered at 400° for 20 minutes.

To make sauce, combine stewed tomatoes, cumin and green onions in small saucepan. Season to taste with salt, pepper and hot pepper sauce. Heat well and spoon over chicken to serve.

TRIPÚI CHICKEN IN CILANTRO SAUCE

Seventeen miles south of Loreto, at Puerto Escondido is the Tripúi Trailer Park. Considered possibly the best in all of Baja, the park boasts an excellent continental restaurant, top-notch facilities and a marina. (It burned almost to the ground in 2004, but has since been largely rebuilt.) This light and ultra-simple chicken dish was created during a quick stopover near Tripúi, where we camped on a deserted beach. This recipe uses the distinct flavor of cilantro to great advantage. You'll love it. Close your eyes and transport yourself to our private beach with the dramatic, sharp-faced mountains of Loreto behind you and majestic Isla Danzante rising out of the sea in front of you. Serves six.

6 boneless skinless chicken breasts
2 tsp oregano
Salt and pepper to taste
3 tbsp red wine vinegar
4 tbsp corn or canola oil
1 large onion, chopped

4 cloves garlic, minced

Cilantro Sauce
1 bunch cilantro, stems removed
1 large onion, quartered
3 tomatoes, quartered
1 poblano or Anaheim chile, seeded and quartered
1 - 2 yellow guero chiles, with stem and seeds removed

Marinate chicken breasts in mixture of oregano, salt, pepper and vinegar for about an hour. Heat oil in skillet, add chopped onion and garlic and cook until translucent.

Combine cilantro, quartered onion, tomatoes and chiles in food processor and blend until smooth. Add mixture to sautéed onions in skillet and cook two minutes. Add chicken pieces. Cover with water and simmer until chicken is tender, about 30 minutes.

* ★ ★

CHILES EN NOGADA

Suzanne lives next to a chile field in Todos Santos where poblanos are grown every year. After the chiles have been harvested in early June, she's invited to pick any leftover chiles for herself and her friends. Terry and I visited in mid-June and she made us this amazing creation for dinner. There were no pasas (raisins) anywhere in town, so we bought a box of Raisin Bran and fished out enough raisins to make this famous and elegant Mexican dish. The next

morning she took me out and we had a field day (literally) picking chiles. We filled giant grocery bags with fresh chiles. I went home and went on a poblano binge! This is Suzanne's recipe and it serves four.

8 poblano chiles
4 tbsp butter
2 white onions, finely chopped
1½ tbsp flour
½ tsp white pepper
½ tsp nutmeg
6 cups chicken broth
1/3 cup raisins
1 green apple, peeled and cut in chunks
½ cup mango, peeled and cut in chunks
½ cup pineapple, peeled and cut in chunks
1¼ cup crema media ácida or sour cream
6 cups cubed cooked chicken
1½ cups chopped walnuts blanched in boiling water for 2 minutes

If you have a gas stove, lay the chiles over the open flame and char skins well, turning with tongs frequently until they're uniformly blackened and stop snapping. The more charred they are, the easier it is to remove the skins. If you have an electric stove, place chiles in a large skillet on high heat. Turn frequently as above. Remove chiles to plastic bag, close it and let stand for 10 minutes. Remove from bag, place in ice-cold water and remove the skins, veins and seeds. Do not remove stems.

Melt butter in frying pan at medium heat. Add onions and cook until limp. Stir in flour, pepper and nutmeg and stir until bubbling. Add chicken broth, raisins and apples. Cook, stirring until softened. Add mango and pineapple. Gradually stir in media crema. Add chicken and heat thoroughly.

Place two chiles on each plate, or arrange all chiles on a platter. Fill each chile with chicken and sauce mixture. Sprinkle walnuts over top and serve.

POLLO CON SALSA ALCAPARRA - CHICKEN WITH CAPER SAUCE

This sauce is perfect served with chicken, but it's also delicious with grilled or broiled fish. If using fish, cook it separately and serve the sauce on the side. Its unique flavors and textures will make it a family favorite for years to come! Martina and Oscar, the chefs at Hotel Buena Vista Beach Resort, bring it to you. This recipe will serve four people and takes about an hour and half to prepare.

1/8 tsp saffron threads
1½ cups warm chicken broth
5 tbsp vegetable oil
¾ cup shelled raw pepitas (pumpkin seeds)
1½ tbsp olive oil
1 small white onion, chopped
3 garlic cloves, minced
1 small crusty roll, cut into slices
½ tsp ground cloves
¼ tsp ground cinnamon
½ tsp oregano
¾ cup capers
4 boneless, skinless chicken breasts

Salt and freshly ground black pepper to taste

Crumble saffron threads into chicken broth and let steep a few minutes. Preheat oven to 325°.

Heat one tbsp vegetable oil in medium-sized skillet over medium-high heat until very hot but not quite smoking. Add pumpkin seeds and cook, stirring constantly, until they are puffed and have a nutty fragrance, about 30 seconds. Don't let them burn or they'll ruin the flavor of the dish! Drain on paper towels.

In same skillet heat olive oil over medium heat until very hot. Add chopped onion and garlic and cook, stirring, three to five minutes. Add sliced roll and cook, stirring until golden brown on both sides. Add cloves, cinnamon and oregano and cook, stirring, another two or three minutes. Add capers with brine and stir well to combine. Simmer, uncovered, for five minutes on low heat. Add chicken stock with saffron and simmer another five minutes.

Place contents of skillet in blender and blend until well puréed, about 30 seconds. Add pumpkin seeds and purée another 30 seconds. Preheat oven to 350°. Heat remaining three tbsp vegetable oil in large skillet over medium heat. Season chicken breasts with salt and pepper and brown well on both sides, about three minutes each. Remove from pan and place in shallow 9 x 13 baking dish. Pour sauce over chicken, cover with foil and bake until chicken is tender, about 40 minutes.

SESAME-CHILI CHICKEN

Toasted sesame seeds, pumpkin seeds and spices give an almost Thai-type peanut taste to this unusual chicken dish. The chef who first prepared this dish for me at a long defunct restaurant in San José del Cabo back in 1983 had recently moved there from the incredible Caribbean diving resort of Cozumel. When I complemented him on it, he claimed that the sauce had its origins deep in the jungles of the Yucatán, way back in the days of the Mayans. I believed him, and you will too. It's definitely exotic, unusual and a treat for the taste buds! Serves six.

4 tbsp sesame seeds
¾ cup unsalted shelled pepitas (pumpkin seeds) or sunflower seeds if unavailable
6 cloves garlic, minced
3 tbsp corn or canola oil
½ tsp ground cinnamon
¼ tsp ground cloves
1 tsp American chili powder
1 cup chicken broth
6 boneless, skinless chicken breasts
Juice from 4 limónes (Mexican limes) or key limes
½ head lettuce, shredded
½ cup sliced green onions
1½ limónes (Mexican limes) or key limes, cut into 6 wedges

Combine sesame and pumpkin seeds, garlic and oil in skillet. Stir over medium heat until sesame seeds turn pale golden brown. Remove from heat and add cinnamon, cloves and chili powder. In food processor, purée mixture until smooth, adding broth a little at a time.

Heat sauce over medium heat, stirring, until it begins to bubble and thicken. You can cover and refrigerate sauce for several days. Bake chicken breasts at 350° for 25 minutes. Heat sauce and add lime juice, stirring constantly until hot. Spoon over hot chicken, surround with lettuce and garnish with onion and lime wedges. Squeeze lime over chicken to taste.

ANITA-CONCHITA'S CHICKEN MOLE

The use of chocolate in the sauce makes this typical Mexican chicken dish unique. I tasted Mole (Moe-LAY) for the first time on a weekend trip to Ensenada when I was in grade school. Because of the dark, almost black color, I thought it was pretty weird back then. But as I grew older, I began to appreciate the subtle, multi-faceted and unexpected flavor of the chocolate. I look forward to my first bite the way I look forward to a swim on a really hot day. It's that good....

Mole is a very special meal in Mexico; one that is served with tenderness to cherished loved ones. I was told this by the salesman, Ernesto, in a Cabo San Lucas store specializing in Huichol Indian art. These Indians live in the mountains behind

Puerto Vallarta on mainland Mexico and create masks, suns, moons and wild animals like jaguars and wolves made exclusively of tiny, multi-colored beads. Nina fell in love with an expensive sun and Ernesto offered it to her for considerably less - if I would go to a timeshare presentation (I didn't have to buy, he assured me - and I didn't) the next morning. He further bribed me by promising me his grandmother, Conchita's Mole recipe, (how could I pass that one by?) which I've integrated into mine.

I've used boneless, skinless chicken breasts to make it less hearty and more suitable for today's eating styles. Why not serve it to your loved ones, accompanied by your favorites from some of the other sections of this book? Serves six.

6 boneless, skinless chicken breasts
½ cup butter or margarine
1 onion, finely chopped
½ green poblano or Anaheim chile, finely chopped
½ tsp pepper
4 cloves garlic, minced
1 - 17½ ounce can tomato purée
1½ cups beef broth
2 tbsp sugar
1 tsp American chili powder
¼ tsp ground cinnamon
¼ tsp ground nutmeg
¼ tsp ground cloves
1 tsp sesame seeds
1 tbsp ground almonds
1 - 2 tsp hot pepper sauce
1 dark chocolate candy bar (about 4 ounces)

4 tbsp cold water with 2 tbsp cornstarch

In large skillet, brown chicken in butter until golden brown on the outside, but not done on the inside. Remove chicken and add onion, poblano, pepper and garlic. Cook until tender. Add tomato purée, beef broth, sugar, chili powder, cinnamon, nutmeg, cloves, sesame seeds, almonds, hot pepper sauce and chocolate. Add chicken, cover and reduce heat. Simmer until chicken is tender, about 30 minutes. Remove chicken to a serving platter and keep warm.

Slowly blend cold water into cornstarch. Pour into sauce and cook, stirring constantly until sauce is thickened. Spoon over chicken and serve.

POLLO LA BALANDRA

At the far end of La Paz Bay, just after you pass Pichilingue and the ferry docks and right before you get to Tecolote Beach there used to be a famous rock formation known as La Balandra. It was shaped like a mushroom on a really long, skinny stem and it sat out in the light green water of a shallow bay right offshore. Several years back it was knocked off its pedestal by vandals, right after the road was put through. Incredibly enough, some local engineers got together and hoisted La Balandra back up onto its perch, where it stood majestically and precariously until a hurricane took it out for good a few years ago.

This wonderful, delicate casserole dish of chicken with green chile was created on a camping trip on the beach closest to La Balandra, where there also used to be a few ready-made campsites (meaning there were a few palapas scattered around on the deserted white sandy beach and some fire pits). We swam and kayaked out into the bay and marveled at La Balandra, never suspecting we'd never see it again. Then we made this for dinner. When you try it, be forewarned. Make enough! People are guaranteed to want seconds and it's easier than easy to make! Serves six.

6 boneless, skinless chicken breasts
Salt and pepper to taste

¼ cup butter or margarine
8 poblano chiles, blistered, or 2 - 7 ounce cans whole green chiles, cut in strips
¼ cup corn or canola oil
1 large onion, thinly sliced
½ tsp salt
2/3 cup milk
2 cups crema media ácida or sour cream
¼ lb cheddar cheese, grated

Season chicken breasts with salt and pepper. Heat butter and oil together in skillet and sauté the chicken fillets for two minutes on each side, until they're lightly browned. Set aside.

To blister chiles: If you have a gas stove, lay the chiles over the open flame and char skins well, turning with tongs frequently until they're uniformly blackened and stop snapping. The more charred they are, the easier it is to remove the skins. If you have an electric stove, place chiles in a large skillet on high heat. Turn frequently as above. Remove chiles to plastic bag, close it and let stand for 10 minutes. Remove from bag, place in ice-cold water and remove the stems, skins, veins and seeds. Cut into strips.

In same skillet you cooked the chicken, add oil and onion and cook until translucent. Set aside two poblanos or one can of green chiles. Add rest of chile strips to onions and cover. Cook over medium heat for five minutes. In food processor, blend reserved chiles until smooth with milk and salt. Add crema or sour cream and blend for a few seconds longer.

Arrange half the chicken fillets in a 9 x 13 inch baking dish. Cover with half the chile strips and half the sauce. Repeat. Sprinkle cheese over the top and bake at 350° for about 30 minutes, or until chicken is done and cheese is melted.

⋆ ⋆ ⋆

PICHILINGUE CHICKEN IN NUT SAUCE

Next to the ferry dock on the east end of La Paz Bay is a lovely beach called Pichilingue. It has a restaurant and plenty of palapas on the beach to laze around under. On a trip my folks made with Aunt Hope and Uncle George many years ago, they had to wait several hours to catch the ferry to Mazatlán as it was running late for some reason or another. They decided to have lunch and go for a swim at Pichilingue.

My mom brought me this recipe back from there and encouraged me to try it. I did. The combination of the chipotle chile salsa, chicken, potatoes and almonds makes it truly unforgettable. It's another easy meal to prepare and one that will leave you hankering for a trip south. As a precaution, be advised that the chipotle salsa makes this dish fiery, so it isn't recommended for the more sensitive palates. Serves six.

6 boneless, skinless chicken breasts
4 cups cubed potatoes
2 tbsp corn or canola oil
2 cups salsa fresca (Salsa section)
1 cup salsa chipotle (Salsa section)

1 cup chicken broth
1 cup almonds, finely chopped
Black olives for garnish

In skillet, brown chicken and potatoes in hot oil. Set aside. In saucepan, stir together salsas, chicken broth and almonds. Bring mixture to boiling. Lightly grease 9x13 pan, place chicken and potatoes in it and top with sauce. Bake, covered at 350° for 30 minutes. Garnish with black olives and serve.

⋆ ⋆ ⋆

MISSION TURKEY BREASTS WITH CHIPOTLE SALSA

Baja is rich in history from the Missionary Era, which began in the early 1500s and ended 300 years later when all the missions were secularized by the Mexican government. While Cortez, Ulloa, Vizcaíno and Cabrillo all explored Baja, it wasn't until Father Juan María Salvatierra, a Jesuit priest landed in Loreto in 1697 that a permanent settlement was established in Baja. The Jesuits built a total of 20 missions from 1697 - 1767 when they were expelled.

At that point, Father Junipero Serra, a Franciscan, was assigned to care for the California mission system. He established only one mission in Baja before moving north to San Diego and Alta California. The Franciscans ceded the Baja missions to the Dominicans in 1773 and in the next six decades, the Dominicans built nine more in

Baja. By then, however, the population of native Indians had shrunk (due to death by warfare and disease) to only a fraction of its original number, so there was no longer any economically feasible reason for the existence of the missions. By 1846 the era of the missions was over. Most remain at least semi-intact today, and many function as active parishes.

This dish is practically effortless to make. The aromatic, smoky flavor of the chipotle salsa complements turkey wonderfully. This entree is not for the timid, however! The chipotle chiles make it quite spicy. Try this and perhaps you'll be able to picture yourself sitting in a mission courtyard, shielded from the hot sun, eating your midday meal with the padres and the Indians. Serves six.

6 - 4 to 6 ounce turkey breast cutlets
Salt and pepper to taste
½ cup flour
1½ tbsp coarsely ground black pepper
6 tbsp butter or margarine
1½ cups chipotle salsa (Salsa section)

Pound turkey cutlets until ¼ inch in thickness. Season with salt and pepper and lightly dust with flour. Melt butter in skillet and sauté turkey breasts for three to four minutes on each side, or until done. Heat salsa in saucepan until just boiling. Spoon over turkey breasts and serve.

CHICKEN ENSENADA

This delectable dish is named after Ensenada, busiest tourist town in all of Baja norte - which wraps itself around the grand bay of Todos Santos. Legend has it that the Spanish padres who first discovered Ensenada sat by the fire brainstorming one night, trying to come up with a name for the bay. They went through one saint's name after another, before finally throwing up their hands and just naming it after all the saints! It was simply too big and too impressive to hang a single saint's name on! The majestic bay extends from El Mirador on the north to Punta Banda on the south and it's a bustling seaport, the busiest on the west coast of Baja. We traveled all the way through Ensenada and around Bahía Todos Santos on our way to La Bufadora, and so always got to view it from every vantage point.

In the winter and early spring, gray whales and their calves frolic in its waters. My kids witnessed the site of the season one year driving home from La Buf. They saw a huge whale throw itself up into the air, breach and then slam its mammoth body back down into the water. They oohed and aahed about it for weeks! Where was I? I was driving. I missed it completely. I've seen plenty of whales breaching since then, but that would've been my first.

Chicken Ensenada is similar to a Russian Chicken Kiev with a chile con queso sauce.

I tasted it first at a now defunct Baja bar and grill in downtown Ensenada and couldn't wait to get a chance to experiment with making it. Serves six.

6 skinless boneless chicken breasts
1 - 7 ounce can diced green chiles
1 - 7 ounce can sliced black olives
1 cup red bell pepper, finely diced and blanched in boiling water for one minute
Garlic powder to taste
Salt and pepper to taste
3 cups chile con queso (Appetizer section, or buy at the store)

Pound chicken breast fillets until ¼ inch in thickness. Put one teaspoon each of diced green chiles, black olives and red pepper on top of each fillet. Season to taste with garlic powder, salt and pepper. Roll and place seam-side down in greased baking dish.

Bake at 325° for twenty minutes. Meanwhile, prepare chile con queso according to recipe. When chicken is done, spoon sauce over the top of each fillet and serve immediately.

ARRACHERA POSADA LA POZA

Arrachera exploded onto the Mexican cuisine scene in the late '90s. Before that, marinated flank or skirt steak was called carne asada and either of type of meat was used. Now skirt steak (thinner) is for carne asada and the thicker, juicier flank steak cut is used to make arrachera. The marinade is similar as both dishes had origins in Tampico. Nowadays every traditional Mexican restaurant in Baja has arrachera on their menu. It's not served chopped and in a taco like carne asada, but is served as a steak, with sides of beans, rice, guacamole and perhaps a light salad.

It's all in the marinade ... so Terry (being a serious carnivore) has spent the last year or so doing a taste test of every arrachera he could find in Baja. His favorite comes from Posada La Poza in Todos Santos, where we spent our honeymoon (in advance) in 2002. Juerg's marinade rocks, and so does his arrachera. Serves four.

1½ lbs top grade arrachera (flank steak)
1 cup pineapple juice
½ tbsp salt
2 tsp black pepper
2 tsp garlic salt
2 tsp onion salt
2 tsp hot paprika
1 tsp celery salt
½ tsp ground nutmeg
¼ tsp herbs de Provence
1 large or 2 small white onions, thinly sliced

1 tsp corn or canola oil
2 tbsp Dijon mustard
1 tbsp honey mustard
1 tbsp water
Salt and pepper to taste

At least two hours before serving, remove fat from meat, cut into ¾ inch strips and place in 9 x 13 pan. Put pineapple juice, salt, pepper, garlic and onion salt, paprika, celery salt, nutmeg and herbs de Provence in a small bowl and mix thoroughly. Pour over meat. Stir every 15 minutes.

Heat coals on barbeque grill to very hot. In skillet, stir fry onions about five minutes in mustard, water and salt and pepper. Then cover and simmer over low heat for ten minutes while cooking arrachera. For medium rare, broil the strips about three minutes on each side. Serve the arrachera on heated plates over a bed of onions. Juerg recommends sweet potatoes to finish off this dish.

* ⋆ ✦

FLANK STEAK SAN IGNACIO

This is dinner party material. If you have someone special coming to dinner, serve Flank Steak San Ignacio (created on a trip to the exquisite mission town midway down Baja). Although San Ignacio isn't on the ocean, there's plenty to see and do. There's the Jesuit mission to visit - arguably the most beautiful in all of Baja. There are hundreds of prehistoric cave paintings in the nearby mountains. Thirty miles southwest is San Ignacio Lagoon, one of the premier whale-watching destinations in the world. From late December through March, here and in Laguna Ojo de Liebre (also known as Scammon's Lagoon to the north by Guerrero Negro) adventurers flock to visit with the gray whales - up close and personal - and to frolic with them and their newborn calves. If you ever have the opportunity to take a trip to see the gray whales, do it. You'll never forget it! Serves six.

Marinade
¼ cup olive oil
¼ cup red wine or Balsamic vinegar
6 cloves garlic, finely minced
2 tbsp cilantro, chopped
Salt and pepper to taste

Steak
1½ pounds flank steak, butterflied
(sliced lengthwise through the middle of the steak, leaving a hinge at far end)
1 red bell pepper
1 yellow bell pepper
3 tbsp cilantro, chopped
1 cup Chihuahua or jack cheese, grated
½ cup fresh basil leaves, chopped
Salt and pepper to taste
Cilantro sprigs for garnish

Make a marinade for the meat by combining olive oil, vinegar, garlic, cilantro, salt and pepper in a bowl. Add steak and marinate for two hours at room temperature or in the refrigerator overnight.

Halve the bell peppers, remove stems and seeds and place in a shallow baking dish. Bake at 400° for 20 minutes until thoroughly softened. Purée bell peppers in food processor and combine with cilantro, cheese and basil in bowl. Set aside.

Lay marinated steak on counter top with flap opened. Spread pepper-cheese mixture evenly over both halves of the steak. Roll the steak up tightly, like a jellyroll and place seam down, in baking dish. Pour remaining marinade over steak.

Bake at 350° for 30 minutes, basting occasionally. After removing from oven, let rest a few minutes before cutting into ½ inch slices. Garnish with cilantro sprigs.

ROSARITO RIBS DE FIERO

Straight from Rosarito Beach - party haven for college students from all over Southern California - and located just fifteen minutes south of the international border, come these spicy, delectable ribs. When I was newly single, the furthest south I dared venture on my lonesome was to Rosarito. I first tried these ribs at a roadside eatery claiming to specialize in carnitas. Carnitas? Can you figure that one out? I couldn't - so I asked. The proprietor told me that when they opened the restaurant their specialty was carnitas. It was only later, after his mother-in-law passed on that he and his wife decided to change their specialty. They just hadn't gotten around to changing the name yet. The logic was pure Baja. Anyway, who cared what the sign said? The ribs were awesome. I told him so and he was so delighted, he gave me the recipe.

A few interesting tidbits of trivia regarding Rosarito: It became a destination for Hollywood celebrities fleeing Prohibition in 1927 when the famous Rosarito Beach Hotel was opened. The city has grown steadily over this century as nowadays decorators from the US flock there to buy authentic, rustic and colonial Mexican furniture, leather and wood equipales, pottery, and folk art. There are upscale furniture stores that can recreate masterpieces from a magazine photo! Rosarito is a well-known surfing mecca and the site of the Rosarito to Ensenada 50-Mile Fun Bike Race, which attracts huge crowds every September and April. Several years ago, Hollywood revisited Rosarito in a major way when Fox Studios Baja was built just south of town next to the ocean, changing not only the face of the landscape, but also transforming the economics of the region. Did you know that Titanic was filmed there? And Pearl Harbor too ... among other movies.

Caution is in order here. These ribs have quite a bite. Save them for your friends who adore spicy foods. Or else invite me over for dinner! Serves four.

6 pounds pork ribs (you can substitute 10 pounds beef ribs)
3 cups water
1 medium onion, finely chopped
2 cloves minced garlic
1 tbsp butter or margarine

1½ cups catsup
1/3 cup A-1 Sauce
¾ cup honey
1 tbsp Worcestershire sauce
1 can beer
1 tbsp seasoned salt
As much Tabasco or other hot pepper sauce as you can handle
1 - 4 tsp cayenne pepper

Boil ribs in water for one hour. Meanwhile, sauté onion and garlic lightly in butter. Add catsup, A-1 sauce, honey, Worcestershire, beer, seasoned salt, hot pepper sauce and cayenne. Bring to boil. Reduce heat and simmer 30 minutes.

Drain ribs and bake at 350° for 30 to 40 minutes or until brown, basting frequently with sauce during the last 15 minutes.

ALBONDIGAS EN CHIPOTLE

These meatballs are seasoned with spicy, smoky chipotle chiles. Originating as a country Mexican dish, this dish has become popular north of the border recently in the Baja Cuisine restaurant scene. Not overly hot, it deserves a try because the combination of flavors is truly spectacular. It's a robust meal that will warm up those cold, winter evenings. Serves six.

Meatballs
¾ pound ground pork
¾ pound ground beef
2 small zucchinis, finely chopped

2 eggs
¼ tsp oregano
½ tsp ground pepper
¾ tsp salt
¼ tsp ground cumin
1 small white onion, finely chopped

Sauce
6 - 8 tomatoes
3 cups water
3 - 5 chipotle chiles en adobo
3 tbsp corn or canola oil
¾ cup beef broth or 1 tbsp powdered
beef bouillon in ¾ cup water

To make meatballs, combine pork, beef and zucchini. In food processor, blend eggs, spices and onions. Mix well into meat and make 24 meatballs, about 1½ inches in diameter.

Core tomatoes and place in boiling water in Dutch oven and cook about five minutes. Drain. Skin tomatoes and blend with chiles to make a smooth sauce. Heat oil, add sauce and bring to boil over high heat. Cook for five minutes.

Add beef broth and reduce heat. Add meatballs, cover and simmer for 50 minutes or until meatballs are done.

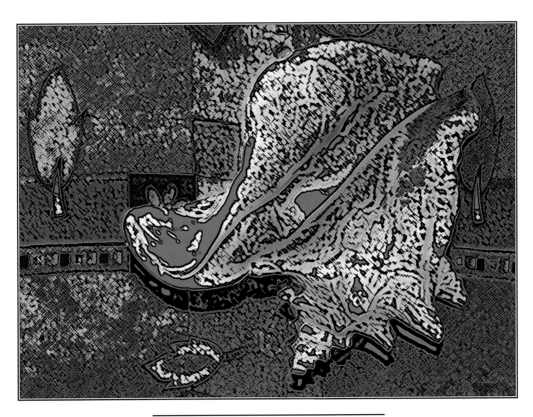

TERRY'S BOMBERO CHILI

Terry created this recipe back when he was a fireman in Palm Springs. He makes it a lot. In fact he gets requests to bring it to nearly every potluck we go to these days. Super Bowl, yeah. Los Barriles Art Festival, yeah. Parties at our house, always. He's not sure I should share it with the world, but it's so good that I have to. It's really popular and it's really easy too. Now everyone will know his secret! Actually, he makes it a little different every time. Sometimes he adds prepared salsa; sometimes different fresh chiles. Takes about two hours to make, but he says to tell you the longer it cooks, the better tastes. This will feed eight to 10 people, if you're lucky.

I remember when he made it for our housewarming party here in Buena Vista. Jesus "Chuy" Valdez, owner of Hotel Buena Vista Beach Resort, scraped the last bit of chili out of the pan and into his bowl for seconds or thirds, I don't recall. We ran out way before people's appetites did!

2 tbsp olive oil
1 large red onion, chopped
1 large white onion, chopped
6 cloves garlic, minced
2½ lbs ground beef
2 green bell peppers, chopped
4 to 6 serrano chiles, stems removed and finely diced (remove seeds if desired)

4 cans Snappy Tom or any other Bloody Mary mix
3 medium tomatoes, diced
2 tbsp American chili powder (or more, depending on how hot you like it)
1 bunch fresh cilantro, chopped and stems removed
Salt and pepper to taste
2 - 1 lb, 11 oz cans kidney beans (drained) or 1 lb bag dried kidney beans, soaked overnight and drained
Saltine crackers and grated cheese for garnish

In large Dutch oven, heat olive oil to medium heat. Add onions and sauté until translucent. Add garlic and continue cooking. Add ground beef and cook until browned. Drain off excess fat. Add bell peppers, serranos, Snappy Tom, tomatoes, chili powder, cilantro, salt and pepper. Heat to boiling. If using soaked beans, add at this point. Cover and reduce heat to low, letting simmer for at least an hour and a half. If using canned beans, about 30 minutes before serving, add them, discarding all but about a third of the liquid from the can. Serve with crumbled saltine crackers and grated cheese on top and get ready for the compliments! Serve leftovers over eggs the next morning.

EXPATRIATE PEPPER STEAK

A La Bufadora original, I dreamed this up over Christmas vacation one year and named it after my expatriate buddies, Jim and Sue. My pepper steak is slightly different from the cracked black peppercorn version you may be used to, but it's definitely tasty. The flavors of the cilantro, wine and mushrooms blend with the green peppercorns to make a subtly different but delectable sauce. This makes a perfect holiday dinner. I remember when I first created it. I served it to a few friends (including the expatriate duo) on New Years Eve, before we went out to Los Gordos, one of our favorite local hangouts for their big New Year's bash. My daughter Gayle was allowed to stay up until midnight for the first time that year. Her favorite memory of the party was of hiding behind a tall, handsome hombre out on the patio at Gordos and watching all the caballeros (Mexican gentlemen) empty their six shooters into the New Year's sky as the moonlight flickered on Papalote Bay. Only in Baja ... and only in the boonies! Serves six.

¼ cup butter, margarine or corn oil
6 medium New York steaks
¼ cup butter, margarine or corn oil
6 green onions, chopped
½ cup chopped cilantro
½ pound fresh mushrooms, sliced
¼ cup green peppercorns
½ cup white wine
Salt and pepper
Lemon and tomato slices to garnish

Heat half the butter or oil in skillet. Fry steaks three to five minutes on each side and remove to hot platter. In same skillet, add remaining butter, add onions, cilantro, mushrooms, green peppercorns, wine, salt and pepper and cook until mushrooms are tender. Pour sauce over steaks. Garnish with lemon and tomato slices.

MEDALLIONS OF PORK MULEGE STYLE

We spent some time in Mulege when I was 11. This is what I remember from that trip: 1) The Audubon Society was there. Famed author Roger Tory Peterson was there and let me and Nina tag along on bird-watching expeditions at sunrise and sunset along the Río Mulege and through the hillsides. 2) We paid the bird-watchers back by performing a water ballet just for them in our hotel pool. 3) Nina sat on a jumping cholla that trip and it took Mom over an hour to pluck out the nasty thorns. 4) We flew in and out in a friend's private plane. When we got ready to leave Mulege, the plane was so overloaded that the pilot had to abort take-off, go back and dump a bunch of weight. When we tried to take off the second time, it was a real white-knuckler according to our mom (who had flown with some real World War II hot shots in her time and wasn't a fearful flyer by any stretch of the imagination). She said we came way close to stalling and barely cleared the mountain at the end of the runway. Whoa!

The orange and wine flavors work feats of

magic with the pork in this recipe, transforming it into an elegant entrée. Our old friends Mike and Carol, who used to live in Mulege, brought me this one few years ago. It will truly convince you that you are seated amid a palm grove along the river, in the exotic, tropical oasis of Mulege. Or at least you'll wish you were! Enjoy with a chilled Sauvignon Blanc from Monte Xanic in the Guadalupe Valley. Ah yes! Serves six.

3 pork tenderloins
2 tsp dry mustard
Salt and freshly ground pepper to taste
2 tbsp butter or margarine
2 - 3 cloves garlic, minced
½ cup dry vermouth
½ cup dry white wine
1 cup orange juice
1 tbsp flour
2 tbsp water

Garnish
Cilantro sprigs
2 tbsp chopped cilantro
2 tbsp zests of orange rind
1 orange, sliced thinly

Trim fat and sinew from pork tenderloins and cut in ½ inch thick slices. Combine dry mustard, salt and pepper, and lightly rub into meat.

In large skillet, melt butter over medium-high heat. Add pork slices and garlic, browning for three to five minutes on each side. Add vermouth, wine and orange juice, and reduce heat. Simmer, covered for eight to ten minutes or until meat is tender. Remove medallions to warm plate and cover.

Make a paste of flour and water. With flat whisk, stir the paste into pan juices and simmer to thicken.

When ready to serve, return the medallions to the hot pan with the gravy for a minute, then arrange on a warmed serving platter. Cover with gravy. Sprinkle with chopped cilantro and zests of orange rind, placing sprigs of cilantro and slices of orange around platter.

TAMALES

This is a basic, easy recipe for tamales. There are so many variations on these you would be amazed. While they are traditionally wrapped in cornhusks, you can also wrap them in banana leaves. This presentation is usually saved for special occasions, like Christmas. They can be made with most any kind of meat or vegetarian filling. You can even make fruit tamales for dessert! You can make these ahead of time - even a few days ahead of time. They refrigerate well. Be sure to begin steaming them about an hour before you're ready to sit down and eat. This delicious recipe will delight your friends and family. Be sure to serve with some salsa fresca on the side for those who love to spice things up a little! Makes 24 tamales.

Basic masa de harina for tamales
6 cups packaged masa de harina
2 tsp baking powder
4 cups beef broth
1 1/3 cups solid vegetable shortening

Combine masa and baking powder in large mixing bowl. Mix in broth. Beat shortening in separate bowl with electric mixer until slightly fluffy. Add to masa mixture and beat until it develops a somewhat spongy texture.

Beef filling
4 lb chuck roast
4 cups water
10 dried red ancho chile peppers, lightly toasted
1 tsp ground cumin
¼ cup pepper
4 cloves garlic, peeled
¼ cup salt
1 large package cornhusks - about 24

Early in the morning, place the roast and water into a large pot or crock-pot and slow cook four to six hours, or until the beef shreds easily with a fork. Remove the meat from pot. Place in large bowl, add salt and shred, reserving broth for later.

Remove the seeds and stems from chiles. Boil in a pan with one cup water for about five minutes. Transfer chiles to food processor and add cumin, pepper, garlic and enough of the chile broth to make a paste when all spices are blended together.

Add spice paste to shredded beef and mix thoroughly. Add as much of the remaining broth as necessary to make a delicately moist, but not watery filling.

Making tamales
Now comes the fun part. Divide the masa into 24 balls. Open up the cornhusks and tear a ¼ inch wide strip off each husk for tying up the tamales. Lay a cornhusk on your counter and pat dry with paper towel. Place a ball of masa on it and flatten into a square shape. Put a heaping spoonful of filling inside.

Pick up the two long sides of the husk, fold them over into the middle and enclose. Roll the flaps of the husk in the same direction around the tamale. Fold the small, pointy bottom end up to close off the bottom and secure the tamale by tying it up in a bow. Repeat for all 24 tamales. These can keep in the refrigerator for a few days before being steamed. To steam, line a steaming pan (Mexican, vegetable steamer or double boiler) with extra cornhusks. Put about two inches of water in the bottom of the pan. Gently place tamales inside and cover pan. Simmer until steaming hot - about an hour. (Short cut: You can also microwave them, a few at a time for about three minutes.)

BIRRIA

Birria is offered throughout Baja at little roadside stands. The mamacita behind the counter is stirring a big pot of bubbling birria, while customers sit on stools in front of her scarfing down big bowls of the spicy soup. It's not difficult to make, but it does take most of the day. I fully maintain that it's worth it if you're cooking for a crowd on a birthday or other special day. It is served in big bowls, garnished with cilantro, onion and fresh limón and will keep several days in the fridge. Serves 12.

Adobo Paste
6 ancho chiles, lightly toasted
10 guajillo chiles, lightly toasted
4 cups water
15 cloves garlic
2 large white onions cut into large chunks
1 tsp ground cumin
½ tsp ground ginger
1½ tbsp oregano
½ tsp ground cloves
1½ tsp ground allspice
1 tbsp ground cinnamon
½ tsp ground thyme
4 bay leaves
1 tbsp salt
2 tbsp cider vinegar

Remove seeds and veins from toasted chiles. In medium saucepan, simmer chiles for about 20 minutes. Drain, reserving water. Purée chiles with garlic,

onion, cumin, ginger, oregano, cloves, allspice, cinnamon, thyme, bay leaves, salt and vinegar to form a very thick paste. If too thick, add a little of the chile water.

Lamb
1 banana leaf
1 tbsp oil
1 - 6 to 7 lb leg of lamb, cut into three-inch chunks
½ cup solid shortening or lard
2½ lbs fresh masa (see tamale recipe)

Cut banana leaf into six or eight pieces so they're small enough to fit into a deep roasting pan. Brush with oil, stack and wrap in foil. Roast at 425° until they're soft and pliable, about 15 minutes.

Rub lamb chunks all over with shortening or lard and let stand for 20 minutes. Then spread adobo paste over all the chunks, coating all pieces thoroughly.

Line bottom and sides of roasting pan with ¾ of the banana leaf pieces. Place lamb chunks in pan and top with remaining leaf pieces.

On floured cutting board, roll out masa until it's almost the size of the roasting pan. Gently move the masa into the roasting pan. Cover with lid.

Fill a slightly larger, shallow pan with water and place on lower oven rack so that it will be below the lamb. Bake lamb at 350° for three to four hours, or until tender.

Soup
5 large tomatoes

1 tbsp corn or canola oil
6 cloves garlic
2 medium white onions, chopped
2 tsp oregano
4 quarts chicken broth
Salt to taste

Garnishes
2 white onions, finely chopped
1 cup cilantro, stems removed and finely chopped
8 limónes (Mexican limes)
or key limes, cut in half

Roast tomatoes in large skillet with oil until softened and slightly blackened, about 20 minutes. Set aside to cool. In food processor or blender, purée tomatoes with garlic, onions and oregano. In large saucepan, add tomato mixture to chicken broth and simmer for 30 minutes.

Remove roast lamb from oven, uncover and discard masa and banana leaf pieces. Shred lamb. Drain pan juices and add to soup.

To serve, divide shredded lamb among 12 big soup bowls. Pour soup over the lamb and garnish with onion, cilantro and lime.

CHILE COLORADO LOS GORDOS STYLE

When we had our house in La Bufadora, Friday nights at Gordos' Restaurante y Cantina were mandatory. It's only open on weekends and everyone who's in town pretty much shows up. The drinks are cheap and strong, the company great and chile colorado amazing. Chuy, the owner and head chef would never give me his salsa recipe, but he would give me leftovers on Sunday afternoon before he headed back to Tijuana for the week. He wouldn't give up this recipe either, so after much experimenting, this is as close as I can get! Serves six to eight.

10 ancho chiles, lightly toasted
6 chiles de arbol, lightly toasted
2½ cups water
2 large white onions, chopped
6 cloves garlic, chopped
3 tbsp corn or canola oil
3 pounds beef bottom round, cut into 1-inch chunks
1 tsp ground cumin
¼ cup fresh basil, finely chopped
1 tbsp caldo de res (beef bouillon powder)
1 tsp pepper
2 bottles beer

Remove seeds, stems and veins from chiles. Rinse and place in a saucepan and with boiling water. Cook for about 10 minutes. Drain, reserving chile water.

In a blender or food processor, purée chiles, reserved chile water, onions and garlic. In large skillet heat oil at medium high heat. When oil is hot, add beef and cook until evenly browned on all sides. As meat is browned, transfer using slotted spoon to a bowl.

Return meat and accumulated juices to pan. Add chile mixture, cumin, basil, bouillon powder, pepper and beer. Bring to a boil over high heat, stirring frequently. Reduce heat, cover and simmer, stirring occasionally, until meat is very tender, about three to four hours.

BAJA BEACH BURGERS

In case you don't know this, the Sea of Cortez does not boast the hot wave action that the Pacific side of the peninsula does. While it can get really windy and the seas can get plenty rough on the east coast of Baja, the water overall is not only much warmer, but much calmer. One can barely body surf here; much less wield a surfboard successfully. So - when I first heard there was a decent surfing beach in Los Cabos and another on the East Cape south of Cabo Pulmo, I was more than skeptical. I didn't believe it at all. I thought this person's synapses were misfiring and that he'd gotten himself more than a little confused - enough to mistake, say the big waves at Todos Santos for the belly busters on the East Cape. Then he took me to both beaches and I saw that he was right on. I was the one who was mistaken!

The easiest to reach beach is located on the south end of San Jose del Cabo, just to the north of the elegant Palmilla resort and every time I drive by there I check out the break. More often than not it's close to perfect - the water light green and glassy - the waves close to six feet. There are usually plenty of surfers out there too, and boogie boarders and body surfers too. The warm water makes wet suits unnecessary most of the year, to be stored in the surfers' VW vans and saved for the cooler waters on the Pacific.

They call this beach Zipper's and there's a restaurant by the same name right there. It's a famous meeting, greeting and eating place for the surf set. It's situated right smack in the middle of their beach, after all. The menu there was gringo all the way and everyone in my group that first day ordered cheeseburgers! Naturally, being Parrot Heads and Jimmy Buffett fans for over 30 years, Nina and I did not fail to make the connection between his famous ballad, "Cheeseburger in Paradise" and our current situation. As we reflected on our lunch, this beach, Jimmy's song and the abundance of hamburger and cheeseburger-serving restaurants all over Baja, we realized that this cookbook wouldn't be complete without a cheeseburger recipe. Because, if you've been out of the US for any length of time, you'll discover, like all expatriated Americans do, that the food you crave the most is - yeah, you got it - a cheeseburger!

This is Terry's latest version of the Baja

Beach Burger. He perfected it when we moved to Buena Vista and we love it. It's really juicy, flavorful and totally satisfies our burger cravings! Serves six.

Burgers
2 lb lean ground beef
1 cup white onions, minced
4 cloves garlic, minced
2 tbsp Worcestershire or A-1 Sauce
Salt and pepper to taste
6 hamburger buns
6 slices cheese (be as creative as you want here)

Trimmings
Lettuce
Sliced tomatoes
Sliced dill pickles
Sliced red or white onions (sometimes he grills them with the burgers)
Mayonnaise, mustard and catsup

In large bowl, mix meat with onion, garlic, Worcestershire or A-1 Sauce and salt and pepper. Form into six patties and cook on a griddle or in a skillet for approximately five minutes on each side. During the last minute, top each burger with a slice of cheese. Arrange the buns around the edges of the grill to lightly toast. Then slap a burger onto each bun, let everyone load theirs up with their favorite toppings and dig in!

HOTEL CALIFORNIA LAMB BURGER WITH GORGONZOLA CHEESE

I had this lamb burger one sultry June day on the patio at La Coronela Restaurant and it rocks! The combination of lamb, pungent blue cheese, the sweetness of caramelized onions is divine. Chef Dany also recommends trying it with chevre, pine nuts and mango chutney. Oh yeah! Makes four burgers.

Burgers
1 lb ground lamb
4 cloves garlic
6 basil leaves
6 mint leaves

1 egg
Salt and pepper
4 pats Gorgonzola or Roquefort cheese almost the size of the burgers.
4 roasted garlic or rosemary bun or any quality homemade bun
Lettuce and tomato on the side for garnish
Dijon flavored mayonnaise
½ cup mayonnaise
2 tbsp Dijon mustard

Caramelized onions
1/3 cup olive oil
1 white onion, thinly sliced
1 tbsp honey

Heat oil in large skillet over medium-high heat. Add all onions. Sauté until pale golden, about 30 minutes. Mix in honey. Sauté until onions are deep brown, about 15 minutes.

To make burgers

Finely chop basil, mint and garlic and mix with the ground lamb. Add the egg, salt and pepper and form four equal patties. In a large skillet or on a griddle, fry about five minutes on each side. Top with cheese about two minutes before done. In small bowl, combine mayo and mustard. Toast the bun lightly and spread with the mayo mixture. Place a burger patty on a bun, top with caramelized onions and serve with lettuce and tomato on the side, and other burger condiments if desired.

BAJA STREET HOT DOGS

There is a strange phenomenon here in Baja. I first noticed it on a trip down the peninsula with my old friend Kit in 1998. Every night in every town we visited we saw hot dog carts on nearly every street corner. The hot dogs were amazing - wrapped in bacon and served with a white sauce, sliced jalapeños, chopped tomato and onion. Kit went so far as to eat a hot dog at every stand we passed in search of the very best Baja street hot dog. He found it in Santa Rosalía at a stand near the famous El Boleo Bakery. The buns were perfectly steamed, the bacon slightly crisp and the toppings fresh and plentiful.

Now you may be asking like we did: Why do they only come out at night? Terry and I have had hot dog cravings around lunchtime on countless occasions, but had no luck finding a cart. The answer is pretty simple. These street vendors all have day jobs. I have never ever seen a hot dog cart before sunset! Serves six.

6 strips bacon
6 hot dogs
6 toothpicks
6 hot dog buns
½ cup mayonnaise
½ cup crema media ácida or whipping cream
2 cups chopped tomatoes
2 cups chopped white onions
2 cups sliced pickled jalapeños from can
Catsup and mustard

Cook bacon strips until about half done but still pliable. Wrap each strip around a hot dog and secure with toothpick. In double boiler, steam hot dogs for 10 minutes. For the last few minutes, add buns. Mix together mayonnaise and crema or whipping cream and put into a squirt bottle. When hot dogs are done, place in buns and squirt with white sauce. Serve with tomatoes, onions, jalapeños, catsup and mustard.

BREAKFAST & BRUNCH

There's a saying in La Bufadora that applies only to newcomers. It's called, "getting boofed." Exactly what does that mean? Let me give you a little background.

There are a few (the number changes frequently) restaurants on the main drag, which is next to a shopping arcade full of curio shops, folk art shops, taco stands and more restaurants. There are stands that sell churros (long, skinny, deep fried donuts dipped in cinnamon sugar) and stands where you can buy fresh fruit in a cup or an ear of corn smothered in butter, hot sauce and Mexican cheese. On Wednesdays, Fridays, Saturdays and Sundays this "mall" as it's called, swarms with tourists. They come in by the busloads from Ensenada to see La Bufadora, one of the biggest blowholes in the world. Local legend has it that the name means "Buffalo Snort," which is exactly the sound the water makes as it's sucked into an underground tunnel, a moment before it explodes from the rocks and bursts sky high, drenching onlookers.

People come to see the Blowhole, but they don't spend the night. There are a few houses to rent in La Bufadora, but there are no hotels. Unless you know someone, or unless you're a diver who doesn't mind camping in the dirt, you never get any further than the touristy part of town. You come in, you shop, you eat, perhaps you stop into Gordos for a shot of Rattlesnake Tequila, or you have some nachos at Celia's. On your way out of town, you may decide to have chips and salsa with a beer at Restaurant La Bufadora. But you don't stay. (After all those drinks, perhaps you should!)

 Nina and John are divers. In 1993 they rented a house in La Bufadora and invited me and my kids to spend Memorial Day weekend there. The first morning we were there, we all walked through Toscano's ranch to Gordos. After all, breakfast was advertised for $1.50 so how could we go wrong? I ran into Kit, an old friend from San Diego on the patio there and he invited us up. As we sat on the deck in the early morning sunlight, my eyes drifted out over the bay. It was beautiful, peaceful, festive, lonely, comforting and magical. My heart stirred, my eyes misted up and in an inexplicable way, I felt I'd come home. Home to somewhere I'd never been before. Bingo. I was boofed. What happened to me? I can only tell you that it reminded me of the Baja I'd come to love as a kid - and forgotten existed in the intervening decades!

I stayed an extra night that trip. I came back again, again and again that summer. I couldn't stay away. I was growing there - happy there - free there - me there. Nina and I ended up buying a house there after the summer passed. I dedicate this section of my cookbook to being boofed. Whether it happens to you in La Bufadora or somewhere else in Baja, it's when the magic of the place zaps you, captures you, sits you right down and makes you its own. You become a part of it and it a part of you.

HUEVOS VERACRUZANOS

Huevos Rancheros are a traditional Mexican breakfast. You can get them in just about any restaurant in Baja that serves breakfast. They're terrific with frijoles, buttered tortillas and fresh fruit and a round of Bloody Marys if you're so inclined. This recipe from Pancho's in Cabo San Lucas is just a bit different than huevos rancheros. The addition of the sliced green olives gives it a Caribbean Veracruz twist that really jazzes it up. Serves four.

Salsa Veracruzana
2 green bell peppers, thinly sliced
2 white onions, thinly sliced
2 lb tomatoes, thinly sliced
2 tbsp olive oil
3 ounces sliced green olives
1 tbsp oregano
2 bay leaves
Salt to taste

Eggs
8 eggs
4 tbsp butter or margarine
Salt and pepper to taste
4 corn tortillas
½ cup corn or canola oil
2 cups Chihuahua or jack cheese, grated

In large skillet, sauté bell pepper, tomato onion until done. Add olives, oregano, bay leaf and salt. Cover and simmer on low heat for fifteen minutes.

Fry eggs sunny side up in butter in another skillet. Season to taste with salt and pepper. Fry tortillas flat in corn oil in small skillet until only slightly crisp. Drain on paper towels. Place two fried eggs on each tortilla. Top with salsa Veracruzana and grated cheese. Place under broiler for one minute or until cheese is bubbling. Serve immediately.

TROPICANA BREAKFAST RELLENOS

Brad and Diane from Washington, who are friends of Nina and John, spent a week at the Tropicana Inn in San Jose del Cabo over Thanksgiving recently. We ran into them there and both were raving about the breakfast rellenos. They said they ate them every morning. Nina and I made a vow there and then to get the recipe for Baja Magic Dos. We highly recommend staying at this hotel if you go to San Jose. It's centrally located, spectacularly built and decorated and the restaurant and bar are as good as it gets! Be sure and try this for breakfast. Better yet, try it tomorrow and then start planning your trip! Serves four.

4 poblano chiles, blistered
3 cups salsa ranchera (Salsa section or use Salsa Veracruzana from preceding recipe)
1 tsp epazote
Salt and pepper to taste
½ lb jack cheese, shredded
2 tbsp butter
8 eggs
½ lb queso Chihuahua, shredded

To blister the chiles: If you have a gas stove, lay the chiles over the open flame and char skins well, turning with tongs frequently until they're uniformly blackened and stop snapping. The more charred they are, the easier it is to remove the skins. If you have an electric stove, place chiles in a large skillet on high heat. Turn frequently as above. Remove chiles to plastic bag, close it and let stand for 10 minutes. Remove from bag, place in ice-cold water and remove the skin, veins and seeds. Do not remove stems.

In saucepan, heat ranchera sauce. In medium bowl, scramble the eggs. Add crushed epazote, salt and pepper. Melt butter in skillet and cook the eggs until done. Make a slit in each chile and stuff with ¼ of the eggs. Put on a cookie sheet and top with combined cheeses. Broil for a minute or until cheeses are bubbling and almost brown on the edges. Move to warm plate and cover each relleno with ranchero sauce. The Tropicana serves this with fried potatoes or beans on the side.

ANITA'S HOT-CHA-CHA OMELET

My friends, Larry and Hal owned a restaurant years ago in Encinitas, CA. They made the best omelet I had ever eaten, but I had a little complaint. There wasn't any hot sauce to go with it, what with their food falling into the California Cuisine category and all. So what did I do? I brought a bottle of Huichol Hot Sauce with me in my purse one Mother's Day for brunch. Hal told me he was renaming the omelet in my honor. (Of course, it was just a joke, but I took him up on it here!) Believe me, the only thing that's hot is the sauce. Everything else is still as Larry conjured it up back then - and it's purely divine. Serves four to six.

1 dozen eggs, lightly beaten
1/3 cup milk or half and half
1 tbsp garlic powder
Salt and pepper to taste
½ cup butter or margarine
2 avocados, peeled and thinly sliced
8 slices bacon, cooked and drained
2 cups Chihuahua, Muenster, jack or Brie cheese, (or combination thereof) crumbled
1 tbsp chili powder to sprinkle on as garnish
Salsa fresca or hot pepper sauce to taste (Salsa section)

Beat eggs with half and half or milk. Add garlic powder, salt and pepper. Heat an omelet pan to medium heat. Melt one fourth of the butter or margarine to cover the bottom of the pan.

Pour one fourth of the egg mixture into the pan and cook until lightly browned on bottom, about two minutes. Add half an avocado, sliced, two slices of bacon and half a cup of grated cheese. Cover pan and continue heating until cheese is melted. Fold omelet in half, garnish with chile powder and serve immediately. Repeat for each omelet serving. Serve plenty of salsa on the side for those who desire it.

✴ ⭐ ✴

CHILENO BAY OMELET

One of my all-time favorite Mommy memories is of the first time I took Gayle snorkeling in Chileno Bay. We sneaked out before breakfast and dove into the warm water right after the sunrise. We held hands as we kicked through schools of yellow and gray striped tiger fish, spiny brown spotted blowfish and rainbow-colored parrotfish. "Umph, umph!" we'd grunt through our mouthpieces as we pointed to the reef below. I remember diving. Seaweed waved at me. Fish stared and swerved from my path. My ears crackled. I swam on, searching the cracks between rocks for those devious, darting flashes of fluorescent blue, yellow and turquoise - those tiny, exotic tropical sea creatures that are the most spectacular of all. Moments before my air ran out, I found two and turned toward the surface and pointed. I heard Gayle's water-muffled laughter as the fish burst forth to gleam briefly in the ripples of reflected sunlight.

When she got tired, we caught a gentle wave that beached us at the shoreline. We took off our snorkels and sat together as the waves lapped at our legs. Then we walked down the beach. I told her stories from my childhood, about this land of endless uninhabited coastline, simple folk and incomparable majesty.

I remember seeing it through her eyes, as though for the first time. It was my favorite time of year in Southern Baja - October. The usually barren landscape was alive with color. There had been an inordinate amount of rain and the hillsides to our back were alive with color. Flowering shrubs twined themselves seductively around the tall, many-armed cardon cacti. Stocky, over-built elephant trees lounged next to red-blossomed, lush-leafed ocotillos. The desert had been transformed into a tropical thorn forest of jungle greens, perfumed with fragrant crimson, yellow and purple blossoms. We passed a washed out riverbed. Whenever the rains unloaded on the mountains behind us, the waters would race to meet the sea, ripping up vegetation and tossing the debris of the hillsides on these now tranquil shores.

Her growling stomach turned us back around and we returned to the Hotel Cabo San Lucas for breakfast. This recipe was inspired by that magical Baja morning. It makes six two-egg omelets, but can serve four if you prefer three-egg omelets. The fresh ingredients and fiery chiles make it a winner in my book.

✴ ⭐ ✴

1 onion, finely diced
½ bunch cilantro, with stems removed and finely diced
2 tomatoes, diced
4 cloves garlic, minced
1 - 3½ ounce can diced green chiles

¼ to ½ cup diced jalapeños (optional)
Salt and pepper to taste
½ cup butter or margarine
12 eggs, lightly beaten
1/3 cup milk or half and half
2 cups Chihuahua or jack cheese, grated

Place diced onion in microwave cooking dish. Cook on high for two minutes, or until onions are wilted. Mix with cilantro, tomatoes, garlic, diced green chiles and jalapeños. Add salt and pepper to taste. Microwave on high for an additional minute, or until all ingredients are hot.

Heat an omelet pan to medium heat. Melt one fourth of the butter or margarine to cover the bottom of the pan. Pour one fourth of the egg mixture into the pan and cook until lightly browned on bottom, about two minutes. Add one fourth of the onion, cilantro, tomato mixture and one fourth of the cheese. Cover pan and continue heating until cheese is melted. Fold omelet in half and serve immediately. Repeat for each omelet serving.

QUESO FUNDIDO CON JAMÓN

In English we call this a "puffy cheese bake." It's a rich and spectacular brunch entree I learned to make from an old friend, Debbie who was one of my original camping buddies in Baja back in the '70s and '80s. We explored both coasts of northern Baja together and for years it was our Christmas morning specialty. Serves six.

4 tbsp melted butter or margarine
8 slices sour dough bread, buttered
6 eggs
2 cups whipping cream
1 tsp salt
1 tsp dry mustard
½ tsp paprika
Cayenne pepper to taste
3 cups cheddar cheese, grated
3 cups ham, cut into chunks with fat removed

Butter a 9 x 13 dish. Line the bottom and sides of the baking dish with buttered bread. Beat eggs slightly and add all remaining ingredients. Mix well. Pour into baking dish and bake, uncovered at 350° for 40 to 50 minutes or until cheese is bubbling and golden brown.

SUNRISE MACHACA CON HUEVOS

The tallest hill right on the coast at Buena Vista on the East Cape isn't all that tall. In fact, it only takes maybe twenty minutes to hike to the top of it. When you get there, you'll find a concrete monument that must be at least 100 feet high. Around it is a courtyard of sorts. General Augustín Olachea, the governor of Baja Sur back when it was a territory (not even a state) built the original structure that became Hotel Spa Buena Vista. He was actually governor twice, once in the '50s and once in the

'60s. What is now the old part of the hotel was his vacation retreat, and the natural hot springs on the property helped ease his pain from rheumatoid arthritis.

General Olachea was a great promoter of education. Back then, villages and ranchos were very isolated and the only way he could educate the children was to build boarding schools for them. Of those he built, only the school in La Ribera is still operational. The others were replaced by traditional elementary schools as the area grew. General Olachea was also chief of the armed forces in Mexico, and built El Monumento on the hill behind the resort.

Every time he was in Buena Vista, he would present the honors and raise the Mexican flag over his home.

A few years back, my kids and I got a collective bug in our bonnets and decided to get up before dawn and hike up there to watch the sunrise. Derek set his watch alarm for 5:15 and off we trucked. We got back in time for the fisherman's breakfast buffet. As we raved about our adventure in line to get our food, I happened to notice that a new friend of ours, an aerospace engineer named Steve who'd taken a real shine to Gayle and Derek, was eavesdropping on us. Later on in the day, while playing water volleyball, he mentioned that he'd like to climb that hill himself and watch the sun swoop up over the Sea of Cortez. I laughed at him and said, "Hey, just show up at our door tomorrow morning at 5:15 and we'll do it again!" I didn't think anymore about it till the next morning at 5:15 when he came pounding on our door.

If you ever stay at the Buena Vista Beach Resort, by all means haul yourself out of bed and go see the sunrise. It has the feeling of a sunset played backwards, because the sky lights up with wild red, orange and magentas which fade out as the burning ball of light slips up over the horizon and into the sky. If you do climb that hill, you'll get to see the town of Buena Vista come to life. You'll count upwards of 70 fishing boats bobbing quietly in the bay, waiting till all those gringos finish their breakfast and are ready to grab their poles and hit the decks!

This is a tried and true, quick and easy Mexican-style family breakfast from our fisherman's buffet line that can be served with a glass of orange juice and milk or coffee. Serves eight - and hey, don't forget the salsa!

¼ cup corn oil
2 cups shredded beef (Taco section)
8 eggs, lightly beaten
1 onion, finely diced
1 to 1½ cups salsa fresca (Salsa section)
8 large flour tortillas

Heat the oil in a large skillet. Add shredded beef, eggs, onion and salsa. Cook until the eggs are done and all other ingredients are hot. Make burritos with the machaca by placing filling inside a flour tortilla, folding one end over and rolling. Place seam side down on plates and serve immediately.

BAJA AH-HA BREAKFAST TACOS

Breakfast tacos could almost be considered the Border region's counterpart to french toast. The tortillas are dipped in egg batter, fried and stuffed with all types of breakfast treats. You can vary the ingredients depending on your mood. Kids and adults alike will love helping you assemble and devour these.

And why do I call them Baja Ah-Ha Breakfast Tacos? Because my dad made them for Nina and me once when we were kids, camping on a lonely hillside at the edge of the Pacific. We'd already been out body surfing and shell hunting and it was past 8:00 a.m. and we were seriously hungry. The smell of those tacos assaulted our olfactories as we hiked up onto the bluff with our dog, Victoria. As you munch our stateside version, you'll be able to feel yourself barefoot on that isolated piece of Baja real estate, your toes crusted over lightly with golden dust and your hair damp from swimming. Imagine the sun easing up over the hills to the east, the coffee perking on the Coleman stove - and take your first bite. You'll be there! Really. These Baja Ah-Ha Breakfast Tacos will definitely alter your perspective on the day. Serves three to six.

6 tbsp butter or margarine
6 eggs
Salt and pepper to taste
6 corn tortillas
1 cup crumbled bacon (or 1 cup chopped ham or 1 cup crumbled sausage)
1 cup cheddar or Monterey jack cheese, grated
1 avocado, chopped and sprinkled with lime juice
1 - 3½ ounce can diced green chiles
1 large tomato, chopped
4 green onions, chopped
1 cup media crema or thick sour cream sauce
1 cup salsa fresca

Melt half the butter in an omelet pan over medium heat. In a medium sized bowl combine slightly beaten eggs, salt and pepper. Dip a corn tortilla in the egg batter and fry one side of the tortilla about half a minute, or until golden brown.

Turn tortilla over and place bacon, ham or sausage, cheese, avocado, chiles, onions, tomatoes and a dollop of crema or sour cream sauce inside the tortilla. Fold over and cook until cheese is melted. Repeat for all tortillas, adding the rest of the butter to pan as necessary. Serve with salsa on the side for those who wish it.

CHORIZO

No Baja cookbook would be complete without chorizo. It originated as a spicy Mexican sausage and has become an integral part of our regional cooking. It can be served as a breakfast sausage, can be added to potatoes, soups, eggs, tacos - just about anywhere you want to add a spicy, delicious, definitely Mexican sausage. This recipe makes about four cups and it's GOOD!

1 large onion, finely chopped
6 cloves garlic, minced
½ pound lean ground beef
1½ pounds lean ground pork
2 tbsp red chili powder
2 tsp oregano
¾ tsp ground cumin
½ tsp cinnamon
½ tsp ground cloves
1 tsp salt
1 - 2 tsp hot pepper sauce
5 tbsp vinegar
1½ cups enchilada sauce (Salsa section)

Combine all ingredients except enchilada sauce. In a large skillet, brown meat mixture lightly over medium-high heat. Break meat apart as it cooks. Add enchilada sauce and boil rapidly, uncovered, until liquid has cooked away. Skim off accumulated fat. Store, covered in refrigerator up to a week. Can be stored in freezer for much longer period.

✦ ✦ ✦

CHORIZO QUICHE IN CORNMEAL CRUST

Imagine that you're sitting on the outdoor terrace of the famous, remote, fly-in resort (or drive-in via the rutted, washboard dirt road) just north of Los Barriles ... Punta Pescadero. It's early morning and the sky is still rosy in the afterglow of sunrise. A flock of pelicans are gliding around the bay in front of you. More are perched on the rock formations jutting up out of the water. Every so often a bird spots his breakfast in the warm sea below and explodes downward into the water like a just-launched torpedo. A second later, Señor Pelícano pops back up to the surface, floating a moment duck-like, as he scarfs down his meal. Then he's off to hunt again.

I've never (yet) stayed at Punta Pescadero overnight, but to me it's one of the most romantic spots in all of Baja. A perfect honeymoon hideaway ... a perfect romantic getaway, period. The food and service are superb, the setting spectacular and the snorkeling, shell hunting and beach and water sports are as good as they get. Anywhere.

This quiche was inspired by a brunch to which my family was invited at Punta Pescadero one year. My mom and I couldn't wait to start experimenting when we got back to the States. The combination of the spicy chorizo, the eggs, cream and cornmeal make it an extraordinary regional delicacy. Serves six.

½ cup cornmeal
¾ cup sifted flour
½ tsp salt
1/8 tsp pepper
1/3 cup vegetable shortening
4 to 5 tbsp cold water
6 slices Chihuahua or jack cheese
½ pound chorizo (see previous recipe)
½ cup green onions, chopped
4 eggs
2 cups crema media ácida or whipping cream
Salt and pepper to taste

To make cornmeal crust, sift together cornmeal, flour, salt and pepper. Cut in shortening until mixture develops texture of coarse crumbs. Add water, one tablespoon at a time, stirring lightly until mixture forms a ball. Turn out onto lightly floured board and roll dough to a 13-inch circle. Fit loosely into a 9-inch pie plate or quiche pan. Fold edge under and flute.

Place cheese slices on bottom of cornmeal crust. Fry chorizo until cooked and crumbly in skillet. Drain off fat. Sprinkle chorizo on top of cheese, then top with green onions.

Lightly beat eggs in bowl. Stir in crema or whipping cream, and season to taste with salt and pepper. Pour over cheese and chorizo mixture. Place on bottom rack of oven and bake at 450 degrees for 15 minutes. Reduce heat to 350° and bake for 25 to 30 minutes longer. Let stand 10 minutes before cutting.

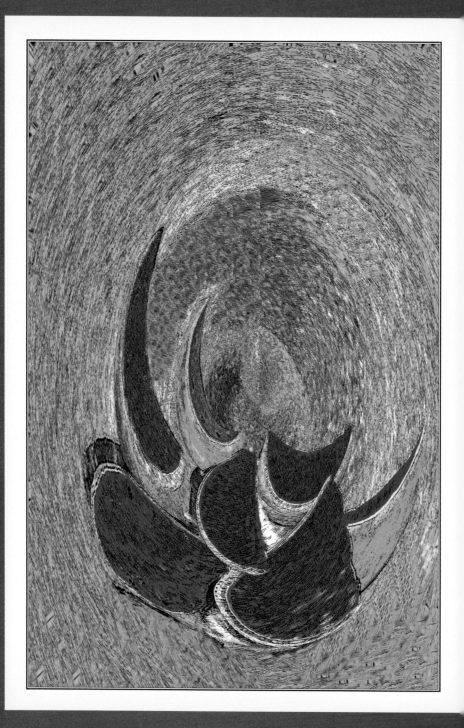

AGUAS FRESCAS - "FRESH WATERS"

The Mexican beverages known as aguas frescas are an inspiring complement to Mexico's cuisine. They're wonderfully unique and refreshing ... plus they provide a perfect balance to the spiciness of the food.

Huge glass containers of aguas frescas can be found at street stands all over Mexico, usually featuring whatever fruits are currently in season. Super healthy and oh-so-simple to make, these drinks only require three essential ingredients: fruit, water and a bit of sugar. How much easier can it get than that? Don't let the simplicity of these recipes fool you. The flavors will amaze you, and you just may find yourself as hooked as I am. (For the record, jamaica and horchata are my favorites.)

Following are recipes for five aguas frescas. Each of them is new to Baja Magic Dos. However, if you can't find the ingredients in your hometown or you feel like cheating, you can buy already made drinks or mixes at www.mexgrocer.com.

HORCHATA - CINNAMON RICE DRINK

Although horchata (or-CHAT-ah) is not really a fruit drink, it's served in the same way, and on the same occasions as the other aguas frescas. The unusual blend of rice, sugar and cinnamon makes this a preferred drink of many Mexicans. You can often find horchata in Mexican restaurants made fresh daily. This recipe must be made in two parts, over a six to eight hour stretch. The first part of the recipe takes five minutes, max. Then after waiting six to eight hours, you take the second step. This takes about 20 minutes to prepare and an hour or so to chill. Makes 1½ quarts.

3 cups long-grained white rice
3 cups water
3 quarts low or non-fat milk
1 cup sugar (or sugar substitute) or to taste
3 tsp vanilla
1½ tsp ground cinnamon

Place the rice in a bowl with enough hot water to cover it completely. Seal bowl with plastic wrap and let stand, at room temperature, for six to eight hours, or overnight. The next day, strain rice through a colander, discarding water. Place 1½ cups water and ½ cup milk in blender with 1½ cups of rice. Blend until liquefied. Pour into a pitcher. Repeat with other half of milk, water and rice. Pour through a strainer to remove extra rice pulp. Mix in sugar, vanilla and cinnamon and stir until sugar is completely dissolved. Chill thoroughly before serving. Pour into tall, ice-filled glasses and serve.

AGUA DE JAMAICA - HIBISCUS FLOWER WATER

Jamaica (Hah-MIKE-ah) is a plant native to Baja. Often confused with the hibiscus flower, this annual is very similar, but has leathery flowers and a single stem without any leaves can produce a dozen flowers. It has a deep burgundy color and a slightly bitter flavor that reminds me of cranberry juice ... only better. I make a jug at least twice a week. Actually there is a glass of it on my desk now. A former iced tea junkie, I am now hooked on Jamaica! It's a mild, natural diuretic, so here in Mexico it is often used to combat high blood pressure. Makes about a half gallon.

1 cup dried jamaica flowers
4 cups water
1/3 cup sugar (or sugar substitute) or to taste
4 cups ice

Rinse and drain the jamaica flowers in a colander. In large saucepan, bring four quarts of water to a boil. Add hibiscus flowers and sugar. Boil for 15 minutes. Mixture will be dark red in color.

Remove from heat. Strain thoroughly, discarding all flower petals. Pour into an ice-filled pitcher and stir. Chill thoroughly before serving in tall, ice-filled glasses.

AGUA DE MELÓN - CANTALOUPE WATER

Delicious. Refreshing. Easy. This is one of my favorites when it's hot out. This recipe takes about 20 minutes to prepare and another hour or so to chill. It makes about a half gallon.

1 cantaloupe, diced, with seeds and rind discarded
6 cups water
½ cup sugar (sugar substitute can be used) or to taste

Place half of diced cantaloupe in blender, along with two cups of the water. Blend until liquefied. Pour into a pitcher. Place remaining cantaloupe in blender, along with two more cups water. Blend thoroughly and pour into

pitcher. Add remaining two cups of water and sugar. Stir until sugar is completely dissolved. Chill thoroughly before serving. Pour into tall, ice-filled glasses and serve.

AGUA DE SANDÍA - WATERMELON WATER

Agua de sandía (sahn-DEE-yah) is a particular favorite with kids! This recipe takes about 20 minutes to prepare and another hour or so to chill. It makes a half gallon and is a wonderful, healthy change of pace for birthday parties and other kid-friendly special occasions.

2 cups diced seedless watermelon, with rind removed
6 cups water
½ cup sugar (or sugar substitute) or to taste

Place one cup diced watermelon in blender, along with two cups of the water. Blend until liquefied. Pour into a pitcher. Place remaining cup of watermelon in blender, along with two more cups water. Blend thoroughly and pour into pitcher. Add remaining two cups of water and sugar. Stir until sugar is completely dissolved. Chill thoroughly before serving. Pour into tall, ice-filled glasses and serve.

AGUA DE TAMARINDO - TAMARIND-FLAVORED WATER

Tamarindos are used frequently in both Thai and Indian cooking. In Mexico they're hugely popular and are regularly used to make aguas frescas. They're also used to make dulces de tamarindo, or tamarindo candies. The pods of the tamarind tree are what flavor this delicious, unique drink. This recipe takes about an hour to prepare and another hour or so to chill. It makes about a half gallon.

20 tamarindo pods
2 quarts water
1½ cups sugar (or sugar substitute) or to taste

Peel the tamarindo pods, removing the veins that run along the sides. Leave the seeds.
In medium saucepan, bring one quart water to a boil. Add peeled tamarindo pods. Boil over high heat for approximately 15 minutes, or until the pulp is soft.

Remove from heat and let cool until the pulp is ready to handle. Remove seeds from pulp and discard, along with any remaining bits of peel. Empty the remaining contents of saucepan into a blender. Add sugar and blend until liquefied. Run the mixture through a strainer, discarding extra pulp. Pour into a pitcher and mix with remaining quart of water. Chill thoroughly before serving. Pour into tall, ice-filled glasses and serve.

Beachfront Cantina at Rancho Buena Vista

FROM THE BAR

Have you heard those awful stories about folks who went to Baja, got rip-roaring drunk and ended up either sicker than a dog or in some kind of trouble? Well, I certainly have. And I've known a few of them in my lifetime. The summer before my senior year of high school, my parents had to bail a friend of mine out of jail, because he thought he had every right to bring his own beer into Hussongs Cantina in Ensenada. Not!

"Would you have done that in the US?" my dad asked him the next day, right after he emerged from the Ensenada jail - filthy, frightened and exhausted. (Let me clue you in on something - he was only 19 and unable to even walk inside a bar stateside.) My father must have told Nina and me this a hundred times: "Remember you are a guest in a foreign country. Treat the Mexican people with dignity and respect. Behave at least as responsibly as you do north of the border and you will never have any problems." I wrote that in my heart and I've never gotten into trouble here.

Uh Oh. I just looked at the clock and it's 5:30. My guests will be arriving shortly. It's time to finish the last minute preparations, put ice in the ice bucket and get ready for cocktail hour. What am I serving tonight? Margaritas? Nope. I'm not in the mood. How about Sangría? Red or White? No. Not Sangría either. Well, then, what about Renegade Rum Drinks? I don't know. I'm confused. Too many choices....

"Hey, Terry! Help me decide something, will you please?" I holler into the living room. We pore over recipes and together we choose what we will serve this fine Baja evening.

You know, even though the following drinks (except Traditional Mexican Chocolate) are all cocktails, it's possible to create them without alcohol. I drank "Virgin Margaritas" and "Virgin Mary's" when I was pregnant. Both of my children have been regulars at the swim-up bar at the Hotel Buena Vista Beach Resort since they were toddlers. I can just see them now - gliding through the water, pulling themselves onto their submerged barstools and ordering in clear, confident voices: "Ricardo, una piña colada sin rum (without rum) por favor." Or, "Strawberry Margarita sin tequila."

A few years ago, as I was sitting at a sidewalk café on the malecón in La Paz, I started thinking. Mexicans are Latinos. Like the French, Italians and Spanish, they consider the consumption of alcoholic beverages to be a natural part of life. When they drink, it's to celebrate life - but there's also sacredness to the way they drink. Rarely does one see a drunken Mexican - more often, sadly - it's the gringos who overindulge and get out of hand. We gringos seem to think we have carte blanche to misbehave in Mexico, because - like Toby Keith sings - "What happens in Mexico stays in Mexico." Not. Not if you live here or want to be invited back as a houseguest!

Keep that in mind and you'll have great fun making, serving and imbibing in the drinks specified here. There are too many variations of Margaritas to offer them all here, but I've offered you a bunch, along with two types of Sangría, a wine, fruit and brandy-laced punch from Spain, as well as recipes for homemade Kahlua and Irish Cream. And I've started the whole thing off with a lesson on tequila from John Bragg, the Maestro.

Baja Magic Dos has plenty of surprises in store for you in this section, with 10 new cocktail recipes. We have the Booby Juice Margarita along with the history of who really invented the drink. We have the Tequila Sunrise, Agave Sunset, Michelada, Sangrita, Mojito, Baja Blast and the White Jamaican. New restaurant recipes include the Banderita Margarita and Skip and Go Nakeds. What more could you ask? Well, how about some history on the Baja wineries of the Guadalupe Valley east of Ensenada. This area is considered comparable to Napa 30 years ago!

Oh yeah. One last thing. What are you serving tonight for cocktails?

THE TRUTH ABOUT TEQUILA

John Bragg has the largest collection of tequila in the world. As of spring 2005 he had over 500 different types of tequila, pulque and mescal. Since 1990, he and his wife Mary have owned Restaurant Pancho's (one of our all-time Baja favorites) in Cabo San Lucas. When we met them on a trip to Southern Baja before my first cookbook came out, Nina and I hit it off with them immediately.

They invited us to dinner at their restaurant the next night and after we ate, John treated us to one of his tequila tastings. Because tequila is "the essence of Mexico," I think it's only fitting that I should pass some of John's knowledge on to you (since his collection is the largest in the world, you can bet he knows his stuff). According to him, tequila isn't for lightweights - it's for those who, like the Mexicans, are passionate, strong and warm-hearted - people who live life with gusto. While most gringos think of tequila as something to be tossed back with a dash of salt and a lime, or added into a Margarita, serious tequila drinkers are thoughtful, slow sippers.

The Mayans started it all, way before the Spaniards showed up. Their fermented beverage of choice was pulque (pool-KAY), which they made from the Agave Mezcalero and used primarily for medicinal and religious purposes. In those days, drunkenness was a crime punishable by death and only old people and nursing mothers got free access to pulque. Why? Because of its high nutritional value and its tranquilizing effects. To this day, Indians still mix homemade pulque into their herbal medicines to treat diseases. And, as John told us, there are still pulquerías (pulque bars) in various parts of Mexico. He goes on to say that pulquerías generally don't have restrooms - just a trough on the floor in the back of the room - so they aren't for the faint-hearted! Or the ladies!

When the conquistadors and missionaries arrived in Mexico, they tried pulque, but at 30% alcohol, it just wasn't strong enough for their liking. So they did some experimenting and came up with mescal. Then they did some more experimenting with different varieties of agave and eventually came up with tequila. Tequila can be made from one of several types of agave plants. The purest, best tequila, however, comes from the blue agave plant, or the Agave Tequilana Weber. It is considered the most exceptional of all agaves because it produces the most full-bodied, clean tasting liquor. If you pick up a bottle of tequila and it reads, "100% Agave" then it is the real deal. If it's simply designated "tequila," it may contain up to 45% added sugars.

The Mexican government strictly regulates the tequila industry. Ninety six per cent of all tequila is produced in Jalisco, with most of it within 100 miles of Guadalajara. Today, four other states are also permitted to produce tequila. They are Guanajuato, Michoacán, Nayarit and Tamaulipas. In 1997, 100 million liters of tequila were produced annually. Since then, growth has averaged 4 to 6% a year overall and 15% in exported tequilas, the majority of them consisting of super and ultra premium labels.

Agave plants require no irrigation, but they take a long time to mature. Weeding is done periodically to keep grasses from stealing the plants' nutrients. Babies, or pups grow alongside the parent plants and these are removed also and relocated to new fields. When a blue agave is between seven to 10 years old, it shoots a flower-bearing stalk as high as 15 feet in the air. The dramatic yellow bloom will last a month or so, but it signals the agave's impending demise, for it dies soon after. Right before the stalk emerges is harvest time. Field workers remove the agave's core, called the piña, carry it to the fábrica where it's split in half and cooked in a large oven (horno) for about 24 hours. After cooling another 24 hours, the piñas are crushed, strained, mixed with water and put in large vats to ferment. After fermenting for 72 to 150 hours, the liquid is filtered and put into stills. The distillation process is carried out twice, and the final product emerges at 100 to 120 proof. It's then diluted with distilled water until it reaches the proper range of 76 to 90 proof.

There are three types of tequila. The first is a blanco (white) or joven. (HOE-ven means young.) A joven is only aged one or two additional months. The second is a reposado (ray-POH-sah-doh means rested), which is aged in wood for three to 12 more months. John says, "A really good reposado grabs you by the throat and gently lets go." The third type of tequila, añejo (Ahn-YAY-hoe means vintage) has been aged at least a year. Tequila ages quickly, so one that's five or six years old is considered "muy añejo" or very old.

When we did our tasting, most of us preferred the reposados. John served us one called Don Julio and if you want to try your hand at some thoughtful, slow tequila sipping, this is definitely one to try. We also love Siete Leguas, which Umberto, the bartender at the Hotel Francés in Guadalajara, turned us onto a while back. John has one parting thought he'd like to leave with you. If you come to Pancho's with a bottle of unopened tequila, and it's one he doesn't have in his collection, he'll buy the bottle from you and your dinner will be on the house! So, hey, that's worth a serious ¡Olé! Don't you think? (For more information on John Bragg, visit www.panchos.com.)

SANGRITA

Thoughtful Tequila sippers consider Sangrita to be the ultimate accompaniment to a really good reposado. It's a curious but typically Mexican blend of flavors - spicy, sweet, tart and salty - and if you enjoy tequila, then this is a recipe you've got to try! Makes about three cups.

2 cups Clamato juice
1 cup freshly squeezed orange juice
Juice of 4 limónes (Mexican limes) or key limes
2 tsp Tabasco (or to taste)
2 tsp Worcestershire sauce
Dash A-1 Sauce
1 tsp celery salt
½ tsp pepper

Mix all ingredients together in large pitcher or plastic bottle. Refrigerate. Serve chilled, in a shot glass, with a room temperature shot of reposado.

HUSSONGS ORIGINAL MARGARITA

Ever been to Hussongs in Ensenada? Most Baja Aficionados have - at least once in our lives. It's a rite of passage for Southern Californians who turn 18 and don't want to wait another three years before bellying up to a bar. But Hussongs isn't just a bar. It's a landmark ... a legend ... a one-of-a-kind, not-to-be-missed experience. It has this certain mystique. It's famous. People all over the world know about it. Its popularity has never waned in all these years. It's also the place where the Margarita was invented - back in October 1941 by bartender Don Carlos Orozco. He concocted the perfect mixture of equal parts tequila, Damiana (Controy is used now) and lime, served over ice in a salt-rimmed glass for Margarita Henkel, daughter of the German Ambassador to Mexico. Not too many people know that, but it's the truth. (Verified by the Ensenada Historical Society, Margarita Henkel herself and Señor Orozco's granddaughter.)

Hussongs hasn't changed much since 1892. Current owner, Ricardo Hussong, grandson of founder Juan, told me that the only changes he's made to the building since taking it over in 1979 were to replace the sheet metal ceiling and to add a new ice maker! He's maintained the family tradition of serving consistently great drinks, using top quality liquor and charging reasonable prices. It's laid back, friendly, casual and always tons of fun. The dark green interior, wooden floors covered in sawdust and funky art on the wall never change. Mariachis rotate in and out, just like they always have. A guy with a Polaroid cruises by, offering souvenir photos. Another comes in with an electrical box and two cylinders, offering to shock you for a fee. Whenever a song finishes, there's a round of hooting, hollering and cheering.

Is it rowdy? In a comfortable, easy-going way that doesn't take itself too seriously. It was way wilder in the '70s. Ricardo believes things have calmed down because, as he says (and he's about my age), "We're all growing up. The crowd is mellower now. The younger tourists go to Papas & Beer. It used to be that we had about 85% Americans here. Now most of our customers are locals. Business people come in here for a drink before lunch. Men in their 20s and 30s meet their girlfriends and wives here on Friday nights. It's steady." I know. I've seen it. And on weekends the locals are always happy to share their tables with visiting Americans. At Hussongs, everyone is your friend.

So how did it all start, anyway? Is the name Hussongs really German? And, if so, how did a German end up owning the most popular bar in all of Baja? Well, here's the scoop...

Johann Hussong, the cantina's founder, was born in Germany in 1863. When he was 23, he immigrated to New York, where he became John. After a year, he headed west to California. In 1889 the discovery of gold south of the border lured him to Ensenada. Back then Ensenada was barely a blip on the radar screen. There were 1,337 people, three hotels, one bar, a pier, a few shops, a flourmill, a school, a stable and a wine cellar. There was a new telegraph and phone line between San Diego and Ensenada and a steamship line that operated between the two cities. The road between the two was pretty much impassible.

John hunted quail, geese and other wild fowl, which he sold to local restaurants. In 1890 he bought a barbershop and began running a carriage with six horses between Ensenada and the gold rush camp, El Alamo, about 60 miles to the southeast on a very bad road. His carriage flipped one day that June, and he broke his leg. He was brought to J.J. Meiggs' cantina in Ensenada to recuperate. A few days later Meiggs attacked his wife with an axe. He was arrested and she took off for California. The day he got out of jail, Meiggs sold the bar to John Hussong and left to search for his wife. Neither was ever heard of again.

In those days, the cantina was located where Papas & Beer is now. However, the next-door neighbors complained constantly about the noise, so John - who had by then become Juan - moved his bar across the street, where it's been ever since. In April 1892 Hussongs Cantina was established.

Hussongs has always been a place that piques the imagination and whose memory lingers in the mind. My dad told me about his first visit there. It was 1931. He was nine. His dad and some fishing buddies were inside drinking and told him to wait outside. He couldn't handle the suspense. He had to see what was behind those green doors, so he sneaked in, climbed up onto an empty barstool and ordered himself a Coke. Ricardo told me that kids were able to come in and hang with their parents until the early '60s, when the laws changed. That was about the time of my first almost-visit to Hussongs. Like my dad, I was told to wait outside, but I was with my mom and sister so we went next door for tacos. When we finished, we stood out front for a few minutes waiting. I remember the music, the laughter. I remember wanting so badly to be old enough to go inside and see for myself just what all the excitement was about.

★ ✦
✦

I had to wait another ten years ... but I've been coming back ever since. We always stop in on our way up or down the peninsula after grabbing a couple of tacos next door. This is the recipe for a Hussongs Margarita. Serves four.

6 ounces tequila
6 ounces Controy (Cointreau or Triple Sec may be substituted)
Juice from 8 to 10 limónes (Mexican limes) or key limes
Crushed ice to top of blender or ice cubes for the glasses
Margarita salt (optional)

In the Blender
Place tequila, Controy, lime juice in blender. Fill until almost full with crushed ice. Shake well or blend until very slushy. Moisten rim of Margarita glass with a slice of lime and swirl in small dish of salt. Pour Margarita into the glass.

Rocks
Rim glasses with lime and swirl in salt. Fill to top with ice cubes. Pour in 1½ ounces each tequila and Controy and the juice of two limes (equivalent to 1½ ounces). Stir. Serve. ¡Olé!

BEN'S BOOBY JUICE MARGARITAS

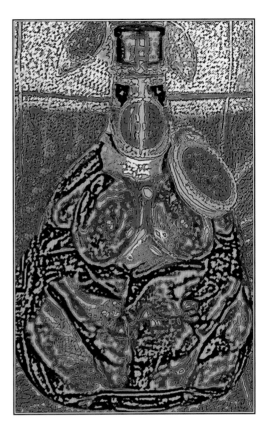

Terry and I named these drinks after a very long afternoon at the Hacienda Hotel pool bar in Cabo San Lucas. With the booby juice (Damiana - so named by us because the bottle looks like a headless pregnant lady with pro-truding breasts) in the Margarita instead of Controy, we learned (the hard way the next day when we woke with hangovers-from-hell) that it gets you way buzzed way too quickly. (Note: Damiana is hard to find in the US and is an alleged aphrodisiac. We did not find that to be true. On the contrary.) This recipe is from our neighbor, Ben. He's famous for these and I guarantee that his recipe is mellower than the ver-sion that put us down for a day. Makes four.

6 ounces tequila
4 ounces Controy (Cointreau or Triple Sec may be substituted)
2 ounces Damiana
Juice from 8 limónes (Mexican limes) or key limes
Dash of club soda for each drink
Crushed ice to top of blender or ice cubes for the glasses
Margarita salt (optional)

In the Blender
Place tequila, Controy, booby juice, lime juice and four dashes of club soda in blender. Fill until almost full with crushed

ice. Blend until very slushy. Moisten rim of four Margarita glasses with a slice of lime and swirl in small dish of salt. Pour Margaritas into glasses.

Rocks

Rim four glasses with lime and swirl in salt. Fill to top with ice cubes. Pour in 1½ ounces tequila, ¾ ounce Controy and ½ ounce Damiana. Add the juice of two limes and a dash of club soda to each glass. Stir. Serve. ¡Olé!

WILD BLUE MARGARITAS from SOMEWHERES -VILLE

Excuse me. Don't I mean Margaritaville? Probably. We play a lot of Jimmy Buffett music in Baja. It fits the place. Like us Baja Aficionados, Jimmy's a bit of an enigma. Until his country crossover CD, License To Chill, he hadn't had more than a couple of hits on the radio in his career (and no MTV videos), yet his concerts continually drew crowds that ranked in the top five nationally. Never heard of a parrot head? Try buying a Buffett CD or two. You'll learn. And Jimmy's music will definitely adjust your internal compass south. Try it. And try this Margarita, but don't forget your flip-flops!

I semi-copied this un-copyrighted (and thus don't claim it's a Buffett original) recipe, which serves two, off a t-shirt I bought at his Chameleon Caravan

Concert in Del Mar, CA back in '93. This is more or less how it goes:

1. Fill shaker with broken ice   -
2. Squeeze two fresh Mexican lime wedges into shaker   -
3. Savor the fresh lime aroma   -
4. Add two ounces of Hornitos or your favorite reposado tequila   -
5. Sniff the cork   -
6. Add ½ ounce of Triple Sec   -
7. Add ½ ounce of good white tequila   -
8. Add 1¼ ounces of Rose's Lime Juice   -
9. Add a splash of Blue Curacao (Oh, baby!)   -
10. Cover shaker tightly and SHAKE vigorously!
11. Flip shaker in midair (three times if you're a pro)   -
12. Strain mixture over ice into chilled, salt-rimmed Margarita glasses -
13. Kick back and turn up the tunes   -

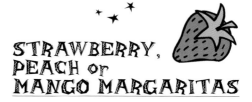

STRAWBERRY, PEACH or MANGO MARGARITAS

These totally tropical, spring or summer Margaritas are easy to make in your blender. Fun, tasty and refreshing, this recipe serves four and it's guaranteed to instantly transport your attitude somewhere south of the Tropic of Cancer! Serves four.

6 ounces tequila
2 ounces Controy (Cointreau or Triple Sec may be substituted)
Juice from 4 limónes (Mexican limes)

or key limes
1½ cups fresh strawberries or 3 peaches (or mangos), pitted and peeled
Crushed ice to top of blender
Sugar to taste (optional)

Put tequila, Controy, lime juice, and strawberries, peaches or mangos in blender. Fill to top with ice. Blend until very slushy and serve immediately. If sugar-rimmed glasses are desired, wet top of Margarita glass with water and swirl in small dish of sugar. Pour Margarita into the glass.

WINE MARGARITAS

Wine Margaritas are perfect for people who prefer a milder version of this potent drink. Restaurants around Southern California without hard liquor licenses invented them - for obvious reasons! The taste is still great, but without the kick of the tequila. Serves six.

1 bottle dry white wine
4 ounces Mexican Controy (Cointreau or Triple Sec may be substituted)
Juice from 8 to 10 limónes (Mexican limes) or key limes
Crushed ice to top of blender
Margarita salt (optional)

Place wine, Controy and lime juice in blender. Fill until almost full with crushed ice. Blend until very slushy. If salt-rimmed glasses are desired, wet top of Margarita glass with lime juice and swirl in small dish of salt. Pour Margarita into the glass.

EL CHILAR BANDERITA MARGARITA

Polo, the bartender at El Chilar in San Jose del Cabo, invented the Banderita Margarita. He named it "little flag" because it's prepared in three layers: green at the bottom, off-white in the middle and red on top, making it a drinkable replica of the Mexican flag. I was a bit skeptical when offered one because the top layer is Cabernet, and I couldn't imagine how the flavors would pair up, but my misgivings were short-lived. I should have known that co-owner and wine connoisseur Ulises would never permit anything to be served in El Chilar that wasn't a perfect blend of flavors. He suggests that you serve it on your terrace on a warm summer night while gazing at the stars and listening to your favorite classical music. Serves four.

4 shots Midori
4 shots tequila reposado
4 shots cabernet wine
4 short straws

Fill four highball glasses with ice. Pour Midori on the bottom. Very gently add a shot of tequila to each glass, being careful not to let it mix in with the Midori. Top with cabernet. Insert a straw and very carefully serve. Guests may stir before they sip, but not until they've properly appreciated the little flag!

SKIP & GO NAKEDS

A little over an hour north of Buena Vista by fishing boat and 45 minutes east of La Paz by road is Bahía de los Sueños (Bay of Dreams). It used to be called Bahía de los Muertos (Bay of the Dead) but the name was changed to make it more palatable to Americans when the new development plan was filed. It calls for 600 upscale homes, a resort with golf course and two marinas. Right now there are less than 10 homes and a beachfront palapa restaurant, the Giggling Marlin Beach Club. Anyone who has been to Cabo (even 20 years ago) has heard of the Giggling Marlin. It's a landmark bar with legendary drinks and a rowdy atmosphere. First timers often find themselves drunk and hanging upside down on the fish scale while their amigos take advantage of the photo op.

The restaurant in Bahía de los Sueños (as of 2005) bears absolutely no resemblance to its Cabo cousin. With breathtaking views of mountains, sea, sand and sky, diners can eat in a tranquil, open-air environment while watching panga fishermen return with the day's bounty of huachinango (red snapper), dorado (mahi mahi) and sierra (sea bass).

The Skip & Go Naked is the Giggling Marlin's signature drink. I've never seen anyone drink a few and run around dancing in the buff, but you never know. It would be far more likely to happen in Cabo than here! Next time you're in Baja Sur, head out to Sueños and enjoy a memorable lunch at the Giggling Marlin. The food is excellent and so is the service. Have one of these too. They're yummy. Makes one drink.

Ice
1 shot tequila
Splash gin
Splash vodka
Splash rum
1½ shots Amaretto
¼ cup fresh orange juice
½ cup pineapple juice
½ banana

Fill tall cocktail glass with ice. Transfer to blender and add all ingredients. Blend thoroughly and serve.

TEQUILA SUNRISE

The Eagles made this drink famous when they sang a song about it. In Baja it's been around for-almost-ever. Some people say it's a morning drink. I say not. But it's great in the late afternoon sitting on someone's patio overlooking the Sea of Cortez or the Pacific. Serves four.

6 ounces tequila
1 quart orange juice (fresh is always best)
Trickle of grenadine
Slice or orange and maraschino cherry
on toothpick

Fill four tall cocktail glasses with ice. Pour in tequila. Fill to top with orange juice. Trickle a bit of grenadine down the side so that it settles at the bottom to give the sunrise effect. Garnish with a slice of orange topped by a maraschino cherry on a tooth pick. Use a paper umbrella if you're feeling really festive!

AGAVE SUNSET

When people ask me, "What is an Agave Sunset?" I tell them two things. First, it's the precursor to a Tequila Sunrise. Second, it was so named because tequila is made from the agave, and I took a photo of one at sunset a few years ago in La Bufadora. I ended up naming my third book after it and using the photo on the cover. After the book came out, my friend Bernie happened to mention that there should be a drink by that name, but we never came up with one. Since I work with Axel Valdez to produce La Buena Vida en Buena Vista - Hotel Buena Vista's monthly online newsletter and we have a contest every month, we decided to allow our readers to submit their own creations for this drink. Suzanna, a longtime hotel guest and good friend, came up with the winning recipe. Here it is. Makes one drink.

2 ounces Hornitos tequila
¾ ounce Controy (or Triple Sec,
Cointreau or other orange liqueur)
Juice of 1 limón (Mexican lime)
or key lime
4 ounces fresh orange juice
2 ounces jamaica (Agua Fresca section,
or cranberry juice)
Maraschino cherry and orange slice for
garnish on toothpick

Fill tall clear 16 ounce cocktail glass with ice. Pour in tequila, Controy, and then squeeze the lime in. Fill to almost top of glass with orange juice and stir well. Add jamaica or cranberry juice, so that it swirls down. Garnish with a slice of orange and a maraschino cherry. This is more refreshing than and not as sweet as the tequila sunrise, so go Agave Sunset! And of course, serve this only at sunset!

PUNTA MORRO STYLE MARTINIS

On the northern edge of Ensenada, hanging right out over the Pacific is the exquisite gourmet restaurant, Punta Morro. It's the kind of place I reserved for celebrations marking special occasions during the decade we had a second home in La Bufadora. It was about an hour from our house, and a perfect place to stop for an early dinner. The presentation of their martini is something right out of Hollywood.

And the hint of scotch they add to it makes it smooth, smooth, smooth! Just imagine yourself sitting back, sipping your martini as you watch those waves crash onto the rocks below you and explode skyward. As the moonlight dances across the ocean's surface, check out the menu and order on of their mouth-watering dinners, served with homegrown vegetables from the nearby Guadalupe Valley. This recipe, shared with me by my waiter, serves two.

1 - 16 ounce tin bucket (this looks like a tiny version of an old-fashioned tin bucket)
1 - 6 ounce pewter carafe
1½ cups ice water
3 ounces gin or vodka
3 splashes vermouth
3 drops scotch
4 pimento-stuffed green olives on toothpicks or plastic swords

Chill two martini glasses in the refrigerator. Fill bucket with ice and water. In carafe, mix gin or vodka with vermouth and scotch. Place in ice bucket to chill. Place a sword or toothpick with two skewered olives into each martini glass. Serve.

Hint: If you have no way of locating the bucket or carafe, you can make these martinis the old fashioned way in a shaker with slightly crushed ice. When thoroughly chilled, pour into martini glasses and serve as above, leaving the shaker on the table so your guests can refill their glasses.

VALLE DE GUADALUPE SANGRÍA

Sangría is a popular summer drink in Spain. It's fruity and tastes somewhat like a delicious wine punch. However, beware that the Mexican version has Controy and brandy, which give it an extra jolt.

This recipe makes a little over a gallon. Sangría may be served in tall glasses filled with crushed ice. It may also be served chilled in wine glasses without ice. Save the "drunk fruit" afterward to use for a quick second batch if you run out, which you may - because it's really, really good! It is my signature drink and I named it after the Guadalupe Valley just to the north of Ensenada and home of Mexico's finest wineries.

1 medium orange
½ gallon burgundy wine
4 cups orange juice
2/3 cup Controy, Cointreau or Triple Sec
½ cup brandy
2 limónes (Mexican limes) or key limes
1 apple
1 pear
2 bananas
Ice

Using a vegetable peeler, gently peel the skin from the orange to make orange zest. Make sure it's very thin. Put the orange zest in a small bowl. Using the back on a spoon, bruise the peel to extract the oil.

In a large punch bowl, combine wine, orange juice, Controy and brandy. Add orange zest into wine mixture.

Separate orange into sections and cut sections in half. Cut the lime into thin slices. Cut apple and pear into small pieces, leaving the skin on. Slice bananas. Add all fruits to wine mixture and chill at least four hours. Serve in clear glasses with just a couple ice cubes in each. Do not remove the fruit!

SANGRÍA BLANCA

Sangría Blanca is a lighter, less potent wine punch that could be best described as the "Los Cabos Sangría." Why? Well, since it's made with white wine, limeade, club soda and pineapple (instead of burgundy, brandy and the more hearty fruits), it's lighter and more tropical in its flavors. It's great for brunches or luncheons. This makes approximately one gallon and will transport you to those little latitudes!

1 - 6 ounce can frozen limeade
1 can water
16 - 20 ice cubes
½ gallon dry white wine, chilled
1 quart club soda, chilled
1 limón (Mexican lime) or key lime, thinly sliced
½ cup chunked fresh pineapple

Place limeade, water and ice cubes in blender and blend until slushy. Pour half mixture into each of two large pitchers. Pour half of the wine and half the club

soda into each pitcher. Garnish chilled wine glasses with lime slice and a pineapple chunk. Serve immediately.

CHIMAYO COCKTAILS

The apple cider used in this authentic but little-known Mexican cocktail makes it a refreshing change from the typical Margarita. While seldom ordered by tourists, a perfectly chilled chimayo cocktail is a real treat to a Baja native - or an expatriated American who's been around a while! But beware - this is just as lethal as a Margarita, so take it easy! This recipe serves four, but if you want to try serving it as a punch, triple the amount of cider in relation to the tequila. It's an excellent, mellower alternative.

12 ice cubes
5 ounces tequila
1 tbsp crème de cassis
½ cup apple cider
2 tbsp lemon juice
4 apple wedges for garnish

Fill a cocktail shaker with ice cubes. Add tequila, crème de cassis, cider and lemon juice. Shake well and strain into four glasses. Add the ice cubes and garnish each glass with an apple wedge.

LOS GORDOS BLOODY MARYS

I like to call these "salad drinks," because whenever my friends and I found ourselves sipping them at sunset on the deck at Gordos in La Bufadora, we felt like we were doing something relatively healthy for our bodies. Believe us when we tell you - nobody, but nobody on Planet Earth makes Bloody Marys as good as Chuy, the owner and bartender at Gordos. You can try. I can try. But to really experience this drink, you have to try the real thing. At the real place. Made by the real guy.

On your first trip into Gordos, which is only open from noonish on Friday through noonish on Sunday - beware of locals who may try to entice you to drink a shot of the famous (infamous?) rattlesnake tequila. (It's identical to the barrel at Pancho's in Cabo San Lucas.) Well - one shot maybe. It's sort of an initiation rite. But if you get going on them, you may have a long, difficult night ahead of you! I recommend the Bloody Marys instead. Have one at sunset for me. Or - hey - have one with breakfast. That's what boofed me, remember? Makes eight drinks.

Margarita salt
Ice
8 ounces vodka
10 limónes (Mexican limes)
or key limes
3 dashes Worcestershire sauce per glass
Pepper to taste

Hot pepper sauce to taste (Tabasco or similar)
3 sprinkles celery salt per glass
½ gallon Clamato juice
8 celery or carrot sticks for garnish

Rub the rims of eight highball glasses with lime and dip in Margarita salt. Fill glasses with ice and to each glass add: one ounce vodka, the juice of one lime, three dashes Worcestershire sauce, pepper, hot pepper sauce and three sprinkles of celery salt. Fill each glass to the brim with Clamato juice.

Garnish with celery or carrot sticks. Distribute among guests. Close your eyes and imagine yourself on Gordos deck overlooking Papalote Bay and take a long swallow. Aaaaaaah.... Wait a minute! Was that a pod of gray whales spouting off the end of Papalote Bay or did I just imagine that? Nope. Thar she blows again! And wow, look at that calf spy-hopping! How cool!

MICHELADAS

Before we moved to Baja for good, Terry and I used to go to Tijuana frequently with our amigos Axel and Gina Valdez. Since they're Mexican, they know all the cool places to go ... ones that tourists do not frequent. They told us that Tijuana has the best restaurants anywhere in Mexico with the sole exception of Mexico City. That is amazing. Many were the times we boogied the night away until at least 3 a.m. We were always the only non-

Mexicans present. It was Gina who introduced us to the Michelada, a spicy, tangy, jazzed up beer. Serves one.

1-12 oz beer (preferably Mexican)
1 limón (Mexican lime)
or key lime, quartered
2 dashes Worcestershire sauce
1 dash soy sauce
1 dash Tabasco (more if you like it hot)
1 dash black pepper
Coarse salt

Rim a tall cocktail glass with ¼ lime, and then twirl rim in salt. Pour beer into glass. Add beer, Worcestershire, soy, Tabasco, ½ lime and pepper. Squeeze in half the lime juice and use last ¼ lime for garnish. Enjoy!

SWIM-UP BAR PIÑA COLADAS
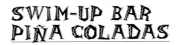

Have you heard Jimmy Buffett's song, "Margaritaville?" (Hasn't everyone?) Does it remind you of hot, sodden days in tropical Mexico? Well - not me. The real scoop is that the tourists in La Paz, Los Cabos, Loreto and every other snazzy resort in Baja drink piña coladas. I know. I've hung out with them at enough swim-up bars around the peninsula! Made from pineapple juice, coconut juice - and of course - rum, the flavor is pure tropics.

This blender-made version is less heavy and calorie-laden than Mexican piña coladas, but it's guaranteed to be just as delicious. Try these and you'll see yourself lounging under a palm tree next to the surf. Or on a submerged barstool somewhere in Baja Sur. Serves four.

6 ounces light rum
2 cups pineapple-coconut juice (found in most grocery stores)
Ice to top of blender
Pineapple slices for garnish
Dash of nutmeg

Pour rum and juice in blender. Fill to top with ice. Blend until very slushy. Pour into tall glasses and garnish with nutmeg and pineapple slices.

EAST CAPE COCONUT RUM COOLERS

You've probably figured out by now that the East Cape is becoming one of the hottest up-and-coming resort areas in Baja. It extends from Punta Pescadero, north of Los Barriles to Buena Vista and then south a ways past from Punta Arena to Cabo Pulmo. It used to officially end there. Nowadays anything north of San Jose del Cabo is included as part of the East Cape. I couldn't dream of a better place to live.

The East Cape rightfully boasts that it has some of the world's greatest sport fishing. In fact, if you see bumper stickers around here that read "¡SUELTAME!" it means, "Release me!" The area has an outstanding record for promoting conservation of the ocean wildlife through this catch and release program, which has kept lots of species (particularly the marlin and sailfish) off the endangered species list. Like I've said before, the East Cape also offers up great diving, wind surfing and any other kind of ocean sports you can imagine.

After a long day fishing or playing volleyball in the pool, order up one of these local delights and you will be amazed at how refreshed you'll feel! The combination of coconut rum, tonic, bitters and lime will delight your taste buds for sure - whether you're stateside sipping them in the back yard on a hot day or whether you're barefoot in Baja! This recipe serves four.

Ice
4 ounces light rum
4 ounces coconut rum (Malibu or Captain Morgan's)
4 dashes of bitters
1 limón (Mexican lime)
or key lime cut into quarters
Tonic water or club soda
4 dashes fruit juice (any tropical punch/combination will do)
4 dashes bitters

Fill four tall glasses with ice. Add light rum, coconut rum and fill to the top with tonic or soda. Put a dash of fruit juice and a dash of bitters in each glass and garnish with a slightly squeezed chunk of lime. Serve immediately.

MOJITOS

The day before Terry and I got married in Buena Vista in 2002 (in front of family and 28 friends), we were all hanging out at the swim-up bar. My college roommate, Laurie was planning a trip to Cuba and had brought a Cuban history book with her. She called me over. "Hey Ann, Check this out. It looks very interesting," and pointed out a recipe for the Mojito, the national drink of Cuba. It sounded interesting all right, so we asked Ricardo the bartender if he could make one. He said, "Claro que sí" and went over to a nearby planter box and plucked some fresh mint off a plant growing there. He proceeded to make us these drinks and we loved them. Here we go! Another swim-up bar favorite! Makes four.

4 shots rum
1 shot simple syrup
Soda water to top of glass
Fresh sprigs of mint for garnish

Fill four tall cocktail glasses with ice. Add a shot of rum, a ¼ shot simple syrup and fill to brim with soda water. Stir and add a sprig of fresh mint.

RUMBAS

From the Palapa Bar at the La Concha Hotel in La Paz comes this light, tropical, fruity drink. I first heard about it over the Internet. I was getting ready to make one last sweep through Southern Baja with Nina to scout up a few special recipes before my first cookbook came out. I put up a notice on the Amigos de Baja web site bulletin board. One of the folks who responded encouraged me to try a rumba (ROOM-bah). It was good! And the bartender was kind enough to share the recipe with me. And now you have to try one yourself. Serves four.

¼ cup fresh papaya

¼ cup fresh cantaloupe
¾ cup pineapple juice
¾ cup orange juice
6 ounces light rum
1 tbsp grenadine
Ice
4 slices orange and 4 maraschino cherries on toothpicks

Put all ingredients except orange slices and cherries in blender and fill to nearly the top with ice. Blend until very slushy and pour into four glasses. Garnish with orange slices and maraschino cherry on toothpicks, if desired. Or drink it plain, pure and simple.

RENEGADE RUM DRINKS

The first summer I spent in La Bufadora I hung out a lot with Kit, an old friend from San Diego (now a restaurateur in McCall, Idaho). Having earned his living as a bartender for many years, Kit taught me how to make some killer rum drinks. I can still see his grin as I navigated the rather treacherous concrete stairs down to the beach at Papalote Bay, carrying a tray of umbrella, pineapple and orange-topped drinks in hot pink and blue plastic cups one late, late summer afternoon. Serves four.

4 16-ounce neon plastic "go cups" (plastic cups)
Ice
6 ounces rum

6 ounces cranberry juice
6 ounces peach juice or any other tropical juice
4 paper umbrellas
4 chunks fresh pineapple
4 slices orange

Fill "go cups" with ice. Add rum, juices and stir. Top with pineapple chunks and orange slices skewered onto the paper umbrellas. Place on tray and serve outdoors with Jimmy Buffett music playing loudly in the background.

ROMPOPE

This drink can be found all over Baja and mainland Mexico in grocery and liquor stores. It's bright yellow in color, features a stunning señorita on the label and is said to have been around at least 600 years. Supposedly, according to local legend, it originated in northern Europe and found its way to Mexico with the padres. The Mexicans have since adopted it as their own and swear it cures colds and the flu, strengthens weak bones and even cheers up the elderly! While it's hard to adequately describe its rich, almost eggnog flavor, let me tell you that it's great with coffee after dinner, over ice cream, or alone - on the rocks - for dessert!

Here's a secret - this recipe makes approximately a gallon - and if you like it as much as the Baja natives do, you just might want to put it into some fancy glass bottles and give it away for Christmas presents. That's what my mom used to do. Makes about a gallon.

2 quarts half and half
3 cups sugar
1 - 4 inch long vanilla bean or 2 tsp vanilla extract
1 fifth of light rum
2 cups egg yolks (from about 2 dozen large eggs)

Heat half and half with sugar and vanilla bean until boiling. Immediately reduce heat and simmer for 20 to 30 minutes. Remove bean and cool.

In blender, beat rum and egg yolks for two minutes. Add half and half mix and whir for another two minutes. Pour into bottles and chill. Will keep up to ten days in refrigerator. Serve warm or cold or in coffee.

KAHLUA

This recipe allows you to make your own Kahlua. It is a traditional sweet, coffee-flavored Mexican liqueur; served most often as an after dinner drink. It can be served in a number of ways (recipes following). The recipe makes approximately half a gallon. If you're unsure about what to do with that much Kahlua, consider doing what we've done with the Rompope ... make it before the holiday season and put it into small bottles to give as gifts to your friends.

2 cups water

4 cups granulated sugar
2 ounces instant coffee or decaf
1 quart 90 proof vodka
1 large (at least 4 inch long) vanilla bean

Boil water in medium saucepan. Mix in sugar and coffee to water. Stir well and cool. Into half gallon bottle, pour vodka, sugar and coffee mixture and vanilla bean. Store for at least 30 days before serving or bottling as gifts.

EL DORADO MEXICAN COFFEE

We locals used to call the El Dorado Restaurant in La Bufadora, "Fred's" because Fred was the owner until he closed it down a few years back. I specifically asked him for his Mexican coffee recipe, because it is the best I'd tasted anywhere. This piping hot drink combines the tastes of tequila, Kahlua, brandy and Rompope - all Mexican originals - with coffee. Topped with whipped cream, it is a dramatic way to end an evening.

Fred told me this coffee is best when flambéed, or served with a flaming sugar crust rimming the cup. I've never attempted flambéing, and I don't recommend that you do either. It can be dangerous if you don't know what you're doing. There are other places in Mexico that serve this drink, so if you ever get the chance to order one of these drinks, do it. It's incomparable. Serves four.

2 ounces tequila
2 ounces Kahlua
2 ounces brandy
2 ounces Rompope (make your own if you can't find it)
4 cups steaming coffee or decaf
Whipped cream to garnish

Heat four mugs by placing in hot water or heating in microwave. Into heated mugs, add half an ounce each of tequila, Kahlua, brandy and Rompope. Top off with hot coffee or decaf and whipped cream. Serve immediately in front of a roaring fire.

BLACK RUSSIANS GUADALUPE VALLEY STYLE

There are remnants of a turn-of-the-century Russian village (the original settlers were White Russians who ran to Mexico to escape persecution) almost at the midpoint of the road that runs between Ensenada and Tecate in northern Baja with a fascinating museum. After you visit, you'll no longer wonder how the Russians and Mexicans got together to concoct this drink. Kahlua and vodka are mixed together and served on the rocks. The taste is great, but the drink is strong. So beware. Serves four.

16 - 20 ice cubes
4 ounces vodka

4 ounces Kahlua
Fill four highball glasses to top with ice. Add one ounce each of vodka and Kahlua. Stir and serve immediately.

WHITE RUSSIANS

A less potent, but sumptuous member of the Russo-Mexican family of drinks, a White Russian is great when you're looking for something sweet and creamy - with vodka in it. Serves four.

16 - 20 ice cubes
4 ounces vodka
4 ounces Kahlua
2 cups milk or half and half

Fill tall glasses with ice. Add one ounce each of vodka and Kahlua. Add four ounces milk, stir and serve immediately.

WHITE JAMAICANS

Terry invented this drink one night in La Bufadora after our neighbor Milo finished off the last of our vodka (not an unusual occurrence). Terry fell in love with it and drinks it to this day. Hint: The reason we named it a White Jamaican is because we were using Mount Gay rum from Jamaica and figured it was only logical. Plus Jamaicans tend to be dark skinned and milk is white! Serves four.

16 - 20 ice cubes
4 ounces rum
4 ounces Kahlua

2 cups milk or half and half

Fill tall glasses with ice. Add one ounce each of vodka and Kahlua. Add four ounces milk, stir and serve immediately.

KAHLUA AND CREAM

Rich, creamy and jammed full of calories and fat grams, Kahlua and Cream is a great after dinner drink for people who aren't counting. Serves four.

16 - 20 ice cubes
8 ounces Kahlua
2 cups whipping cream or half and half

Fill highball glasses with ice. Add two ounces of Kahlua and four ounces cream to each glass. Stir and serve immediately.

BAJA BLAST

A friend of mine whose family hails from Santa Rosalía gave me this recipe. Susie said to pop it back in one quick swallow, but I tend to prefer it savored more slowly! It's a light and pleasant switch from the heaviness of the White Russian and the POW of the Black. Serves four.

16 - 20 ice cubes
4 ounces vodka
4 ounces Kahlua
½ quart soda water

Fill medium-sized glasses with ice. Add one ounce each of vodka and Kahlua. Add soda to top of glass and serve immediately.

ICE CREAM - KAHLUA ESPECIAL

This is truly what I would call a dessert drink. Serves at least eight.

1 cup ice cold, strong coffee or decaf
1 cup vodka
½ cup Kahlua
½ gallon vanilla ice cream or frozen yogurt
At least 8 strawberries

Place half the ingredients except strawberries in blender. Blend until thoroughly mixed. Repeat. Serve in champagne glasses, garnished with strawberries. Repeat.

CARLOS O'GRINGO'S MEXICAN - IRISH CREAM

You say there's no such thing as an Irish Mexican? Wanna bet? Well, what about a gringo masquerading as an Irish Mexican? Oh yeah, sure ... only in Baja ... only in Baja....

Every Christmas for years I made gallons of Irish Cream. People requested it again and again, because they insisted that mine was at least as good as everyone's favorite big name brand! It can be put into small individual bottles and given as gifts. It's also great in coffee and in the other drinks, which follow. This recipe makes a blender-full, or about five cups and will keep in the refrigerator until the expiration date on the half and half.

2 cups brandy or whiskey
1 - 14 ounce can sweetened condensed milk
1 cup half and half
3 eggs
2 tbsp chocolate syrup
2 tsp instant coffee or decaf
1 tsp vanilla extract
½ tsp almond extract

Combine all ingredients in blender. Blend until smooth. Pour into bottles and store tightly covered in refrigerator for one month or until the expiration date on the carton of half and half. Shake well before serving.

IRISH - MEXICAN COFFEE

Irish Cream and tequila go hand in hand here to make a tasty coffee drink with a kick worthy of an Irish Mexican ... or a gringo masquerading as one. Serves four.

4 cups steaming coffee or decaf
4 ounces tequila
4 ounces Irish cream
Whipped cream to garnish

Into four mugs of steaming coffee, add an ounce each of tequila and Irish Cream. Top with whipped cream and serve immediately.

FROZEN IRISH CREAM

Frozen Irish Cream was my sister's and my creation. We invented it one Christmas Eve when my kids were tiny and spent the better part of the night drinking it while catching up on the last few months. It was so delicious that we forgot we were going to wake up in the morning wishing desperately that it wasn't Christmas morning, that we didn't have to get out of bed and that we didn't have to visit relatives all day long. Mostly we wished we hadn't drunk so much of it! Open presents? Oh no, way too much energy.... Be careful. The memory still hurts over 20 years later! Serves four.

2 cups Irish cream
½ cup brandy
Ice to top of blender

Put Irish Cream and brandy in blender. Fill to top with ice. Blend until very slushy. Serve immediately.

TRADITIONAL MEXICAN CHOCOLATE
(Non-Alcoholic)

True Mexican chocolate is sweet, hot and laced with cinnamon. It will please both kids and adults. It's perfect during cold weather when it's served the way the Spanish like it, with hot, cinnamon-sugared churros (Dessert section). You can also order instant Mexican Chocolate Ibarra (my favorite since childhood) at www.mexgrocer.com. Makes 16 servings.

3 quarts milk
15 ounces semisweet chocolate squares
10 cinnamon sticks
1 tbsp vanilla

Combine milk, semisweet chocolate and cinnamon sticks in saucepan. Cook and stir just until chocolate melts. Remove from heat. Remove cinnamon and stir in vanilla. Beat with electric beater until frothy. Place cinnamon sticks into mugs and pour in hot chocolate. Serve immediately.

Baja's Boutique Wineries

The rolling hills and lowlands of the Guadalupe Valley, northeast of Ensenada and only an hour or so south of San Diego are covered in vineyards. The wineries in this area produce nearly 95% of Mexico's wines, and they're top-notch too. It's considered by wine experts to be comparable to Napa Valley in California about 30 years ago.

The winemakers of the Guadalupe Valley are as passionate about making wine as any fussy Frenchman from Bordeaux. In fact, the conditions here are remarkably similar to those in southwestern France. With ideal marine and atmospheric conditions and porous soil of primarily decomposed granite, these wines rival any produced in California. Grapes thrive in the area's coastal valleys framed by rugged, rocky hills. They're tended to lovingly, picked by hand and fermented with the utmost care, using techniques perfected over the centuries. These days they produce an array of memorable wines, including Cabernet Sauvignons, Merlots, Cabernet Francs, Zinfandels, Petit Sirahs, Sauvignon Blancs, Semillons, Chenin Blancs, Fumé Blancs, Blanc de Blancs and Chardonnays.

Winemaking in the Californias actually began in Baja. The Spanish padres planted the first grapes as they worked their way from southern Baja to San Francisco founding missions. The first cuttings arrived at Misión San Francisco Javier near Loreto from Europe in 1699. In 1791 the first vineyards were established at Misión Santo Tomás, 30 miles southeast of Ensenada. Vineyards were planted at Misión Nuestra Señora de Guadalupe del Norte in Guadalupe Valley around 1934. Bodegas de Santo Tomás, the first official winery, was founded in 1888. It has produced wine consistently since then, and was the only major winery in Mexico until fairly recently.

Tours at the Baja wineries are relaxed, casual, intimate and informative. There are no crowds. You're sure to learn far more about the art of wine making there than at any winery up north-and you'll have more fun too. You'll learn that whites are picked at night and reds very early in the morning-and why. You'll learn about the importance of gravity (in lieu of pumps) in keeping the juice pure as it goes into fermentation. You'll taste the wine right out of the barrels as it's aging.

Terry and I did a wine tour of the area in 2000. We began by heading east on Highway 3 to Tecate just north of Ensenada. Our first stop was the Adobe Guadalupe, a romantic bed and breakfast with its own winery right in the middle of the valley. The stark white of its buildings, accented by a red tile roof, stood out dramatically against the backdrop of rock-strewn brown hills and the brilliant green of the vineyards. Standing alone amidst the vines and marking the entrance to the inn was a water tank with a pair of angel wings hovering over it. Subtly but exquisitely painted in hues native to the valley, it gave me chills.

The Adobe has the spacious elegance of a modern-day Spanish hacienda. We strolled through a courtyard designed by a Persian architect who included 125 arches - so that cool Pacific breezes ricochet around inside, creating a natural kind of air conditioning. Hosts Tru and Don Miller, transplants from Newport Beach, began harvesting their own grapes at their winery in 2001, so visitors can now experience wine making up close and personal.

In addition to the inn and winery, there's a chapel and shrine dedicated to Our Lady of Guadalupe. It's adorned with Angel's wings and vaqueros (Mexican cowboys) tip their hats at the virgin as they ride by. Some leave little gifts, a few pesos and candles behind. People have gotten married here.

After a Mexican breakfast of huevos rancheros in the morning, we started off to tour the wineries. For the ease of navigation, we backtracked and began from west to east, beginning just south of the third tollgate on the road from Tijuana to Ensenada, where Highway 3, the road east to Tecate, begins.

The first winery we came to was Casa de Piedra, on the left hand side of the road at San Antonio de las Minas. It was established in 1999 by celebrated winemaker, Hugo de Acosta to produce an "author's quality wine." Apparently he succeeded, because the entire 2000 and 2001 harvests sold out-before they were even fermented. Well-known all over Mexico, these wines are a favorite with young professionals in Mexico City.

Practically across the road is Viña de Liceaga, a winery that produces excellent Merlot, Merlot "Gran Reserva" and Cabernet Franc Blend. Next stop: Mogor Badan, next door to Liceaga to the east. It has been dubbed a "virtual winery" because all their wines are produced at friends' wineries with grapes purchased in the Guadalupe and Santo Tomás Valleys. It's known for its white Chasselas, red Mogor Badan (Cabernet Sauvignon with different varietals each year).

Art on a door at Adobe Guadalupe

Heading east again on Highway 3, we ran into the town of Francisco Zarco, just past a long bridge. Turning left, we drove through. There weren't any signs for the wineries, so it was mandatory to pay attention. The pavement ended and we were on a wash-board dirt road. We passed the Russian museum, which depicts the story of the Russian immigrants who settled this valley in 1907. The sign for Monte Xanic popped up, alerting us to turn right. Five wine lovers, whose sole objective was to make world-class wines, founded this winery in 1988. Under guidance of gifted winemaker, Hans Backoff, they have succeeded. They make an array of excellent red and white wines. Our favorite was the Viña Cristel, a mixture of Sauvignon Blanc and Semillon grapes.

Chateau Camous is visible from Monte Xanic, to the west. It was founded in 1995. Co-owner Fernando Favela, and the winery's Bordeaux-educated winemaker, Victor Torres-Alegre, met us at the front door and gave us a two hour guided tour. Their wines, under the careful supervision of renowned French wine expert, Michel Rolland, have won awards all over the world. Their Gran Vino Tinto, made from a blend of Cabernet Sauvignon, Cabernet Franc and Merlot, has raked in the most honors. Camou also produces a dazzling Merlot, Zinfandel, Fumé Blanc, Chardonnay, Clarete and Blanc de Blanc.

A little further west is Bodegas Valle de Guadalupe, owned by David Bibayoff, who uses a blend of traditional and modern techniques in his wine making.

Back on Highway 3 heading east, the next stop was Casa Pedro Domecq on the left side of the highway. Founded in 1973, this winery is famous throughout Mexico for making both wine and brandy, and is considered the marketing pioneer of Mexican wines.

Last stop on Highway 3 was Vinos L.A. Cetto, just past Domecq on the right side of the road. Founded by Angel Cetto from Italy, this winery offers tastings of wines, cool-ers, brandy and tequila. We, of course, bought a bottle of wine and had an early din-ner-picnicking on the terrace overlooking the vineyards. L.A. Cetto their own wine har-vest festival in early September with wine tasting, grape stomping, dinner, a bull fight, dance show and fireworks.

The next day, we headed south into Ensenada to visit its wineries. The first we hit was Cavas Valmar, founded in 1983 by brothers Hector and Gontran Valentín, along with winemaker Fernando Martain. They produce an excellent Cabernet Sauvignon and Chenin Blanc and their tasting room in Ensenada is located at Avenida Riveroll #1950 at Calle Ambar.

Every year, the first week of August is the Fiesta de la Vendimia or annual wine harvest festival, in Ensenada and Valle de Guadalupe. There are concerts in the vineyards, winery tours, and a street fair and a paella contest with over 100 entrants in Ensenada. It gets bigger and better every year, so check it out if you can.

Fruit Bowl by Janna Kinkade

DESSERTS

Desserts. You may not want to admit it, what with wasted calories and carbs being so unpopular and all, but I bet this is your favorite section. It's mine! Well, maybe it's a tie with the salsas - and the - and the - oh, never mind!

I've included an array of desserts here from Baja and mainland Mexico, plus a few from the Caribbean, Spain, California and New Mexico. Many sound quite sophisticated, but I assure you, they aren't all that difficult to make. Remember, we're not into slaving in the kitchen! We're into being outdoors and having a good time. We're into capturing some of that magic from south of the border and transporting it into your kitchen - and from your kitchen into your heart and your home. There are lots of new ones, including Kahlua Flan, Avocado Pie and Pastel de Tres Leches. You'll also want to try the Mango Mousse and the Jalapeño Brownies - they're new too and they're yummy! Many, like Margarita Pie, have had a facelift!

Remember to enjoy yourself - as you choose a dessert and get ready to prepare it tonight. If you find yourself forgetting what Baja Magic is, or even worse - forgetting what it feels like - open this book and allow yourself to be reminded.

One last thing. Remember? It's an attitude, it's an attitude, it's an attitude. It's an attitude most easily attained by changing the latitude, as Jimmy Buffett has been reminding me for over 30 years. Think south. Think sky. Desert. Big, big blue ocean. Think pelicans. Whales. Margaritas. Street Tacos. Mariachis. Tequila. Friendly folks. Put on some music and get thyself into the kitchen, amigo! Now give me an   -

¡Olé!

¡Olé!

¡Olé!

MARC'S CITRUS FLAN EXTRAORDINAIRE

The day Nina and I met Marc Spahr at his Caffé Todos Santos, he sent this flan out to us as a gift after our meal. In all our years of traveling Baja and mainland Mexico, neither of us had ever, ever tasted flan this good. I consider it a real honor to have been entrusted with this recipe, and now it's yours too.

Marc never had any formal training as a chef until 2004 when he went to Paris. He came to Todos Santos, if you'll recall, to grow tropical fruits - and he's as successful a farmer as he is a restaurateur. Married to a lawyer in La Paz, he's definitely integrated himself into the Southern Baja culture. He likes to tell the story of how he started cooking. His first attempts at baking were in a wood-fired brick oven on his farm. He started selling breads, cakes and cookies to the local gringo community. Pretty soon he was hired as head chef at El Molino Restaurant in Todos Santos. By 1993 he'd taken the big step and opened his own restaurant.

If you ever are so fortunate as to find yourself in Todos Santos, make sure you stop in at Marc's restaurant. Try it for breakfast, lunch or dinner - or anytime in between. Sit in front in one of the hand-painted artsy chairs, or waltz through the kitchen (pure Baja-style) and eat outdoors in the cool, lovely patio. You won't be disappointed. No way José!

Coffee Caramel
½ cup sugar
¼ cup espresso

Flan
2 cups milk
1 cup heavy cream
¼ tsp nutmeg (fresh, grated)
1 cinnamon stick (4 inches long)
1 tbsp citrus zest (lemon, limón and/or orange)
1 tbsp pure vanilla extract
6 egg yolks
3 eggs
1/8 tsp salt
1 cup sugar

Coffee Caramel
In a small copper saucepan, mix sugar and coffee. Cook over medium heat, stirring only until sugar is dissolved. Then cook until syrup forms a soft ball when dropped into ice water. (If you have a candy thermometer, this happens at about 238°.) Pour mixture into mold - a nine-inch round, two-inch deep cake pan works well. Let the syrup set up in refrigerator while making flan.

Flan
Preheat oven to 325°. In medium saucepan, combine milk, cream, vanilla, nutmeg, cinnamon stick and zests. Cook until almost boiling on low heat, stirring, constantly. Pour mixture through fine sieve into a bowl. In another bowl, whisk together eggs, yolks, salt and sugar. Pour

milk mixture slowly into egg mixture, whisking constantly.

Remove mold with caramel from refrigerator and pour flan into it. Set this mold inside a larger mold (a ten-inch round cake pan works) filled a quarter of the way up with water. Bake for one hour. Remove from oven and refrigerate for four hours. To serve, loosen edges with a knife and invert onto a platter. Cut flan into eight wedges.

BUZZARD'S KAHLUA FLAN

San Jose del Cabo is getting a new marina, which will be completed in 2010. That means the road has been paved to Buzzard's Bar & Grill, about five miles northeast of town. This is a quintessential Baja beach bar ... tables set on the sand under a big palapa just steps away from the sea. Of course the food is top notch and the prices are reasonable. Owners Denny and Judie Jones are transplants from Southern California. Judie told me that they were looking for a place to open a restaurant in downtown San Jose, but couldn't find the right thing, so they took the money designated to build their house and built the restaurant and a bed and breakfast. They lived in their camper for over two years during construction ... with a nine year old! That was in the mid '90s. Buzzard's was a success from the get-go, so now they live in an apartment above the hotel.

Check it out next time you're in Los Cabos ... you might even want to the spend the night in one of their four casitas. Enjoy the ambience, the beach and the food! Judie's chef of six years, Lupe invented this flan as a surprise for her. It's their most popular dessert and very unusual in that it calls for cream cheese. Makes eight servings.

1 cup sugar
1 8 oz package cream cheese at room temperature
1 - 10 oz can sweetened condensed milk
3 large eggs
2 cups milk
1 tbsp vanilla
4 tbsp Kahlua
Whipped cream to taste

Dissolve 1 cup sugar in an old omelet sized pan and melt until sugar is dark caramel. Soak pan right away with soap water to make cleanup really easy.

In blender add cream cheese, canned milk, eggs, milk and vanilla. Blend until smooth.

In the bottom of eight 8-ounce bowls, equally distribute the caramelized sugar. Pour flan into the cups on top of the caramel.

Set cups in 9 x 13 baking pan and fill pan half way up with hot water. Bake at 350° for about an hour, or until centers are firm (like Jell-O). Turn off oven and let cool in it. Chill thoroughly. To serve, run knife around edge of flan, set saucer on it and turn over. Garnish with a splash of Kahlua and a dollop of whipped cream.

MARGARITA PIE

Margarita pie is a perfect way to end any elegant meal. Light, unusual and incredibly tasty, your guests will feel the essence of Baja Magic tickling their tongues as they slide that first bite of pie into their mouths. And they'll definitely be back for seconds. Over the years, I've had more compliments on this than anything else in this section. The original recipe featured a graham cracker crust, but at the urging of my friend, Hugh Kramer - president of Discover Baja Travel Club - the crust has been reinvented as a crushed pretzel crust. This way, it captures the salty edge of a real Margarita. Makes two 9-inch pies.

Filling
1 small package lemon pudding mix
1 small package lime Jell-O mix
2 cups water
2 eggs, lightly beaten
1/3 cup lime juice
¼ cup tequila
¼ cup Controy, Cointreau or Triple Sec
1½ cups whipped topping

1 limón, (Mexican lime) or key lime, thinly sliced

Crushed Pretzel Crust
½ lb butter
½ cup sugar
2½ cups finely crushed pretzels

Crust
Melt butter. Stir in pretzels and sugar and mix well. Divide mixture in half and press each half firmly onto the sides and bottoms of two nine inch pie pans. Freeze for at least an hour before filling.

Filling
Combine pudding mix and Jell-O mix. Stir in a ½ cup water and beaten eggs. Blend well. Add remaining water and pour into medium sized saucepan. Cook over medium high heat, stirring constantly until mixture comes to a full boil.

Remove from heat. Stir in lime juice, tequila and Controy and chill two hours. Fold whipped topping into chilled mixture. Spoon into piecrusts and chill until firm, at least two hours. Garnish with lime slices.

CHURROS

Churros are Spanish doughnuts, squeezed out through a pastry bag and fried in long ribbons and dipped in sugar and cinnamon. In Spain they are served with piping hot chocolate. At street fairs in Baja - whether it's during Carnaval (Mardi Gras everywhere else) or during a little town's annual fiesta, you'll find vendors waving them in front of your eyes, offering you a free sample in hopes that they can entice you to buy a bag. You can also buy them as you wait in line to cross the border back into the US. Recipe makes 1½ dozen churros.

1 cup water
¼ tsp salt
1 tsp sugar
½ cup butter or margarine
1 cup flour
4 eggs
¼ tsp lemon extract
1 cup corn or canola oil
½ cup sugar mixed with 1 tsp cinnamon

In a medium sized saucepan, combine water, salt, sugar and butter and bring to a full boil over high heat. Add flour and remove pan from heat. Beat mixture with spoon until smooth and it comes away from the sides of the pan. Add eggs, one at a time and beat well after adding each egg. Stir in lemon extract and cool for 15 minutes.

Put half the dough in a large pastry bag with a large star tip. Heat oil in deep skillet or deep fryer to 400°. Squeeze dough into oil until you have a ribbon about 7 to 9 inches long. Cut it off with a knife. Fry 2 to 3 ribbons at a time for 6 or 7 minutes each. When golden brown, remove from oil and drain on paper towels. Roll in cinnamon sugar and serve warm.

SPIRIT OF ENDEAVOR AVOCADO PIE

In March 2003 Terry, I, Nina, John, our dad, Suzanna, Jeannie, Leslie and Kim all spent a week on the Spirit of Endeavor, a 102-passenger cruise ship that sailed between La Paz and Loreto. (These days it departs from Cabo.) The Spirit of Endeavor is definitely not your average cruise ship. There is no casino, nightclub or swimming pool onboard, but we did enjoy world-class cuisine and roomy, comfortable accommodations. The crew was young, friendly and energetic - most of them wearing two or three hats and

working 12 hour shifts every day. Our waitress, Shanda, cleaned the rooms after serving us breakfast. She also did beach duty, helping passengers in and out of inflatable boats on shore excursions. At dinner, she was back on duty in the dining room - ever cheerful. I wanted to adopt her and take her home.

Every morning we awoke to see the sun rising dramatically over the Sea of Cortez, and every day we were anchored off a different island. For the first time in my life, I was experiencing - up close and personal - places I had only previously seen from 35,000 feet above sea level. We even snorkeled with sea lions at Los Islotes off Isla Partida. Amazingly enough, if we got too close to one of the males, he would blow a circle of bubbles, letting us know where the boundaries of his space were and giving us a big hint to stay outside it!

Wednesday morning found us just off-shore of Loreto as the sun's first rays danced across the sea and lit up the city, accenting its colonial buildings, back-drop of palm groves and the craggy Sierra de la Giganta Mountains - the most ferociously dramatic on the entire peninsula. It was breath taking. On the way to our anchorage at Puerto Escondido, an hour south of town, we were treated to a whale show the likes of which most of the crew had never experienced before. We saw countless blue whales, blowing and rolling and showing their flukes. One even did a belly roll under our bow. Sperm whales showed up too. The first sight we had of them was a monstrous splash of white water off to the starboard. I ran upstairs, knocked on the door of the bridge and begged Captain Dave to let me in. He did. We saw seven or eight sperm whales breeching in the next half hour and it was more exciting than I could've ever imagined.

The next day, as we motored back toward La Paz, I was in my stateroom about 6:45 a.m. contemplating getting out of bed. Over the loudspeaker I heard these words: "Orcas. 4:00." I never got dressed so fast in my life. Out on the bow, I ran back and forth from port to starboard with the other pas-sengers, as killer whales were sighted all around us. An immense pod of dolphin swam, flying in and out of the water at top speed - hell-bent on not being breakfast for Orcas.

The chef, Danny Spani shared this recipe with me. It is unlikely-sounding but inde-scribably delicious. Makes one 9-inch pie.

Graham cracker crust
1½ cups graham cracker crumbs
2 tbsp sugar
6 tbsp melted butter

Pie filling
3 medium or 4 small avocados, peeled and pitted
Juice of 5 limónes (Mexican limes) or key limes
1 - 14-ounce can sweetened condensed milk
1 - 8 ounce package cream cheese
2 small packages gelatin dissolved in ½ cup water

Garnish
1 kiwi, peeled and thinly sliced
1 cup whipped cream or whipped topping

To make crust
Preheat oven to 350°. Combine all ingre-dients in a medium bowl. Press into the bottom and sides of a 9-inch pie pan. Bake until set and golden, about eight minute. Cool.

To make pie
In a food processor, place avocados, lime juice, condensed milk and cream cheese. Purée until completely blended and uni-form in color and texture. Add gelatin and purée again until completely blended. Pour

into piecrust and chill in freezer for two hours. Garnish each slice with a kiwi and a dollop of whipped cream.

JALAPEÑO BROWNIES

I met Suzanna at the Hotel Buena Vista's 25th anniversary party in 2001. Since she's been traveling Baja her entire adult life, we share many passions. She immediately bonded with my family, and has spent every Thanksgiving and my dad's birthday with us in Buena Vista since then. In 2003 we all took a wildlife cruise from La Paz to Loreto and saw every kind of whale imaginable (including Orcas!). We spend a few days with her in Nevada on our way to and from Idaho every summer. So ... yeah ... we're family. This is Suzanna's favorite oddball Mexican recipe. It's spicy, sweet and of course, chocolaty. It's definitely unique and a crowd pleaser. Makes about a dozen brownies.

2/3 cup semisweet chocolate chips
½ cup butter
4 large eggs
½ tsp salt
2 cups sugar
1 tsp vanilla
1 ¼ cups all purpose flour
¼ cup unsweetened cocoa powder
8 large canned jalapeño peppers, minced
¾ cup walnuts, toasted and chopped
¼ cup powdered sugar

Preheat oven to 350°. Lightly oil a 9 x 13 inch pan. Melt butter and chocolate chips together in a double boiler. Set aside to cool.

In a large bowl, beat eggs with salt until foamy. Add the sugar and vanilla and beat until well blended. Add the chocolate butter mixture and stir until just barely combined. Add the flour and cocoa powder and mix until almost blended. Fold in jalapeños and nuts.

Transfer batter to the prepared pan and bake until the top forms a cracked crust and the inside looks slightly moist, about 30 to 35 minutes. Cool, then cut into squares and dust with powdered sugar.

PASTEL DE TRES LECHES - THREE MILK CAKE

This very traditional Mexican cake is not only delicious, but elegant. It will make a perfect ending for any special dinner. Rafaela at Hotel Buena Vista gave us this recipe. It's one of her most requested, and it rocks! Serves eight and takes about two hours to prepare.

Cake
10 eggs, separated
¼ cup sugar
2 cups flour
2 tbsp baking soda
¼ cup warm milk (microwave for 20 seconds)

Crema de Tres Leches
10 oz can evaporated milk
10 ounce can sweetened condensed milk
10 oz. can crema media ácida (no substituting on this one; try Nestle at www.mexgrocer.com if you can't find it.)
1 tbsp vanilla extract
¼ cup brandy
Whipped cream for topping

Preheat oven to 450°. Cream the egg yolks with sugar in medium bowl. Mix in flour and baking soda, then the warm milk.

In a separate bowl, beat the egg whites until stiff peaks are formed. Mix with other cake ingredients. Place in a greased angel food cake pan and bake for 25 minutes. Remove from oven and cool.

Put all ingredients for tres leches except whipping cream in blender and blend until creamy. Remove cake from pan and place on platter. Drizzle the crema de tres leches over the cake. Top with whipped cream.

SOPAPILLAS

Sopapillas have been a New Mexico favorite for hundreds of years. They made their way to Baja during the first half of the 20th century. Derived from Indian fried bread, they are generally served hot with cinnamon and honey for dessert. Light and scrumptious! Makes approximately 20.

1¾ cups sifted flour
2 tsp baking powder
½ tsp salt
2 tbsp solid vegetable shortening
2/3 cup cold water
1 cup corn or canola oil
Honey and/or cinnamon sugar to taste

Sift flour, baking powder and salt into a mixing bowl. Cut shortening in, using two knives until it forms a coarse mixture. Gradually add cold water. Mix together just enough to hold together as you would if making a piecrust. Turn out on a lightly floured surface. Knead gently until smooth. Cover and let dough sit for five minutes. Roll into a rectangle about 12 inches by 15 inches. Dough will be very thin.

Cut into smaller rectangles about 2 inches by 3 inches. Heat oil in a large skillet until a drop of water sizzles when dropped into it. Drop a few sopapillas at a time into the oil. Turn them over three to four times to make them puff up evenly, then fry for two to three minutes on each side, until they are golden brown and puffed up like small pillows. Dust with cinnamon sugar or pour small amount of honey over the sopapillas. Serve hot.

PINEAPPLE SOPAPILLAS

These delightful sopapillas are filled with pineapple. By using the above recipe, and adding the filling, you'll have created a unique dessert that will please adults and kids alike. You don't have to use just pineapple. Get creative and use any kind of canned fruit! Makes approximately 20.

Preceding recipe for sopapillas (without cinnamon and honey)
2½ tbsp granulated sugar
2 tbsp cornstarch
1 - 1 lb 4 ounce can crushed pineapple, undrained (or any other canned fruit)
½ cup powdered sugar

Before frying the sopapillas, make the filling. In a medium sized saucepan, combine granulated sugar and cornstarch. With wooden spoon, stir in pineapple. Cook mixture over medium heat, stirring constantly until boiling. Boil one minute, stirring and set aside to cool.

After sopapillas have been made, and while they are still hot, make a slit along one long side and one short side of each pillow with a sharp knife. Lift up the corner and fill each with a slightly rounded tablespoon of the filling. Sprinkle tops with powdered sugar and serve warm.

MANGO MOUSSE

The pastry chef at Hotel Buena Vista Beach Resort, Rafaela is renowned for her awesome array of desserts. She works magic in her kitchen in the oldest part of the hotel. Every time I walk down the winding path down the hill toward my dad's room, I hear her in there singing. The music is sweet; the aromas even sweeter! She even made our wedding cake and it was pure heaven. This very traditional Baja dessert is best made in July, when the mangos ripen! But you can make it anywhere, anytime if you use canned or frozen mango. Serves eight.

4 mangos, peeled, seeded and cubed or
4 cups canned mango
2 - 1 ounce packages unflavored gelatin
1 cup heavy cream, whipped to stiff
peaks
1 cup sugar or honey (if using canned
mango, reduce to ¾ cup)
1 cup hot water
1 - 14 ounce can sweetened condensed
milk
8 mint leaves

Purée the mango in blender or food
processor. Dissolve the gelatin and sugar
or honey in hot water. Set aside to cool.

Mix mango, condensed milk and cooled
gelatin in large bowl. Fold in whipping
cream. Pour into serving bowl or individual bowls and refrigerate until thoroughly
set, at least an hour or overnight. Serve
garnished with a mint leaf.

WATERMELON - LEMON ICE

Watermelon-lemon ice is an
easy sherbet-like dessert that
you can make with your kids' help. It's
a refreshing after dinner treat during
the hot months and one that will make
you feel that you're barefoot under a palapa in San Felipe, Todos Santos or La Paz.
Makes 1½ pints.

2 cups puréed watermelon pulp (no
seeds)
1 - 6 ounce can frozen lemonade concen-
trate, thawed
¾ cup water

2 egg whites, stiffly beaten

Combine watermelon pulp, lemonade and water. Pour into freezing tray and freeze until mushy. Place in chilled bowl. Add egg whites and mix thoroughly. Return to tray and freeze until firm, stirring twice while freezing.

BAKED PINEAPPLE DELIGHT

Oh yum, yum, yum.
Simple and exquisite, Baked Pineapple Delight combines the tastes of fresh fruit, rum and custard to create a memorable finale to any meal. Serves eight.

Dessert
1 large or 2 medium sized pineapples
Sugar to taste
3 tbsp rum
¼ cup butter or margarine

Sauce
2 cups crema media ácida with 1 tbsp water or 1 pint half and half
¼ tsp salt
¼ cup sugar
1 egg
2 egg yolks
2 tsp cornstarch
1 tsp vanilla

Lay pineapple on its side and take a thick slice from one side. Do not remove green top. Set this slice aside. Carefully scoop out fruit and cut into bite-sized pieces.

Mix pineapple pieces with sugar to taste. Flavor with rum. Put pineapple pieces back into shell, dot with butter and cover entire pineapple with foil. Bake at 375° for 20 minutes.

While pineapple is baking, make sauce by stirring together crema and water or half and half, salt, sugar, egg, egg yolks, cornstarch and vanilla. Cook over low heat, stirring constantly until smooth and slightly thickened. This will take about 10 minutes.

Chill until ready to serve. Serve pineapple warm with cold sauce on top and try not to blush when you get a standing ovation!

FRIED BANANAS MULEGE

Fried bananas were transplanted to Baja from Vera Cruz. Or Cozumel. Or some other exotic spot on the Gulf of Mexico or the Caribbean. I first tried these on an early trip to Mulege - that incredible tropical oasis almost two thirds of the way down the desert peninsula, that marks the entrance to the equally incredible Bahía de Concepción. Both should go on your "to do" list for "must see" places. And this is a "must eat" dessert that my mom brought back with her that trip. She pilfered the recipe from the chef, of course! Fried and lightly spiced with orange and cinnamon, it's a simple dessert that will please everyone.
In case you haven't heard much about Mulege, let me clue you in on a couple of

things. First of all, it has the only navigable río (river) in all of Baja. The riverbanks are lined with groves of date palms, coconut palms and olive trees. Mulege has a lovely mission and some offshore rock islands where colonies of sea lions live. There are prehistoric cave paintings in the nearby hills - and of course - there's Bahía de Concepción. Aside from Los Arcos at Lands End in Cabo San Lucas, Mulege and Bahía de Concepción are undoubtedly the two most-often photographed places in all of Baja. You just have to see them for yourself! This recipe serves four.

4 tbsp butter or margarine
¼ cup brown sugar
¼ cup orange juice
½ tsp cinnamon
4 green tipped bananas, peeled and sliced lengthwise

Melt margarine in skillet with brown sugar, orange juice and cinnamon. Cook over medium heat until sugar dissolves. Add banana slices. Stir and cook over medium high heat for four to five minutes until bananas are golden and liquid is almost caramelized. Serve immediately.

BUÑUELOS

Bunuelos are sugared, fried tortillas. Popular and very easy to make, they're served all over Baja, mainland Mexico and the Southwest. (God forbid ... Taco Bell even has them these days!) Serves ten to twelve.

12 flour tortillas
½ cup corn oil
1 cup granulated sugar
1 tsp cinnamon
½ tsp ground cloves

Slice each tortilla into eight wedges. Heat oil in skillet over high heat until a drop of water sizzles when dropped into the pan. Fry tortilla wedges until crisp. Drain on paper towels.

On flat plate, mix sugar, cinnamon and cloves. Coat tortilla wedges with sugar mixture. Serve warm or cool.

MAYAN MANGO MADNESS

From the deepest jungles of the Yucatán, where the Mayans once ruled, to the produce section at Gigante on the south end of Ensenada, you will never see mangos or papayas any bigger, sweeter or juicier than the ones they grow in Mexico. You can make this dessert with mangos, papayas, strawberries or peaches. It's a truly delectable summer treat that will make you famous. Serves eight.

2½ pounds fresh mangos, peeled and seeded or 1 - 20 oz can mangos
(You can substitute papayas, strawberries or peaches)
1 cup water and ½ cup dissolved sugar or juice from the canned mangos
1 oz brandy
3 - 3 ounce packages ladyfingers

1 pint whipping cream
Sugar to taste
½ tsp vanilla
1 cup pecans, ¾ cup chopped only

Chop mangos into small pieces. Place fresh mangos in sugar and water, or return canned mangos to their syrup. Add brandy.

Dunk ladyfingers into fruit syrup quickly one by one and line the bottom and sides of a 9 x 13 glass pan. Add a layer of chopped mangos.

Beat sugar, vanilla and whipping cream. Place a layer of cream and a layer of chopped pecans on top of the mangos. Alternate layers of ladyfingers, mangos, cream and pecans, ending with whipped cream. Garnish with pecans. Refrigerate three to four hours. Cut in squares to serve.

And enjoy. Enjoy. Enjoy.

Live the magic!

¡Disfruta la mágica!

MEXICAN COOKIES & CANDIES

This section is completely new and was born - like the new section on Aguas Frescas - because of reader demand!

Whenever I took my kids shopping in a Mexican grocery store when they were little, the first place they'd race off to was the bakery. Grabbing round metal plates that looked like pizza pans and a set of tongs, they cruised through the racks of freshly baked cookies and pastries, piling the tray with enticing goodies. Usually, half of them were gone within an hour of our departure from the store! They're that good! The recipes that follow are some of our family favorites.

Don't forget to try out a few of the Mexican candy recipes. If you think Mexican candy is anything like US candy ... boy are you in for a surprise! In fact, most are homemade. San Bartolo, a mountainside community about 20 minutes north of my home, is famous all over Baja Sur for its candies. Buy some cactus candy or cocada next time you pass through on your way from La Paz to Los Cabos. Or try a sandía (watermelon) or mango lollipop with chile in it. They will change your outlook on life!

CRESCENT BALL AND RING COOKIES

This recipe makes two dozen rich, buttery cookies and takes about 40 minutes to prepare.

1¾ cups flour
¼ tsp pinch salt
½ cup powdered sugar
1 cup butter, softened
1 cup finely chopped pecans
1 tsp vanilla

Preheat oven to 325°. In medium sized bowl, mix together all ingredients. Shape into a medley of 24 crescents, balls and rings. Place on lightly greased cookie sheet and bake for 10 to 15 minutes, or until golden brown. Cool and serve.

EMPANADAS DE FRUTA - SPICY FRUIT TURNOVERS

This delicious recipe makes two dozen empanadas and takes about an hour to prepare. A 21-ounce can of your favorite fruit pie filling can be substituted for the fruit filling.

Dough
6 cups flour
1 tsp salt
1 tbsp sugar
¾ cup solid vegetable shortening
1 egg
1½ cups water

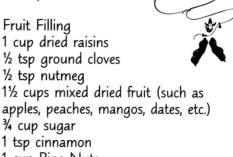

Fruit Filling
1 cup dried raisins
½ tsp ground cloves
½ tsp nutmeg
1½ cups mixed dried fruit (such as apples, peaches, mangos, dates, etc.)
¾ cup sugar
1 tsp cinnamon
1 cup Pine Nuts
1/3 to ½ cup water
2 cups corn or canola oil for frying
½ cup sugar

Mix flour, salt and sugar together in large mixing bowl. Cut in shortening with two knives, scissor style until the size of small peas. Mix well.

In small mixing bowl, beat egg. Add water and mix thoroughly. Add to dry mixture and stir well to make dough. Dough should be soft but not sticky. If it is sticky, add a bit more flour. Shape dough into 24 small balls. Using rolling pin, flatten circles until they are about 5 inches in diameter and 1/8 inch in thickness.

To prepare fruit filling, add enough water in medium saucepan to cover the dried fruit and raisins. Cook over low heat until tender, about ten minutes. Add sugar, spices, and pine nuts. Mix until well blended.

Place a heaping teaspoon of filling on one half of each piece of rolled out dough. Fold dough in half and press edges together to make a turnover. Pinch edges between thumb and forefinger to seal well.

Heat oil in large fry pan or deep fryer until sizzling. Fry each empanada until golden brown, turning once. Drain on paper towels and serve with sugar sprinkled on top. Best served warm.

MEXICAN CHOCOLATE MERINGUE COOKIES

This recipe is worth the time it takes (about three hours). It makes two dozen super yummy cookies.

1 cup slivered almonds
2 cup sugar
10 tbsp Dutch process cocoa powder
6 tbsp cornstarch
3 tsp ground cinnamon
8 egg whites
½ tsp cream of tartar
2 tsp vanilla extract
½ tsp almond extract
4 oz semisweet chocolate

Preheat oven to 350°. Line two baking sheets with parchment paper. Spread almonds in a pie pan and bake for five to ten minutes, or until lightly toasted. Set aside to cool. Reduce oven temperature to 200°.

In a food processor, purée toasted almonds with 2/3 cup sugar. Add cocoa, cornstarch and cinnamon. Pulse briefly, until mixed and set aside.

Separate egg yolks from whites and discard yolks. In large mixing bowl, beat egg whites with electric mixer on low speed until frothy. Add cream of tartar and increase the mixer speed to medium. Beat until soft peaks form. Gradually add remaining sugar, a tablespoon or two at a time, beating until the whites form firm peaks. Add vanilla and almond extracts and beat just until blended. Fold in cocoa mixture into the beaten whites just until blended.

Drop heaping teaspoonfuls of the batter, an inch apart, onto the prepared baking sheets. Place one baking sheet on the top rack of oven and the other on the bottom rack. Bake for 1½ hours, alternating the positions of the baking sheets after 45 minutes. Turn oven off. Leave meringues in the oven to cool for one hour. Remove from oven and peel off parchment paper.

Melt chocolate in small bowl set over a pan of water or in microwave. Use a small pastry brush to apply a thin coating of chocolate to the flat side of the meringues. Wait until chocolate has set before serving. Cookies may be stored in an airtight container for up to four days.

MEXICAN WEDDING COOKIES

This recipe makes two dozen delicate, rich cookies and takes about a half hour to prepare. They're perfect for any special occasion, really.

1½ cups all-purpose flour
1 tsp baking powder
¼ tsp salt
3 tbsp butter, softened
1/3 cup unsweetened applesauce
1½ cups powdered sugar
1 large egg
1 tsp vanilla
¼ cup chopped pecans

Preheat oven to 375°. In small bowl mix flour, baking powder and salt. In large mixing bowl, beat butter and applesauce until well blended. Add ½ cup of sugar, egg, vanilla and pecans. Beat until smooth. Add flour mixture and beat until blended. Dough should be stiff, but not dry. If it is too dry, add a little water.

Divide dough into 24 balls. Lightly grease two cookie sheets. Place balls one inch apart on sheets and bake about 15 minutes, or until they are a light, golden brown. Remove from oven and cool until lukewarm.

Sprinkle half of remaining sugar onto a large sheet of wax paper. Roll each cookie in sugar. With your fingers, pack more sugar all over each cookie to a depth of about 1/8 inch. Place cookies on a rack over wax paper and dust generously with remaining sugar. Allow to cool completely prior to serving. Cookies may be stored in airtight container for four days.

MEXICAN CHEESE COOKIES

This recipe will remind you of a cheese Danish. It makes two dozen and only takes about a half hour to prepare.

½ cup sugar
1/3 cup butter, softened
1 cup jack cheese, grated
1 cup flour
1 tsp baking powder
¼ tsp salt
1 large egg, beaten

Preheat oven to 375°. In medium sized mixing bowl, combine sugar and softened butter. Stir in grated cheese. Add all remaining ingredients except egg.

Shape dough into 24 small tubes. Using rolling pin on lightly floured surface, roll each piece of dough into a stick, 3½ inch by ½ inch in size. Place on lightly greased cookie sheets and press sticks lightly to flatten. Brush top of each cookie with beaten egg.

Bake for eight to 10 minutes, or until lightly browned, around edges only.

Immediately remove from oven and cool on wire racks.

PAN DE MUERTO – BREAD OF THE DEAD

Let's face it. In the US, we're terrified of the Grim Reaper. We see him as a sinister, ugly apparition who snatches us up and spins us off into nothingness. He's the symbol of our ultimate powerlessness over Mother Nature.

Not so in Mexico. In Mexico, the symbol of death is a grinning, fleshless beauty called La Muerte (Lady Death). An elegantly and colorfully clad skeleton wearing a flower-laden hat, created by press artist José Guadalupe Posada (1853-1913), she's an amazing metaphor of life embracing death. You can feel this in her name, for she goes by La Catrina (Fancy Lady), La Flaca (Skinny), La Huesuda (Bony) and La Pelona (Baldy). There's humor here, not fear. What's up with that?

When the Spaniards defeated the Aztecs in the 1500s, they converted the Indians to Catholicism. However, they encountered resistance when attempting to eradicate all native religious traditions. In a compromise sanc-tioned by the Church, Día de los Muertos was merged with two Christian holidays - All Saints Day on November first and All Souls Day on November second. This makes it a thoroughly unique, cross-cultural holiday, effectively blending two very different traditions.

Día de Los Muertos is a celebration, not of death but of the continuum of life. It consists of prayerful reflection, joy and revelry honoring those who came before. In a culture without written family trees, parents and grandparents pass stories on to their children. These are lively, humorous tales about those who came before. Their favorite foods, passions and possessions are discussed, along with their triumphs, their foibles and all sorts of other anecdotal details about their lives - forging a tangible, emotional link between the past and the present.

In celebration of Mexico's Día de los Muertos, this bread is shaped into skulls or round loaves with strips of dough rolled out and attached on top to resemble bones. This recipe will take a little over three hours to make and will make four loaves.

¼ cup milk
¼ cup butter or margarine, cut into 8 pieces
¼ cup sugar
½ tsp salt
1 package active dry yeast

¼ cup very warm water
2 eggs
3 cups all-purpose flour
½ tsp anise seed
¼ tsp cinnamon
2 tsp sugar

In medium saucepan, bring milk to a boil. Remove from heat and stir in butter or margarine, ¼ cup sugar and salt. In large bowl, mix yeast with warm water until dissolved. Let stand five minutes and add to milk mixture.

Separate yolk and white of one egg. Add yolk to yeast mixture, reserving the white for later. Add flour to yeast and egg, and blend well until a dough ball forms.

Sprinkle flour over a pastry or cutting board. Place dough ball in center and knead until smooth. Return to bowl and cover with towel. Let rise in a warm place for about 90 minutes. After an hour, grease a baking sheet and preheat oven to 350°. Knead dough again on floured surface. Divide dough into quarters and set ¼ aside. Roll remaining three pieces into "ropes." On baking sheet, pinch three rope ends together and braid. Finish by pinching ends together on opposite side. Divide the remaining dough in half and form two "bones." Cross and lay them over the braided loaf.

Cover bread with dishtowel and let rise for 30 minutes. Meanwhile, in a bowl, mix anise seed, cinnamon and two teaspoons sugar together. In another bowl, beat egg white lightly.

After 30 minutes, brush top of bread with egg white and sprinkle with sugar mixture, except on cross bones. Bake at 350° for 35 minutes. Cool and serve.

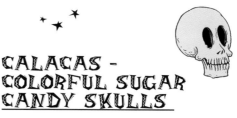

CALACAS – COLORFUL SUGAR CANDY SKULLS

Making these candies is a great activity to do with your kids or grandkids, particularly if you explain the holiday to them and make a small altar in your home, with flowers and candles, a few photos and maybe some things that were special to your loved one(s). Do a little research and you'll be able to impart to them a real appreciation for the continuum of life. The recipe takes less than an hour to prepare. You can do most of the work ahead of time, and then bring it out at the last minute. Then everyone can make their own skulls and paint them together!

2 cups powdered sugar
1 egg white
1 tablespoon of light corn syrup
½ teaspoon of vanilla
1/3 cup of corn starch

Blue, green, red and yellow food coloring
1 fine paintbrush

Sift powdered sugar. Mix egg white, syrup and vanilla in a dry, clean bowl. Mix sugar into wet mixture gradually. Mix with fingers until the mixture forms a ball.

Sprinkle cornstarch on table or board. Put the mixture on the table and shape into smooth, manageable ball. Wrap tightly in plastic and chill until ready to use. (Mixture will keep for months.)

Use plenty of cornstarch when making skulls or other shapes. When the figures are dry, get creative and paint them with wild colors.

NOPALITOS EN ALMÍBAR - CACTUS CANDY

Growing up, Nina and I loved cactus candy. (I still do.) Whenever we went into a store that sold it, we talked our mom into buying us some. Made from the paddles or cactus flowers (tunas) of the prickly pear cactus, known in Mexico as the nopalito, its taste and texture is indescribable - moist and succulent with a sugarcoated crunchy outer skin. I know it sounds weird, but don't knock it till you've tried it! Makes about two cups.

2 cups granulated sugar
1 cup water
4 prickly pear paddles, with spines removed (These are only available in grocery stores with Latino clientele or in Mexico.)

Boil sugar and water for 15 minutes to make a syrup. Cut cleaned cactus paddles into 3 inch by 1½ inch chunks. Rinse the chunks (they're now called nopalitos) under cold water until the mucous-like substance along the cuts is gone.

Add the nopalito chunks to the boiling syrup; turn the heat down until it's barely simmering. Cook for 15 minutes.

With tongs, remove the nopalitos to a plate and spoon some syrup over them. Wait to serve until they have cooled and a solid sugar crust has formed around the candy.

CAMOTE - SWEET POTATO CANDY

This is another one of our family favorites. The unique flavors of the pineapple, sweet potatoes, ginger, anise and cinnamon will knock your socks off! Makes a little over two pounds of candy.

20 ounce can crushed pineapple, well drained
16 ounce can sweet potatoes or yams, well drained
4 cups granulated sugar
1¼ cups all-purpose flour

1½ tsp cinnamon
1 tsp finely grated fresh ginger root
½ tsp anise seeds, crushed
Powdered sugar
Flaked coconut

Put the drained pineapple in the blender and purée. Then purée the sweet potatoes or yams. Put into a large pot and add the sugar, flour and spices. Bring to a boil and stir constantly, cooking until quite dry. Be careful not to allow the mixture to scorch. Remove from pot and form into balls about an inch or so in diameter. Roll in powdered sugar and coconut. Yum!

LIMÓNES COCADAS – LIMES FILLED WITH COCONUT

Rumored to have been a favorite of famed artist, Frida Khalo, these candies combine the tart with the sweet in a uniquely Mexican way. They are easy to be make, even though they need to stand overnight every night for about a week in order to lose their bitterness, and gain the desired flavor ... they are definitely worth the wait.

Limónes (Limes)
16 limónes (Mexican limes) or key limes
1 tbsp baking soda
3 cups granulated sugar
3 cups water

Cocada (Coconut Filling)

1 cup granulated sugar
1 cup water
1½ cups unsweetened shredded coconut

In a medium saucepan, cover limes with water and simmer, covered, until slightly softened, about 20 minutes. Pour the contents of the saucepan into a clay pot. Sprinkle with the baking soda, cover, and let stand overnight at room temperature. The next day, drain the limes. Cut a small slice from the top of each and carefully hollow them out. Discard the pulp and return the limes to the clay pot with enough hot water to cover. Cover with a dishtowel and a tight-fitting lid. Let stand overnight again.

The next day, drain the water and replace it with fresh hot water. Let stand, covered, as above. Repeat this process for three or four days, until the limes are no longer bitter.

Combine the sugar and water in a medium saucepan. Bring to a boil and add the limes, simmering until the syrup is quite thick. This takes about 45 minutes to an hour. Let cool overnight.

To make the cocada, combine the sugar and water in a saucepan and bring to a boil. Stir in the coconut and cook, stirring constantly, until thick. Let it cool completely.

To serve, remove the limes from the syrup and fill with cocada.

A FEW PARTING THOUGHTS ...
LIVING LA BUENA VIDA IN BUENA VISTA

The air is soft. The light ripples across a jade green-dark blue sea. The sky is soft too. The puffs of clouds that hid the sun as it rose over the Sea of Cortez all fiery red and molten gold are gone now. The sky has colored itself a perfect pale shade of periwinkle, spreading endlessly overhead until it's confronted by the jagged mountain range of the Sierra de la Laguna. Layered back in rows, shaded dark to light, the edges of these mountains captivate me, begging me to paint them. They are green this year, unbelievably so after two years of ample rains. Hidden in their nooks and crannies are streams, natural hot springs, waterfalls. There are rancheros scaled up the steep sides of their peaks where every variety of tropical fruit and flower grows in abundance.

As I walk along this beach, my feet crunch against the coarse sand. A warm wave

---

splashes over them and snakes up my legs. I scoop up the tennis ball and toss it into the waves so my dog, Cassie can fetch it. A tiny thing, she flings herself into the face of the wave with the determined force of a dog three times her size. I smile to myself. How blessed am I to live here.

I snorkeled for nearly an hour this morning. I saw three eels, a sea turtle and two stingrays, along with the usual bounty of parrotfish, needlefish, pompano, trig-gerfish and so many others I couldn't begin to name them all. I swam further today than I have before, alone in the sea, delighting in the warm-cool softness of the water, the push-pull of my arms against it, enjoying the tension in my legs as I kicked along. My mask leaked a lot but it gave me the excuse to stop every so often, to look again at the mountains rising up out of the desert - stark and adamant against sea and sky.

For years I dreamed of living in Mexico. It began on a vacation to Puerto Vallarta in 1983. I was 30. My boyfriend and I were at a restaurant named El Set, terraced down the edge of the Pacific to the beach. It was, of course sunset and we were sipping mar-garitas and nibbling on guacamole. At a table near us sat a group of 12 expatriates. They were close to our age. I stared and eavesdropped shamelessly. My boyfriend was appalled, but I couldn't help myself. I had traveled often in Mexico, particularly in Baja while growing up, but it had never before occurred to me that I could actually live here. It was a revelation and the images of that golden group of expatriates never left me. It amazes me still that I became one myself 20 years later.

In October 2003 my husband Terry and I moved to Buena Vista, 45 minutes north of the Los Cabos airport. We're on what's known as the East Cape - one of the pre-mier sport fishing, windsurfing and diving destinations in the world. This is my father's favorite place on the planet. He spends a week a month here every year fishing, and he turned 83 in 2005. My son comes about five times a year with him. My daugh-ter and her three dogs fly in about as frequently. Family holidays are spent here. My mother's ashes are here. When we sold our homes in San Diego and La Bufadora just south of Ensenada it was a no-brainer that we would move here.

Visitors compare the East Cape to Los Cabos a generation ago. It's growing and it's home to a burgeoning community of Americans and Canadians, but the resorts are still small, the restaurants few, the lifestyle easy-going and peaceful, and the scenery spectacular. People don't come here expecting upscale spas, world-class golf, shopping, raucous nightlife and gourmet cuisine. They come for the outdoor adventure experience, for the pristine beaches with perfect swimming water and of course for the fishing - which is even better than in Los Cabos. Back in the '50s and '60s, guys like Chuck

Connors, Desi Arnaz, Fred Astaire, and Ray Cannon came here. They came, the word got out and the East Cape was on the map.

I am not a city girl. The life here suits me. Where I came from, we had eight lane freeways and 20-hour-a-day rush hour. Here we say that three cars in line at a tope (speed bump) constitute a traffic jam. In San Diego I had constant claustrophobia. To quote a Jimmy Buffett song, I found myself always "pacing the cage." Here I am deeply content. There is a view of endless sand, sea, mountains and sky from our living room window. The beach is steps away. I am free, and I am connected to my community in a way I never felt before. Everywhere we go, people know us and we know them, Mexicans and expatriates. Everyone who passes gives a smile and the flat-handed Baja wave - modeled from the Native American "how" gesture. My Spanish improves daily as I plactico (chat) with Mexican friends and acquaintances. Sometimes I find myself going back and forth between the two languages so quickly I don't even notice the transition. I love it.

I always felt more at home in Mexico than in the US and for years I pondered why. Now I know. It's simultaneously simple and complicated, like the Mexican culture. It's also a bit esoteric and more than a bit spiritual - like the story of Mexico's Virgin of Guadalupe. I now know that my heart is Mexican. Mi corazón es Mexicano. That is why I am here.

INDEX

RESTAURANT CREDITS
(in order of appearance)

Pancho's in Cabo San Lucas: Salsa Ranchera Pancho Villa Style

El Corral in Buena Vista: Maria's Salsa de Arbol

Caffé Todos Santos: Marc's Mango Salsa Tropical

Taquería Mexico in Ensenada: Avocado Sauce

Los Barriles Tacos: Chiles Toreados

Hotel Buena Vista Beach Resort: World Famous Nachos

Posada La Poza in Todos Santos: Flautas de Atún Ahumado

El Chilar in San Jose del Cabo: Esquites Callos de Almeja

Caffé Todos Santos: Chicken Flautas

Mr. Azucar's in La Paz: La Cola de la Sirena and Sopa Rompe Catre

El Chilar in San Jose del Cabo: Lobster & Crab Pozole

Pancho's in Cabo San Lucas: Tortilla Soup

Tío Pablo's in Los Barriles: Green Chile

Pueblo Bonito Hotels in Cabo San Lucas: Chile Fruit Salad

César's in Tijuana: Original Ensalada César

Celia's in La Bufadora: Summer Nopales Salad

Caffé Todos Santos: Tenth Anniversary Salad

Chapala in McCall, Idaho: Hot Carnitas Salad

Tropicana Inn in San Jose del Cabo: Ensalada de Camaron y Callo

Hotel Buena Vista Beach Resort: Spa Vegetable Kabobs and Rajas en Crema

Brisas del Mar in San Jose del Cabo: Ground Beef & Potato Tacos

Hotel Buena Vista Beach Resort: Mushroom, Chorizo & Raja Tostadas

Pueblo Bonito in Cabo San Lucas: Enchiladas Baja

Las Olas in Cardiff-by-the-Sea, California: Grilled Chiles Rellenos

Rancho Buena Vista: Catch of the Day (Empanizado y Mojo de Ajo)

Hotel California in Todos Santos: Shrimp & Smoked Salmon Ravioli

Tío Pablo's in Los Barriles: Cabrilla Veracruzana

Isla Loreto: Fish Meuniere

Ray's Place in Santispac: Shrimp Papagayo

Restaurant La Bufadora: Orphan Calamari

Palapa Azul on Tecolote Beach near La Paz: Stuffed Clams on the Grill

Hotel California in Todos Santos: Chevre Stuffed Chicken Breasts

Hotel Buena Vista Beach Resort: Pollo con Salsa Alcaparra

Posada La Poza in Todos Santos: Arrachera

Los Gordos in La Bufadora: Chile Colorado Los Gordos Style

Hotel California in Todos Santos: Lamb Burgers with Gorgonzola Cheese

Pancho's in Cabo San Lucas: Huevos Veracruzanos

Tropicana Inn in San Jose del Cabo: Breakfast Rellenos

Hussongs in Ensenada: The Original Margarita

El Chilar in San Jose del Cabo: Banderita Margarita

Giggling Marlin Beach Club at Bahía de los Sueños: Skip & Go Naked

Punta Morro in Ensenada: Martinis

Los Gordos in La Bufadora: Bloody Marys

La Concha Beach Resort in La Paz: Rumbas

El Dorado formerly in La Bufadora: Mexican Coffee

Caffé Todos Santos: Marc's Citrus Flan Extraordinaire

Buzzard's just north of San Jose del Cabo: Kahlua Flan

Spirit of Endeavor, traveling between Cabo, La Paz and Loreto: Avocado Pie

Hotel Buena Vista Beach Resort: Pastel de Tres Leches

Hotel Buena Vista Beach Resort: Mango Mousse

Top Ten (or so) Favorite Baja Websites

Baja Discovery
www.bajadiscovery.com

Baja Expo
www.bajaexpo.com

Baja Insider - Webzine and Resource Guide
www.bajainsider.com

Baja Life Magazine
www.bajalife.com

Baja Links
www.bajalinks.com

Baja Magic
www.bajamagic.com

Baja Times
www.bajatimes.com

Discover Baja Travel Club
www.discoverbaja.com

East Cape Information
www.eastcape.org

Ensenada Gazette
www.ensenadagazette.com

La Paz Tourism & Hotel Association
www.vivalapaz.com

¡Loreto!
http://www.loreto.com/

Mexico Online
www.mexonline.com

Todos Santos Original Website
http://www.todossantos-baja.com

About the Author and Artists

Ann Hazard is passionate about all things Mexican. She is a third generation Baja Aficionada who lives in Buena Vista on the East Cape of Baja California Sur with her husband Terry and their two Mexican dogs. Ann has followed her grandfather and father's footsteps up and down the peninsula since she was eight. Cooking With Baja Magic Dos is her fourth book. It includes updated versions of all 175 recipes that were in her first cookbook, 80 new recipes and adventure stories and all new art.

Ann's second book, Cartwheels in the Sand, is an insightful novel about four women's odyssey of self-discovery while traveling the Baja peninsula in an RV. Drawing upon personal experiences, Ann has created fictional characters that are entertaining and believable and has sent them on an authentic road trip.

Her third book, Agave Sunsets, is a collection of 50 tales spanning four generations of Baja adventures. Rich in knowledge of Mexican culture and lore, Ann writes about "Bay of L.A. - Aquarium on the Moon," "Boys 'n Beer in Baja," "Expatriated Americans - As the Palapa Turns Down East Cape Way," "Baja's Exotic Wine Country," "Exploring the Baja Cave Paintings" and "Can You Tell Me ...Where is the Second World?" Whether read in one sitting or perused story by story, Agave Sunsets is a memorable journey through Baja.

Additionally, Ann has written articles for publications including: San Diego Union-Tribune, Coastal Living Magazine, Baja Traveler Magazine, the Coast News, the Baja Tourist Guide, Baja Tourist Guide, RV Companion, Western Outdoor News, Discover Los Cabos, Discover Baja, Sister Cities Magazine, La Buena Vida in Buena Vista, and The Mexico File. She contributes to websites including: BajaInsider.com, LosCabosGuide.com, JustSayGo.com, Mexgrocer.com and her own website, BajaMagic.com. She is a member of Mexico Writers' Alliance and North American Travel Writers' Association.

Terry Hauswirth became a photographer in 2000 on a trip to the Mayan Riviera with his wife, Ann Hazard. A good friend of theirs, Antonio Cristerna - an award-winning Mexican photographer - took the two of them on a tour of the Yucatan peninsula. At that time Ann was delving into magazine and newspaper writing. Since her clients requested photos to go with her stories, they had just purchased their first digital camera. Terry and Antonio had identical cameras and shot photos together for three days. By day two, Antonio was copying Terry's photos onto his camera because he said Terry's were better. Terry then discovered that he had "the eye."

After that, his career as a photojournalist took off. Terry's work has been published in Coastal Living Magazine, San Diego Union-Tribune, Baja Traveler Magazine, Sister Cities Magazine, Pacific Coast Sportfishing, Western Outdoor News, The Mexico File, The Coast News, La Buena Vida in Buena Vista, Discover Baja, Baja Tourist Guide, RV Companion Magazine, Agave Sunsets and on numerous Baja and travel websites. Prior to reinventing himself as a photographer, Terry was a firefighter for 27 years.

Janna Kinkade's love of the Mexican people, their culture and landscapes is clearly evident in her

paintings. Her use of bright colors and simple designs are almost childlike. In addition to painting in the Mexican folk art style, she also paints large abstract pieces in acrylic and oils. Janna is mainly a self-taught artist but has benefited from classes taken in her native state of Oregon. Janna and her husband, Martin Davis have wintered in Todos Santos since 1997, where they have been restoring a small Mexican house, using local materials and the same bright colors as are in her paintings. She can be reached at jannakin@hotmail.com.

Gayle Hazard has been traveling in Baja since before she was born. Currently a student of University of San Diego, she has been all over the peninsula, and spent much time during her growing up years in La Bufadora. She visits her mom and Terry every other month with her three dogs, Max, Dooti and Maya. Max (a Rotweiller-Doberman mix) is infamous with both Alaska Airlines and Aeromexico, because he regularly escapes from his cage while airborne between San Diego and Los Cabos. Gayle has been painting since high school. Gayle can be reached at hazardousg14@yahoo.com.

Renegade Enterprises Order Form

Cooking with Baja Magic Dos by Ann Hazard $28.95
Agave Sunsets by Ann Hazard $19.95
Cartwheels in the Sand by Ann Hazard $14.95

Five easy ways to order:
1. US Phone orders: 619-298-1831
2. US Fax orders: 619-298-1432
3. Mexico Phone orders: 624-141-0174
4. Email: Cookbaja@aol.com
5. Mail: Renegade Enterprises
         5422 Napa Street
         San Diego, CA 92110

	Quantity Each	Total Books
Cooking with Baja Magic Dos		
Agave Sunsets		
Cartwheels in the Sand		
Subtotal		
Shipping & Handling $3.95 per book (US)		
Add Sales Tax for delivery to CA: 7.75%		
TOTAL AMOUNT		

Enclosed is my check, money order or credit card information for the amount of:
$_____ Payable to RENEGADE ENTERPRISES

____ Check or Money Order ____ Master Card ____ Visa _____ American Express
Account #_____ Expiration Date_____
Signature_____ Billing Zip Code_____

Send book(s) to:
Name_____
Street Address_____
City/State/Zip_____
Daytime phone_____
E-mail_____